HOW HISTORY'S GREATEST
PIRATES
PILLAGED, PLUNDERED, AND GOT AWAY WITH IT

HOW HISTORY'S GREATEST PIRATES

PILLAGED, PLUNDERED, AND GOT AWAY WITH IT

THE STORIES, TECHNIQUES, AND TACTICS OF THE MOST FEARED SEA ROVERS FROM 1500–1800

BENERSON LITTLE

former Navy SEAL and author of *Pirate Hunting* and *The Buccaneer's Realm*

FAIR WINDS
PRESS
BEVERLY, MASSACHUSETTS

First published in the USA in 2011 by
Fair Winds Press, a member of
Quayside Publishing Group
100 Cummings Center
Suite 406-L
Beverly, MA 01915-6101
www.fairwindspress.com

15 14 13 12 11   1 2 3 4 5

ISBN-13: 978-1-59233-443-8
ISBN-10: 1-59233-443-1

Library of Congress Cataloging-in-Publication Data available

Cover design: Peter Long
Book design: Sheila Hart Design, Inc.

Printed and bound in Singapore

For my parents,
who let me choose my own course.

CONTENTS

INTRODUCTION

I n the history of the world there are few figures more romanticized than the pirate. He—and, yes, even she—has been with us for at least 3,500 years. When we consider that sea trade has existed for at least 8,000 years, and that our ancestors or their cousins probably first launched a canoe or raft upon the saltwaters at least 130,000 years ago, it is likely that piracy is one of the world's oldest professions, right along with hunting, farming, and, as the saying goes, prostitution. Where goods and gold travel, so do thieves.

It should come as no surprise that the pirate has our regard, deservedly or not. Pirates did not follow the common course—they set their own. They lived outside the bounds of mundane day-to-day existence, and sailed the seas instead, making their own rules and society, rebelling against order, and living as they pleased. Their image is irresistible: a rakish ship sweeps swiftly down upon a hapless merchantman. The victim's unlucky crew quakes in fear at the sight of the pirate ship as it hoists its terrible black flag and opens its gunports to reveal a grinning broadside. The pirate fires a broadside, and the merchantman one in return. They blaze away at each other, sending thick plumes of gun smoke across the water between them. Yards and masts shiver and crash to the deck, and soon the ships collide. The pirate crew hurls grappling hooks, then leaps and swings onto the merchantman's decks, cutlasses waving, pistols erupting with fire and lead. Soon, the merchantman's deck is awash in blood, its captain has a sword at his throat, and the victim's colors slowly drift down from the masthead to the deck.

But pirates didn't swing from ship to ship when they boarded, they certainly were not Robin Hoods, and the blood they spilled was a terrible thing to witness. It is well to remember that pirates were thieves, that they lived off of the goods and labor of others violently or by the threat of violence. Yet even acknowledging this does not stop most of us from admiring them, even if only secretly or guiltily. We know pirates are thieves, that often they were cruel, evil men—and cruel, evil women as well—who deserved to die. Nonetheless, we elevate them as heroes, even as far as the heavens themselves. If you look south at night, you can see Jason's *Argo*, the first known pirate and pirate-hunting ship, now sailing the firmament.

To understand pirates, we have to look beyond the enticing images Hollywood and swashbuckling novelists have given us. But not to worry—the reality of pirates does not diminish the image at all, except perhaps of the pirates' purported nobility. They remain fascinating figures. There is no need to invent or reinvent their deeds, or their characters; thus I have kept strictly to the facts, proving that dramatic exaggeration is unnecessary. Their deeds were real, and all who witnessed them would have felt their hearts pounding with excitement and fear. Call it a romantic realism, if you like, for that is what this book intends: to show the great pirates as they really were.

To do this, we need to look closely at what pirates were all about: plundering ship and shore, and getting away with it—and often not getting away with it in the end. This requires that we discover what their tactics were and how different pirates used them. Some pirates used the tried-and-true, relying on the threat of force to strike fear into the hearts of their prey, as Blackbeard, Bartholomew Roberts, and Ned Low did. Others had to work harder, relying on both courage and cunning to seize wealth in the face of great odds, as Henry Morgan and Bartholomew Sharp did, for example. Tactics, after all, were at the heart of their success.

In writing about these notorious men and women, I have looked at them through two avenues. First, I gleaned what I could from extensive research, both scholarly and practical, ranging from the detailed study of written evidence to the extensive firing of a variety of replica pirate weapons. But just as important, I have also looked at pirates through the eyes of my experience at sea, especially that of my seven years as a U.S. Navy SEAL. The pursuit and boarding of great ships by men in small boats is little different today than it was in the age of sail, and the understanding of these tactics gave me great insight into pirate attacks, enabling me to decipher details I might otherwise have missed. I knew, for example, that weapons must be test-fired before an attack, and that when transiting in open boats en route to a target, vital equipment must be secured, and if it were vulnerable to seawater, then waterproofed as well. And sure enough, when I looked carefully, I discovered that pirates did the same—they had to. On a much broader scale, I understood the minds of those adventurers who bear arms on the sea today, and this helped me understand those who did so in the past.

The following should help the reader navigate his or her way through the world of the pirate. In particular, consider not only the different pirate tactics, but also how different pirates used the same tactics, and whether and why they

Original
Jolly Roger

Captain Condent

Modified
Jolly Roger

French Jolly Roger

Captain
Emanuel Wynne

Captain
Edward England

Captain
Christopher Moody

Captain Bartholomew Roberts

were successful. Regarding seagoing language, one should note that a cannon at sea was a *gun* or a *great gun*. A cannon was called a *cannon* only ashore. *Windward* meant the direction from which the wind blew, and *leeward* away from it. The names of ships can sometimes be confusing, because many ships and other vessels had the same ones. In other words, a ship in one chapter is not likely to be the ship of the same name in another chapter. The names of places can be similarly confusing. There was more than one Trinidad in the Caribbean, for example, and more than one Tortuga, and where necessary, distinctions are noted. Further, place-names often changed over the centuries: in this book, for example, you will see Puerto del Principe change to Porto Principe. It is known today as Camagüey. Some places do not even exist anymore. Venta de Cruces, for example, is underwater, lost during the building of the Panama Canal.

These details will not distract you from the pirates, but enhance them instead, for they are an important part of the romance of the sea and of the pirates who plundered upon it. Enjoy the voyages!

A probably nineteenth-or early-twentieth-century illustration of pirate flags flown by early eighteenth-century pirates. In the upper left corner is the original Jolly Roger. The Jolly Roger is actually mentioned only twice in period documents, and only in reference to pirates Bartholomew Roberts and Francis Spriggs. This flag or a similar one was also flown by Edward Low, Charles Harris, and probably John Russel. Beneath it is perhaps the most typical form of what we refer to today as the "Jolly Roger," that of the death's head with crossed bones. The skull and bones was a common mortuary design, for example, on tombstones. The attribution in the illustration appears to have been inadvertently swapped with that of the flag opposite it on the far right, and should be Edward England. The flag at the bottom left, commonly attributed without evidence to Christopher Moody, is actually a Barbary corsair design from the late seventeenth century. Such flags may be the ultimate origin of the "Jolly Roger." At bottom center is a flag commonly attributed to Bartholomew Roberts, although there is no solid evidence for it. At bottom right is another of his real flags. Center right is that of Emanuel Wynne, not Edward England. Above it is a flag of uncertain origin, which may have no basis in fact, although Richard Worley flew one with this design, but white on a black field. Further, there is evidence of a pirate flag with a black death's head on a white field. Top center is a pennant bearing the usual death's head and bones. It is commonly attributed to Christopher Condent, although there appears to be no evidence he actually flew it. At the center of the illustration is the ensign of French pirate Thomas Jean Dulaïen. The original flag was destroyed by order of Louis XV, and it is unknown whether this depiction is based on the original, or an existing written description, leaves room for significant interpretation. Otherwise, all of the depictions in the illustration are based on written descriptions, or were invented by later writers and historians, and have no basis in fact. No pirate flags from this period exist today. The earliest description of the "skull and bones" being flown by the "pirates of the Caribbean" dates to 1688. The flag was red, with a white skull and crossed bones beneath.

INTERFOTO/Alamy

CHAPTER 1

☠

KHEIR-ED-DIN BARBAROSSA,

A.K.A. REDBEARD

1470s–1546

TWO BROTHERS AND ONE LEGEND WHO CREATED FEAR AND MAYHEM THROUGHOUT THE MEDITERRANEAN

There were four of them originally. They were all brothers, all pirates at first and then corsairs, which was simply the Mediterranean word for privateer—a pirate with a license to steal. From a single small brigantine they had expanded to a small fleet of galliots, as their light galleys were called. But Elias was long dead now, killed by the corsairing Knights of Rhodes in an attack near Crete, the same attack that left Aruj, the eldest, a galley slave until he was finally ransomed as much as a year later. Isaac, governor of Djerba, Tunisia, was busy building the light galleys necessary for a great expedition. Hizir, the youngest, was a fierce, capable corsair captain.

Yet it was Aruj, the first of the brothers to become a pirate, who was so far the most successful sea rover of them all. Called Barbarossa—Redbeard—by the Italians for the "perfectly red" hair that grew on his face and head, he was now known by this name across the Mediterranean, from the Pillars of Hercules to the Levant. Some, though, said his nickname derived first from the Spaniards who mistook Baba Aruj, as he was known among his followers, as Barbaroja.

In late 1512, Aruj, bloodthirsty "only in battle and cruel only when disobeyed," saw off his brother Hizir and the nine galleys he gave him to command. Aruj could not lead the cruise, for he was still recovering from a near-mortal wound received while trying to wrest Bougie, a piratical port city in modern-day Algeria, from the Spaniards, who had violently dislodged its ruler. The ousted sultan beseeched the corsairs to restore the city to him, and offered them a reward. After days of bombardment, the force of Turks and Moors finally breached a castle wall, leaving a passage blocked only by men whose blood could easily be spilled by cold Damascus steel. But just as Aruj charged at the head of his Janissaries and North Africans toward the shattered wall, a cannonball carried most of his left arm away and crushed his body and his warriors' spirit. The corsairs retreated.

Hizir was doubtless glad of his brother's faith in him. Earlier that year, Aruj had installed him at La Goulette, the fortress of Tunis, which lay next to the salted ruins of Carthage. In retaliation for the capture of a rich Genoese galliot, an overpowering force under the command of forty-four-year-old veteran pirate hunter Andrea Doria made a surprise attack of reprisal on La Goulette, forcing Hizir and his men to flee. Hizir did not lose his Christian slaves, or much else of value except the six galliots he sank so Doria could not capture them, but Aruj was nonetheless furious with his brother. The Genoese had destroyed the fortress, recaptured the rich galliots, and burned or

The Barbarossa brothers, Aruj and Hizir, the latter of whom would become known as Kheir-ed-Din—Defender of the Faith. These corsair brethren refined pirate galley tactics and developed North African privateering and piracy into a serious threat across the Mediterranean. The illustration, from a late-seventeenth-century Dutch compendium of naval heroes, was engraved more than a century after the brothers' deaths and is probably inaccurate. We do know that Aruj's hair was red, thus the name Barbarossa meaning "Redbeard." Hizir's hair was auburn, although he is said to have colored it red with henna after his brother's death.
Private Collection / The Bridgeman Art Library International

captured any other vessels. The loss of the galleys hurt the corsairs, for they needed them not only for attacks at sea but also to make great expeditions ashore. Only after Hizir sailed to Djerba, the corsairs' new home port, and ordered three fine new galleys to be built, was his brother appeased.

"Allah speed us!" the crews of the nine vessels shouted as the galleys pulled away from the port of Djerba, or at least the warriors did. The oars of the light raiding galleys were probably still manned with freemen, warriors all, although within a few decades this would change. Still, the corsairs usually had a larger galley or two manned with slave oarsmen in their company. These slaves, chained to their benches, did only what they were told—and if they were told to shout blessings, doubtless they did. Some may have shouted good wishes out of sincerity. But many oarsmen were captured Christians put to work propelling the larger corsair galleys across the Mediterranean, just as Christians often put captured Muslims to work on their galleys. They wished for nothing more than to be home again.

"Allah give you many prizes!" shouted well-wishers on the shore amid the loud crack of cannons fired to announce the cruising voyage and wish it much success. Among the spectators were fishermen, laborers, owners, and outfitters, as well as soldiers and sailors not departing with Hizir's expedition. They shouted not only in Turkish and Arabic but also in Lingua Franca, the mix of tongues used by Christians, Muslims, and Jews for trade in the many ports of the Mediterranean. The Ottoman Turks would soon expand into the corsair ports of the Barbary Coast, and the corsair brothers were the cutting edge of the curved conquering sword, although they did not know it yet.

The galleys moved swiftly across the near-placid sea, their brilliantly colored, exquisitely appointed ensigns and banners denoting what these galleys were and what they were after. They were larger than the common small galleys that the Barbary corsairs often used for raids. The corsairs referred to their small galleys as frigates, but the Christians called them brigantines, for they were small craft manned by brigands. Though Hizir's galleys were larger than the Barbary frigates, they were still smaller than the large heavy Christian galleys, and for this reason the Christians referred to them as galliots rather than galleys. Hizir's rakish galleys were low, swift, and well-manned. Further, holy men, investors, outfitters, and even corsair wives had blessed the voyage with prayers, incense, and myrrh, and astrologers had sought signs in the heavens that the cruise would be profitable.

But it is sea fighters who actually make a voyage, not those who are left behind. Hizir's mixed crew, of Turkish Janissaries lured to Barbary by the prospect of riches and a smaller number of local Moors already well acquainted with the riches to be had in the western Mediterranean, were disciplined and experienced, as was Hizir himself. From his brother he had learned to command and fight a galley, and by his side he had bloodied the decks and plundered the holds of European and North African merchant vessels.

The Barbarossa brothers, led by Aruj, attacking one of two papal galleys in 1504 in this somewhat fanciful nineteenth-century American engraving. The illustration conveys a sense of the difficulties and dangers of boarding a ship under fire. Not only were there the hazards of enemy polearms, swords, arrows, crossbow bolts, and stones, but also of falling into the sea and drowning or being crushed between the two vessels. Typically, an attacking galley would have driven its boarding prow into the side (specifically, into the rails and outriggers) of its prey, rather than "laying it aboard alongside" as is depicted here.

DECEPTION, SPEED, AND VIOLENCE

The brothers first great prizes had come not as their first captures had, taken by mere speed of oar and force of arms. Cruising for plunder in 1504, Aruj, perhaps not yet thirty years old, and Hizir, perhaps only twenty-one, lay in wait near the island of Elba, in a single galley, probably flying the colors of Genoa or Marseilles, or of some other Christian port. The island rests between the mainland of northwestern Italy and the island of Corsica, along the trade route from Genoa to the south of Italy. The day was fair, the Ligurian Sea quiet, perfect for vessels swift under oars.

It was not long before they sighted two great Italian galleys flying papal colors—they were obviously vessels of Pope Julius II, sailing from Genoa to Rome and doubtless richly laden. Aruj ordered his men to arms and then waited to see what the leading galley, which rowed distractedly and even "careless, indolently supine, and, according to custom, in very indifferent order," would do. Given that it lay a fair distance, surely two miles (302 km) or more, ahead of the second, Aruj was cert s could capture it before its consort caught up.

But many among his crew were not as certain. They complained to their captain of the size of the papal galley, and of their own small force, and suggested they would be better off rowing swiftly away than fighting what was doubtless a well-armed galley, for riches were always well protected. Worse, if there were any resistance at all, would that not give time for the second galley to come alongside and slaughter them? Who can fight and win when attacked in force on two sides?

"God forbid," Arij is said to have thundered at his reticent crew, "that I should ever live to be branded of such infamy!" Immediately he ordered them to throw half or more of their oars overboard, leaving just enough to send the light galley alongside their papal prey. Flight was now impossible, and the lead galley was on a course to intercept the corsairs.

At first, the papal galley rowed casually. It was soon obvious that it had made no preparations for battle and saw no threat in the approaching corsair vessel. Indeed, the papal crew had no idea what it was. Few could recall when Turks and Moors last raided in these seas, and why would pirates venture into these waters where powerful Christian warships were common?

It is difficult to see good detail in faces, clothing, and arms until very close, within 200 or 300 yards (180 or 275 m) even, and in those days the telescope was not in use. Only at close range did the papal galley's captain and crew discern turbans and scimitars and realize who they faced. Quickly the Italian crew began

The first of two pages of illustrations, numbering twenty-two in all, of Barbary corsair methods of torture and execution, from *Histoire de Barbarie and des Corsaires* by Father Pierre Dan, 1637. Such cruelties were not limited to Barbary corsairs. Most states and peoples practiced torture for a variety of reasons, ranging from religious and political intolerance to intelligence collection to the search for plunder. Abuse depicted in this illustration includes impalement on spikes; quartering by four vessels; being used for target practice by archers; burning torches inserted in wounds created for the purpose; internment, leaving only the head exposed; being rolled in a barrel filled with nails; beatings of five or six hundred blows; strangulation by garrote; having one's bones broken with an iron rod and being left to die; being tied to the mouth of a cannon so that the body is torn apart when the piece is fired; and mutilation of the nose and eyes.
© Mary Evans Picture Library/Alamy

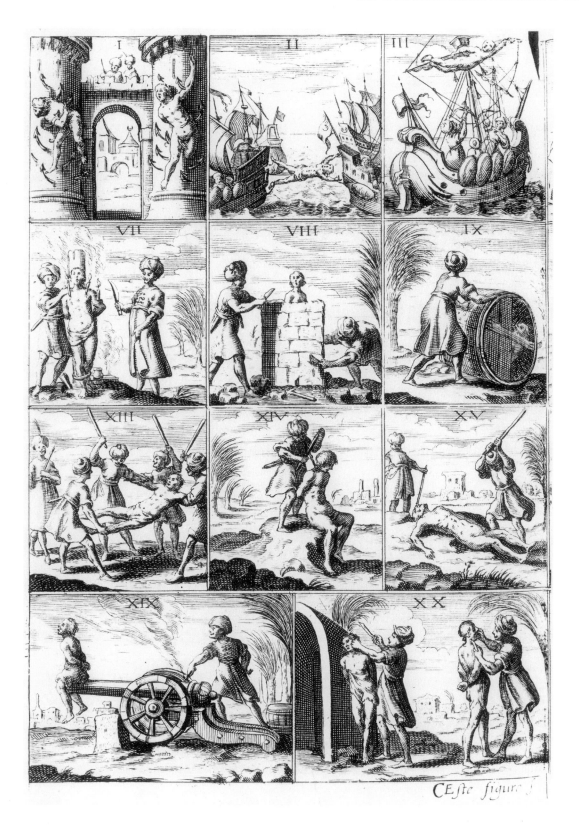

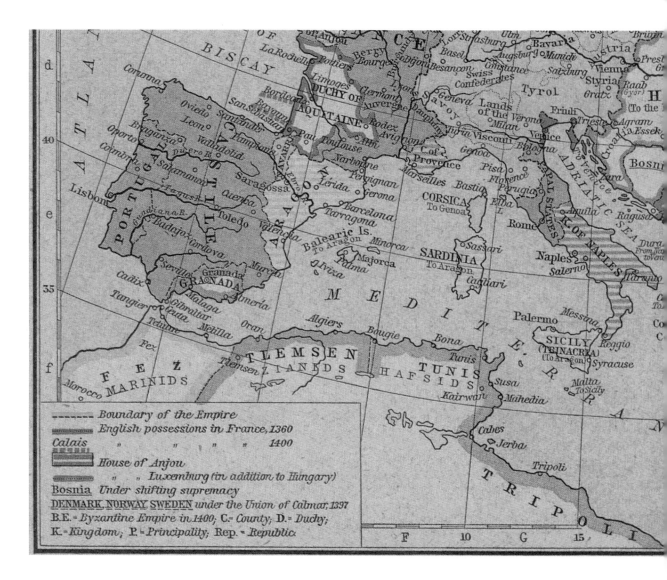

A map depicting the Mediterranean during the late Middle Ages and Renaissance. The Barbary Coast—shown here as the area from Tlemsen to Tripoli—was ideally situated for sea roving. Barbary corsairs had easy access to the coasts, islands, and trade routes that ranged from Spain to Greece. The Barbarossa brothers were based first at Tunis, but later established themselves as rulers of Algiers. From this location they could attack vessels entering or leaving the Mediterranean, and could easily launch expeditions against Spain, France, and the Italian states.

to make ready for an engagement, but Barbarossa had already ordered his men to attack. They hoisted their true colors, probably Tunisian, and the Islamic crescent created even more fear among the Italians. As quickly as they could, the corsairs rowed their galley with their remaining oars across the short distance. Within 100 yards (91.5 m) they opened fire, sending waves of harquebus lead and arrows into the mass of exposed crew and oarsmen. With these swift projectiles they "killed some Christians, wounded many, and terrified all the rest."

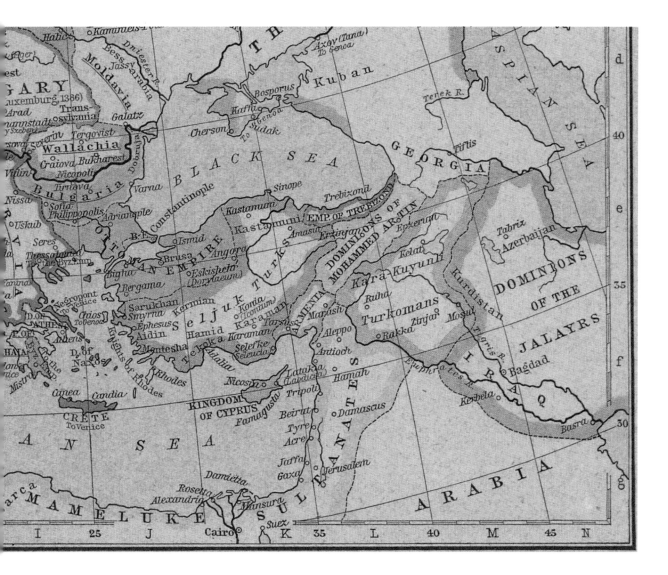

Confusion reigned aboard the papal galley as the bow spur of the corsair galley slipped over the extended oars and pierced the outrigger. The corsairs surged over the spur and aboard the prey vessel, their sleeves drawn up to their elbows, their scimitars in hand, their voices shouting "Allah!" and hurling war cries and promises of bloody slaughter. They gave no quarter to anyone, and would not until the galley surrendered, as was their practice. Both victor and victim were covered in blood as the naked blades rang against opposing arms and armor, as sharp steel carved flesh from bone and limb from body. The broad strokes of the Turkish scimitars and North African swords cut easily, for their sharply curved blades were made for such cutting. The blades need not be drawn or pulled through their living targets in order to cut: the curve of the blades did this for them.

Axes and pikes entered the bloody fray as well, and even stones. Arrows fired at close range from powerful Turkish bows struck one side of a chain-mailed warrior or hapless oarsman and passed right through to the other. It was not long before the crew of the papal galley cried for quarter. By now, the second galley was fast approaching—and this one, seeing the fight, should have been prepared for battle.

Barbarossa immediately, and over the opposition of some of his crew, tried an old trick, one that almost never failed. He ordered the prisoners to be secured below where they could not be seen, released and armed the Turks and other Muslims among the slave oarsmen, and had his crew dress in the clothing of the papal soldiers and crew. His own galley he took in tow, as if it were a papal prize. The approaching galley was unaware of what had happened, although by the time its crew saw the corsair galley in tow, they would have known what was up—or at least what they thought was up.

Within 100 yards (91.5 m) the pirates opened fire, sending waves of harquebus lead and arrows into the mass of exposed crew and oarsmen. With these swift projectiles they "killed some Christians, wounded many, and terrified all the rest."

If the crew of the second galley had armed itself, it relaxed its guard. If it had not armed, or if it thought about doing so, it was reassured at the sight of the "defeated" galliot in tow. Congratulations were in order, not bloody battle! But fortune forever inclines to the side of the daring and typically scorns those who take things for granted.

As soon as the second galley came near, the corsair sped forward, drove its boarding prow onto the deck of the papal galley, and boarded. The Italians were unprepared for the onslaught, and like the crew of their sister galley, soon surrendered. The capture of both galleys had probably taken less than two hours. Turkish and Moorish corsairs had been known in the Mediterranean for centuries, as had Christian ones. But of late the large European galleys had considered themselves invulnerable to attack by the light brigantines and galliots of the Barbary corsairs. Barbarossa and his brothers had just shown them how wrong they were. And it was only a hint of what was to come.

Later that year the corsair brothers "scoured the coasts of Sicily and Calabria, taking several vessels, and a considerable number of slaves." In 1505 they captured a large Spanish galley filled with pieces of eight—a new Spanish silver coin—intended for the Spanish garrison at Naples. The galley was leaking badly, its crew exhausted from pumping, its 500 soldiers seasick. It could neither run nor fight effectively. The plunder of silver and slaves increased the renown and naval might of Aruj and his brothers. It was not long before Aruj commanded a fleet of eight galliots, two of whose captains were his brothers. With such a fleet, the brothers quickly grew wealthy, and their fleet and followers even larger. The shares paid out from successful cruises drew as many experienced fighting men as they could use. As common soldiers, Janissaries were paid in small silver coins called akçes. But as successful corsairs, they discovered they could be paid far better, and often in heavy Spanish pieces of eight.

PLUNDERING THE CHRISTIAN COASTS

By the time Hizir took the flotilla to sea in his brother's place eight years later, in 1512, he had more than a decade, and perhaps as many as two, of experience as a successful corsair—or, as his Christian enemies and even some of the Moors he had raided would say, as a successful pirate. After all, one man's pirate was another's corsair. And the fact was, even corsairs, both Muslim and Christian, often stole from those they were not authorized to, if they thought they could get away with it.

From Djerba, Hizir led the nine galliots to the Andalusian coast of Spain, quite possibly seeking profitable revenge for the Spanish shot that took Aruj's arm, which had now been replaced by one of silver. Along the Spanish coast, Hizir "spread terror wherever he showed himself." He sacked a town or village and moved quickly on to sack another while Spanish forces raced about, unsure where he was. Those who believed that Andrea Doria had broken the Barbary corsairs were mistaken, although, for now, Hizir would not venture into Italian waters.

As he raided the Spanish coast, his tactics were those of Mediterranean corsairs for centuries before and after, but Hizir had a talent for the timing necessary for surprise. Unless well defended, ships and other vessels at anchor or becalmed were easily taken by these "eagles or queens of the sea," as corsair galleys were known. With no wind, the prey could not flee.

While attacks ashore were based on surprise, Hizir's tactics at sea were those of ruse whenever possible. Galleys could row swiftly when necessary, but not for long periods, making a long chase almost impossible except under sail.

However, galleys were difficult to spot at sea or along a coastline. They were low vessels, unlike the large, and now often cannon-armed, "round" sailing ships that were spreading across the seas as merchantmen and men-of-war. They had but to lower their sails and they became nearly invisible against the background of the coastline or at even medium distances across the water. And this was a great advantage, as Hizir and his crew knew.

Often, to lure the prey closer, the corsairs lowered the sails of all but a single vessel. A well-armed, well-manned carrack of great tonnage, which towered far above oared vessels, did not fear to approach a solitary galley. It was easily a match for a pirate galley under any circumstance, no matter how many men the pirate had aboard, or how many scimitars were flashing in the sun. The carrack's sides were high and its crew could rain slaughter down upon attackers. Further, its broadside of cannon, if it were big enough and if the crew were enough to manage it, would simply shoot oars, oarsmen, and pirates to pieces with its bombards, culverins, serpentines, and perriers, as its various iron ordnance were named.

But the corsairs had an answer. Several corsair galleys lay in wait, most with their sails down so they could not be seen until too late. The solitary galley with its sail hoisted raised false colors. When the merchantman came within striking range, suspecting little if anything, the corsair captain ordered his galleys to row quickly into the wind, toward their prey, which could flee only slowly to windward, and never in the direction of the wind, unlike the galleys. The galleys shot their harquebuses and bows and tried to board it under their cover. In most cases this worked, and the ship was quickly boarded and captured. But today this did not work—the iron and stone shot of the ship's ordnance could kill and wound too many warriors. The galleys had to attack from the stern.

One after the other the rakish vessels rowed astern of the ship, firing the small stone-throwing swivel-mounted cannon, called perriers, in their bows, hoping to kill and maim men or shatter the ship's rudder. After one galley fired its guns, the next took its place, each in turn shooting at the ship, shattering and shivering its hull and crew until it surrendered or could be boarded and forced to do so. With harquebus and bow, the corsairs kept up a constant fire, harassing the ship's crew, forcing them to keep under cover.

But the merchant captain had tricks up his sleeve as well. He suddenly turned his ship and fired his small broadside. Gunports were still a new innovation, and most ships did not yet carry cannon on their lower decks. He was lucky enough with his first ragged volley of culverins and perriers—it turned one galley's oarsmen into a bloody mass, some killed outright, some dying, some crippled for life. But he could not destroy enough men in enough galleys. The galleys were too many for a single ship to fight, and too swift, and they could row in any direction.

If there were any slave oarsmen aboard, they would go down with the sinking galley, chained to their benches, except for the few lucky enough to find their benches torn free and be left floating as jetsam above the galley's grave.

The merchant captain tried to escape downwind, for the light galleys could never catch him if he got a good lead with a good wind. But they cut him off. He tried to ram one of the galleys, something a galley captain lived in fear of. The longer a galley was, the slower it turned, and if its captain and crew were not careful, they might find the hull of a great ship bearing down upon them. The large round hull of a merchant sailing ship could snap oars and disable a galley, and might even bulge its hull or force its gunwale below the water, quickly flooding and foundering it.

If there were any slave oarsmen aboard, they would go down with the sinking galley, chained to their benches, except for the few lucky enough to find their benches torn free and be left floating as jetsam above the galley's grave. Any corsairs who survived the sinking might be left adrift to drown or die from the scorching sun and the deadly thirst it can quickly inflict upon a man. Those who were lucky enough to be plucked from the sea might have been hanged. If they were not, they would likely end their lives as galley slaves. Yet though a merchantman might ram a single galley, it was unlikely to destroy them all. The reality was that the average merchantman caught in a calm or trapped to windward of even a single galley would likely be captured, as was this merchantman. Its crew was not large enough, nor was its broadside. Hizir captured many before he returned—twenty, according to one account.

CAPTURING AN ENTIRE VILLAGE

To attack ashore was more dangerous, but was also more profitable, for people were the plunder and there were many more to be had ashore than at sea. Following the common tactics, Hizir first headed out to sea, over the horizon, where his galleys could not be seen from the shore or by coastal vessels. Then, when the moon was new and thus the nights dark enough, he would bring several galleys ashore, preferably into a creek or small inlet some distance from his target, leaving a small number of men to guard them. Given the size of his flotilla, doubtless he left a couple to patrol at sea as well, to give warning of an attack while he was ashore, not to mention to defend against one. He could not bury his vessels in the sand, as some corsairs did with their tiny frigates. His vessels were much too large, and too numerous.

Barbary corsairs nearly always had renegades aboard, not only Europeans who had converted to Islam to escape slavery and get rich as corsairs, but also Moriscos, or Spanish Moors. Moriscos were Spaniards who converted to Islam while the Moors ruled most of Spain, and then left or were thrown out after Spain was "reconquered" and the Moors were expelled in 1492. Renegades and Moriscos provided Hizir with the intelligence he needed: where to attack, where to land, and how to get there without getting lost or running aground. Some corsairs, and probably Hizir as well, sent the Moriscos ashore days or weeks ahead, where they dressed as Spaniards, spoke the language, and learned all they could about local defenses and local plunder.

Leading his men ashore on the coast of Andalusia, Hizir marched at their head quickly toward the target, capturing and interrogating locals as they came across them, demanding to know what forces—and what riches—were in the area. Often they marched several miles (kilometers) inland, or even more. They attacked swiftly, with great surprise. As quickly as possible they rounded up and bound men, women, and children, and marched them just as quickly back to the shore where the galleys were waiting. Corsairs captured whole villages in this manner, carrying an entire population to the Barbary coast as slaves, some of them to be ransomed, but most of them to provide labor. Many of the women would end their days as wives of Turks, Moors, Moriscos, or renegades.

Having plundered the coast, Hizir sailed to Minorca to replenish his provisions. He had made arrangements with merchants there, having done business with them in the past. They received him, as usual, with open arms. But Hizir was no fool. Something about the Minorcans' manner gave them away, and he realized he and his retinue were being led into a trap. He avoided it, returned to his galleys, and took a troop of well-armed men to punish the locals. Following a shepherd fleeing with his flock, they discovered the path to a small coastal castle. With thirty men Hizir besieged it, leaving the remainder of his force behind to protect their rear. The fight was fierce, and the Minorcans killed several of Hizir's men. Rallying the remainder, he led them in a charge against the main door. Hizir himself took an ax to the heavy timbers, chopping a breach into the portal. Their lust for blood and plunder heightened by the fear and adrenaline of the close fight, the corsairs surged into the castle, captured it, and carried away forty prisoners as slaves.

Elated by the success of his punitive raid, Hizir sent the slaves to his galleys and led another expedition ashore, manning it with those who had earlier been his rear guard. Soon he found another small castle worthy of his blood and ax blows. But the resistance was greater this time, and he had no time for a long siege. The defenders knew what their fate would be if they failed; many would have rather died than been carried away as slaves. Soon, the corsairs realized they "might be taken between two fires"—a force of sixty mounted men, supported by a troop of armed men afoot, was at their backs. Hizir was trapped.

Hizir was no fool. Something about the Minorcans' manner gave them away, and he realized he and his retinue were being led into a trap.

He attempted to lead his men away, the cavalry and infantry in hot pursuit, taunting the fleeing corsairs. "O damned Turks!" they shouted, "don't run away! Turn your faces toward ours! Do not believe you can escape us! This land will be your downfall!"

Hizir arrested his flight and turned to face the Minorcans. Nineteenth-century historian Charles Farine wrote that he and his corsairs were of "firm heart, resolved to sell their lives dearly." They would fight as if they were already dead, for paradoxically in such extremes is victory often snatched from long, almost impossible odds. "There is no God but Allah, and Mohammed is his prophet," they prayed, and with these words hurled themselves at their pursuers. Their arms were light—harquebus and bow, scimitar and lance, ax and dagger—but they were enough to turn the ground as dark and bloody as the dirt floor of an abattoir. Hizir saw a gap in the Minorcan force and immediately led his men in a headlong charge into it, and with their scimitars they carved a breach and slipped through it to freedom.

The corsairs retreated safely to the galleys. Hizir swore revenge, but soon a slave informed him that a Spanish fleet had been signaled from a mountaintop, and if he did not soon depart he would be trapped. He was no match for a force of large carracks fitted out as warships and accompanied by great war galleys. He led his light galleys away, first vowing in writing, it is said, to return and enslave the Minorcans' wives and daughters. He wrapped his threatening missive in silk, attached it to a horse, and sent the horse toward the village. But his vengeance had to wait another day.

Still, as already suggested, fortune is perverse and has a way of smiling on the daring, no matter their purpose. En route home to Djerba, Hizir espied four merchant ships somewhere along the Italian coast. In some accounts they were Spanish, in others Genoese. Swiftly his galleys pulled toward them, but the merchant crews did not put up a fight. They took to their ships' boats and escaped, wisely abandoning their ships and cargoes to the plundering Barbary corsairs. Today, at least, these seamen would not be captured and bartered in the slave market at Tunis. Doing their duty, and hoping their ships and cargoes would be recovered as well, they gave warning and soon word reached the Genoese, who dispatched a pirate-hunting flotilla.

Eight Christian vessels, Corsican some accounts say, were soon on the heels of the Muslim corsairs. Hizir engaged them; the fight was long. Two of his galleys were captured. Hizir led his galley against the flagship, but neither vessel gained the upper hand. In the end, both squadrons retreated, but the corsairs were able to recover their two captured vessels.

When Hizir finally returned to Djerba from his cruise—and in some accounts he had made as many as three cruises, one each in the fall, winter, and spring, while in others he had made no cruise at all—he was said to have captured more than two dozen vessels and 5,600 prisoners, an incredible haul. He divided the plunder among his crews, but kept the prisoners as slaves for himself, Aruj, and Isaac. By making great raids along the Christian coasts, the corsair brothers had begun to change the face of the Mediterranean.

BARBAROSSA II

With their newfound wealth and power, the brothers, Aruj in particular, resolved to attempt Bougie again in 1514. Without doubt they intended to make it their own, their alliance with its former ruler notwithstanding. But it would be no easier this time than it was when Aruj lost his arm. With a dozen galliots and 1,100 of their own men, plus Moors from the area surrounding Bougie, the corsairs attacked. The siege went well at first, and the outer fortifications fell. But the city walls were another matter, and even as the corsairs thought they might prevail, a Spanish relief force of five galleons arrived with troops for the garrison. Almost simultaneously, fall rains lured many of the local Moorish warriors away to their fields. After fewer than two months the corsairs were again forced to retreat from Bougie.

To truly understand the brothers, one must understand their goals, and thus their persistence in attacking Bougie. Beginning as pirates, they had slowly graduated to legitimate corsairs. But their goal, once they had established themselves on the Barbary coast, was no longer to merely profit from the sea, if that was ever their goal at all. They wanted and needed a permanent base, as this was the only way to reap great profit from theft at sea and upon shore. The Barbary coast at the time was in flux, a hodgepodge of port cites held variously by local chiefs or Spanish garrisons, often at odds with and even at war with inland tribes. To rule a port city was to have a base not only from which to raid both land and sea but also from which to rule both coastal and inland peoples, and thus profit from them as well. It is well to remember that, whatever their faith or nationality, sea rovers were foremost about profit via plunder. And the three remaining corsair brothers knew that to control their sea-roving destinies to greatest effect they had to first control a port city.

In 1516, King Ferdinand of Spain died, and the Moorish inhabitants of Algiers, a city held by Spain, decided the time was ripe to overthrow the Spanish garrison. Nearby ruler Sheik Selim agreed to help, and in return he would rule Algiers. Having neither cannon nor ships, he made a pact with Aruj, and together they defeated the garrison and retook the city. Aruj, however, had other plans, and quickly his scimitar was slick with Selim's blood. The city now belonged entirely to the corsairs. Aruj quickly consolidated his power, defeating both a Spanish attack and a Moorish rival who intended to expel the interloping Turkish corsairs.

But Aruj did not long enjoy his newfound kingdom. History records that Spanish Lieutenant García de Tineo is said to have struck him down with a pike thrust as Aruj fought, one-armed, against an invading force in 1518. De Tineo also struck off Barbarossa's head, the image of which was forever after borne on the de Tineo coat of arms. Isaac, by some accounts, was killed in the same battle. Now only Hizir was left to carry the crimson mantle wrought in blood by the corsair brothers.

Immediately, in honor of his brother, Hizir took for his own the nom de guerre the Italians had given Aruj. Hizir's hair was auburn, perhaps close enough to red to bear the name, but others say he dyed his hair and great beard red with henna. Barbarossa might be dead, yet Barbarossa still lived.

Barbarossa was the pirate who became the government who authorized the pirate.

For more than a decade afterward, Hizir, known as Barbarossa, raided the Mediterranean, a pirate who had become a corsair by becoming pasha of Algiers—a corsair, after all, was but a pirate with a license from an established government. Barbarossa was the pirate who became the government who authorized the pirate. The strategy was both cunning and effective.

In 1532 he led the Ottoman navy victoriously against Andrea Doria, and was soon after appointed admiral of the Ottoman navy. Barbarossa quickly improved the navy by teaching the Ottomans how to build effective fighting ships, and also how to handle them in a single fight or in a fleet engagement. Over the next decade he led the new Ottoman navy to a string of great victories. Perhaps his most notable victory was over the now seventy-year-old Andrea Doria in 1538 at Preveza, Greece, in which Barbarossa's ability to remain clear-headed and patient until the time for aggressive action arrived proved to be the critical factor. Here he wisely avoided engaging Doria's heavily armed ships until the wind died, and then he struck victoriously, destroying thirteen ships and capturing thirty-six, without the loss of a single Ottoman vessel. Hizir could do what many could not: he could take the tactics, strategies, and lessons learned in one form of combat and apply them to another, and on a greater scale. He took what he learned as a corsair, whose warfare was unconventional, and applied it to conventional tactics on a great scale. His victory at

Preveza gave the Ottoman Empire control over the western Mediterranean waters until its defeat at Lepanto (now the Gulf of Patras, Greece) in 1571.

But the battle of Preveza was also an omen. At one point, Barbarossa sent a large number of galleys to overwhelm the isolated great "Galleon of Venice." They surged forth, intending to overwhelm it with numbers. The galleon's admiral, Condalmiero, waited until they were within harquebus range, then opened fire. His great guns shattered the approaching galleys as they came within point-blank range. One sank, and many others were crippled. Barbarossa pulled his galleys back and ordered them to attack in waves, firing their great guns at longer range, then withdrawing, as several galleys might do when attacking a single ship. Even then, the Galleon of Venice could not be captured or sunk. The days of the galley as a great warship were numbered. The marriage of large cannon in large numbers to large ships began to doom galley attacks on sailing ships, even those of many against one.

Hizir was sixty-three years old, or even older perhaps, when he died of a fever in 1546, this man, this Barbarossa II, who was born on the island of Lesbos, the son of a retired Janissary, probably Albanian, who became a potter, and a Greek woman who was said to be the widow of a Christian priest. As a pirate, corsair, and naval commander, Barbarossa ranks as one of the greatest in history. None surpasses him in deed or renown. He was known by many names and titles, including Arch-Pirate, Arch-Corsair, Pasha of Algiers, Ruler of Algeria, and High Admiral of the Ottoman Empire, but he was known best, including by many of his enemies, as Kheir-ed-Din, Defender of the Faith, a title bestowed upon him by the ruler of the Ottoman Empire.

Ultimately, he was also one of the few who succeeded in making the transition from sea rover to navy admiral, and from commander of warriors to effective ruler of people—from common sea thief to corsair captain to empire builder. Yet Barbarossa will always be known foremost as a corsair, as a swift, deadly, plundering warrior of the sea. For almost three centuries after his death, Turkish and Barbary corsairs practiced his tactics successfully along Christian coasts as far as the North Sea. Although his corsair galliots and galleys are long gone, and also the fear that stirred in many at the sight of them, the wake they left behind is not.

CHAPTER 2

GRACE O'MALLEY

1530?–1603

THE WARRIOR PIRATE WHOSE GUERILLA-LIKE TACTICS WERE FEARED THROUGHOUT IRELAND

As the Algerian corsair drew close aboard, its great guns, swivels, and muskets all spitting fire, the captain of its intended prey, an Irish galley, lay in the cabin at the stern, recovering from giving birth to a baby boy the day before. Hopefully the newborn was deep in sleep near his mother, and took no note of the loud violence above.

The galley's master, fearing defeat, even if only as a remote possibility, respectfully beseeched the woman to come on deck so that her presence would inspire her crew. The "Algerine" corsairs, better known as Barbary pirates, would be thrust aside only with great violence sustained by great courage, and courage is always more likely with an inspiring example. Muskets played heavily on the Irish galley, and the corsairs not handling artillery or firearms waved their scimitars fiercely, a signal to surrender as well as a threat of what would come to pass if they did not.

Based on accounts of similar battles—as this one is lost to history—both vessels were almost certainly pirate galleys, although in fact neither crew would acknowledge such crime in themselves, but only in others. The Irish galley, for example, was regarded as a pirate by everyone but those who sent her to sea, that is, the O'Malleys and their people. Likewise the Algerine: a pirate in everyone's eyes except those of the Ottoman Turks and North Africans of the Barbary coast. For this Irish captain and crew, the sea was a great part of their lawful "maintenance," and their "thefts" at sea were merely the harvesting of what they believe was by right theirs to take. For this Algerian captain and crew, a fair number of whom were probably renegade Europeans, a similar attitude reigned.

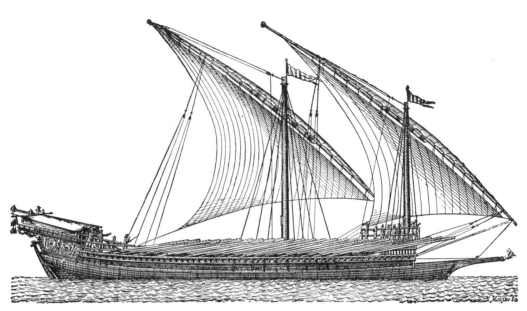

GALLEY RUNNING BEFORE THE WIND.
(*Jurien de la Gravière*.)

Only those vessels whose nations paid tribute were exempt from attack, and sometimes not even then. Profit was often put before honor, especially if no one was looking.

The Irish galley may have been making a mere transit from one place to another, rather than cruising for prey as often it did. Its captain, or perhaps she was its admiral, was pregnant when they put to sea, not a condition for a cruise in which violence was intended. This is not to suggest that potential prey would have been passed up—the O'Malleys were not known for their timid disposition and would be unlikely in almost any circumstance to pass up the chance to steal a poorly defended merchantman.

The Barbary corsairs—variously called "Salley rovers," Turks, Moors, and Algerines—often ranged into the Atlantic, and attacks on English and Irish shores were not unknown. Slave raiders primarily, they used their galleys as the Irish did: to attack weak merchant shipping, and to make quick raids ashore for prisoners and other booty.

At a distance, there was little to tell the galleys apart, other than their sails. The Irish sail was square, the Algerine lateen, or triangular. The Irish had thirty oars or fifteen banks, the Algerine eighteen to twenty-four banks,

Pictured is Mediterranean galley of the sort Grace O'Malley might have fought against in her action against a Barbary corsair. At the bow is a long boarding prow or spur, and at least two great guns, as cannons were called at sea, would have been mounted just aft within the forecastle. Little is known of the appearance or construction of Irish galleys, but they were probably similar yet simpler: sturdy square-rigged two-masted vessels lacking boarding spur and great guns.
The Story of the Nations, 1890, by Stanley Lane-Poole

and was larger overall. The Irish probably had a single mast with a fighting top, and a small deck or "castle" aft, and perhaps one forward as well. The Algerine also had a mast, or perhaps two, a platform astern, and a sharp boarding prow forward. The Irish galley was sleek, narrow, shallow-drafted, and swift—like the Algerine. The Irish might have had swivel guns on its rails where they could be fitted between the oars, and possibly at least one great gun, or cannon, in the bow, although there are no records of such artillery. The Algerine assuredly had swivel guns on its rails, and may have had two or even more great guns in the bow.

Chances are, each vessel mistook the other for prey. It was a rule among pirates and privateers to chase everything, at least until you discovered it might be too much for you. In this case, in the phrase of the day, each galley "catch'd a Tartar"— the prey turned out to be predator, and the outcome was anyone's guess.

In the stern cabin the Irish galley's master waited for an answer. Soon enough he got one. "May you be seven times worse off this day twelve months, who cannot do without me for one day," the woman cursed him, then wrapped herself in a blanket, and stepped into action on deck.

Immediately her presence rallied her crew. They might not have feared the enemy, but doubtless many feared defeat, for enslavement would be the result, and most did not have money enough to buy their freedom from Algerian slavery. Even the bravest, most skillful of fighting men might fight better when encouraged, and the weaker when encouraged might fight as the cornered lion rampant. Cursing as fluently as the best of boatswains could, the woman urged her crew to row harder, shoot faster, shout louder. She took a musket, discharged it at the Moorish galley, and shouted at its Barbary crew to "take this from unconsecrated hands!" Women, after all, were expected to remain at home, or at least within doors, after they had given birth, until they had been "churched," or blessed.

The Algerine corsairs were surely taken aback by her female yet martial appearance. Even so—and it quite possibly was—the corsairs nonetheless quickly got over their surprise. An armed woman could be killed by a bullet or cut down by a sword just as an armed man could, and Barbary corsairs were known for their dogged determination in battle.

If the seas were fairly high, oars were useless and the galleys fought under sail, each trying to wear down the other with musketry and artillery until a successful boarding was assured. But we will assume that the Irish seas and airs were calm and light, and so the galleys fought as galleys ought, with men pulling at the oars, drawing their vessels swiftly through the water, making them seem as light as birds of prey on the air, as sleek as sharks in the sea. By now the galleys might have been broadside to broadside, each hoping to kill enough of the other to be able to board and with steel at close range overwhelm those who remained. Each crew loaded and fired its matchlock muskets as quickly as it could, sending lead one galley to the other. The Irish also shot arrows and, when in range, hurled steel- or bronze-tipped darts, which wailed as they flew through the air. In return, the Algerines launched arrows and crossbow bolts. The Irish galley may have put an effective tactic into play: its crew displaced three or four banks or oars, and in their place made "a bulwark with gowns, beds, sails, and other things that no shot" from the Algerine would penetrate. It was difficult to place fighting men between the banks of oars, for there was little room. Although moving men from the three or four banks of oars would slow the galley down, it did make room for musketeers and archers to ply their slaughter upon the enemy.

The Irish crew worked its bloody duty on the Algerine crew. The Turks were known for their savagery in battle, and if they boarded they would fight until no one was left standing. But the Irish may have had an advantage. Equally fierce in battle, they were all fighters, unlike the Algerines, who now manned the oars of their corsair galliots and galleys with slaves, many of them Christian. Only their smallest of vessels, the brigantines of fourteen banks or smaller, were still rowed by warriors, and these were too fragile to make the journey to Ireland.

If it came to boarding, every Irishman, even the oarsmen, would fight, and they might well have outnumbered the opposing Turks and Moors. As many as 100 "good shots" were aboard the Irish galley, armed not only with muskets but also probably bows and darts, long axes, short swords, shields, spears, pikes, and long knives called skeans. If the Moors came alongside, the Irish would fire bullets and arrows into the Algerines, fling darts at their warriors and oarsmen, and thrust and jab with spears, pikes, and perhaps even fire-pikes to keep the Moors at bay. But the Irish did not intend to let the Algerine galley get that close. In battle there was no distinction between fighters and oarsmen, whether they were one and the same or were free and slave: the Irish shot at them all, thinning their ranks and slowing their oars. The Moors hurled threats across the short span of water, mingling them with the cries of wounded warriors whose blood was draining from the deck into the sea.

Soon the Algerine pulled away, its brilliant, richly appointed banner of expensive fabrics and threads still flying, its crew uncowed, its captain perhaps both angry and resigned. Like him, the commander of the Irish galley was no fool; she probably let the Algerine escape, although tradition has it that she captured the Moorish vessel. Both captains' crews were foremost after plunder, not hard knocks. Each would discover more profitable prey another day.

The woman warrior left the galley in its master's hands and returned to her perhaps sleeping, perhaps wailing, son wrapped in a blanket in the stern cabin. For her this may have seemed as no change at all in roles. Fighting a naval action and breastfeeding an infant were each a vital, natural part of her life, and she may have neither seen nor made any separation between them. The English would later say that she "imprudently passed the part of womanhood," but this was not the case at all. She was indeed woman triumphant.

The year was 1567, or near enough, and the season summer, or near enough, when the seas were not so rough and galleys could fight under oars. The infant's name was Theobold, but he would become better known as Tibbet-ne-Long, or "Toby of the Ships," given the circumstances of his birth. His mother's name was Gráinne Ní Mháille—Grace O'Malley, in English—but she would become better known as Granuaile, the Pirate Queen.

A "NOTORIOUS WOMAN" COMES OF AGE

Grace O'Malley was more than merely a woman in a man's role: she was a master of men in a profession invariably reserved for men. Not merely a sea captain, she was a pirate captain who took to arms and not only used them as well as a man did but was also as willing as a man to use them. The sole child of Dubhdara "Black Oak" O'Malley and his wife Margaret, Grace was born around 1530 into a powerful maritime clan. Dubhdara was the hereditary lord of Umhall, which the English called the "Owles," a territory adjoining the tortuous, island- and inlet-ridden waters of Clew Bay on the west coast of Ireland. Their motto was "Powerful by Land and Sea," and indeed they were. Dubhdara's galleys, along with those of the allied O'Flahertys, ruled the western waters of the Emerald Isle.

The O'Malleys, like many pirates throughout history, had multiple related trades. Not only were they pirates—or more likely in their minds, honest sea rovers following an ancient tradition—but they were also maritime mercenaries. For pay they ferried soldiers in support of local clan wars, and they made many

Western Europe circa 1560, Grace O'Malley's bases on the west coast of Ireland provided protection as well as an ideal location from which to strike, even as far as France and Spain. Anyone who dared sail along the west coast of Ireland had to be well-armed, lest they find themselves the prey of Grace's galleys. To the east were the Irish Channel and the English Channel, both of which were significant "choke points" along major trade routes, making them vulnerable to attacks and profitable to pirates. (The dotted line indicates the route of the Spanish Armada in 1588.)

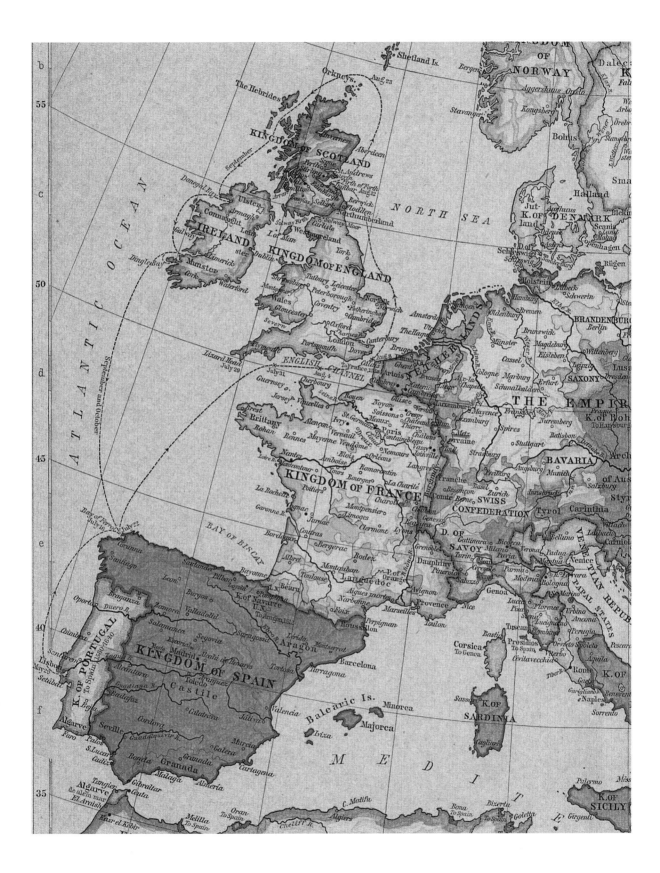

trips bringing the Scottish Gallowglass mercenaries to fight in Ireland. For pay they attacked the shipping and raided the villages of a warring clan. Ruling the local seas, they granted licenses to fish in these waters, and captured those vessels that had no license. Perhaps most commonly, the O'Malleys themselves fished the Irish waters in leather-hulled boats called curraghs and exported the catch.

The O'Malley clan's most notorious trade was an ancient one: Irish pirates had been around since the days of the Romans and probably long before. During the Viking Age, the Norsemen were not the only ones to commit plundering slave raids on the Irish and English coasts: "Afterwards Griffith and those Irish pyrates, joining their powers together, passed over the river Wie, and burn[ed] Dumenham, and slue man, woman, and childe, leaving nothing behind them, but bloud and ashes ... the Irish returned home merrily, loaden with spoyle."

Grace O'Malley probably did go to sea as a young girl. According to legend, when her father first told her she could not because her long hair would catch in the rigging, she cut it, giving her the anglicized nickname Granuaile (pronounced "granya-wail"), whose Irish version meant she had cropped hair. And there may be some truth to the legend, for sailors usually wore their hair short or braided in a queue so that it would not be caught in a block as rigging was drawn through it.

But O'Malley's first rise to power was not aboard an Irish pirate galley, or in any circumstance of sword or storm at sea. She was married at fifteen to an O'Flaherty chieftain named Dónal, and within a few years and at the behest of O'Flaherty clansmen, she for all practical purposes usurped her feckless husband's role as clan leader. When Dónal was killed after recapturing Cock's Castle from the Joyces, who had stolen it from him, O'Malley led his clan in its defense. So diligent was she that she and her followers routed the Joyces. Reportedly, the fortification was renamed Hen's Castle in her honor.

With the death of her first husband in 1560, another O'Flaherty was appointed in his place, leaving O'Malley largely powerless, at least according to law and custom. But where they denied it to her, she simply seized power, recruiting O'Flaherty warriors and returning to her father's lands, where, with O'Malley galleys and 200 men, she began to wage a piratical campaign.

Without doubt she was a superb mariner who understood not only seamanship but also combat at sea, and she was successful as a pirate. She proved many times that she was a superb warrior ashore, and she was a courageous one both on water and on land. Her appearance is unknown, but she may have looked as the typical

Irish woman was described: "comely, tall, slender, and upright," with fair skin, freckles, and blond hair. Certainly, she was physically and mentally tough—she had to be—and was physically strong as well, for the weapons of her day required strength to wield. Taken all together, this can account for much of her success, but certainly not all of it. Although there are ancient examples of warrior queens among the Celts (and among the Britons, too), O'Malley's society was patriarchal and male dominated. Doubtless, as a female leader of male warriors, she had to display not only competence in martial skills and leadership but also exceptional prowess to earn the respect of her followers, beyond what a male commander would have been expected to prove in arms, tactics, and courage.

Part of her success as a *female* leader certainly lay in her relationship with her male warriors. That she cared for those who followed her is undoubted, for she said that she "would rather have a shipful of Conroys and MacAnallys than a shipful of gold." She led them to success, and she did all she could to avoid failing them. They were more than mere crewmen; as members of her clan, they were extended family.

However, beyond this loyalty earned in part by devotion, clan ties to her crew, and success, it is likely that Grace O'Malley's male crews fought even more stoutly for her than they would have for most male captains, helping ensure her success. In a male-dominated society, men serving in battle under a woman probably felt they had something to prove, particularly if the woman bore arms under fire and led from the front, swinging a cutting sword and splitting skulls as she did. Indeed, in most endeavors traditionally considered masculine—warfare, the practice of arms and military arts in general, seamanship, exploration, hunting, and physically demanding sport, as well as trades demanding significant physical labor—men have a tendency to want to prove at the very least their inherent physical superiority. Often they go to great lengths, quite amusing at times, to avoid being bettered by a woman. And often enough, to even greater amusement, these great lengths fail.

That O'Malley, a woman, was a match for any of her followers, and superior to most, most likely inspired their respect and loyalty, as well as a desire to prove themselves worthy by striving to keep up with her, no matter how skilled she may have been. Perhaps some were even shamed into exceptional courage in battle. A crew fired up in this way would fight to the death for a captain like Grace O'Malley. She would soon be known—and feared—throughout Ireland and as far away as Scotland, England, France, Portugal, and Spain.

A MOST FAMOUS FEMININE SEA CAPTAIN

The pirate's purpose was always plunder—profit, that is. And the best way to do that was to be a wolf among sheep, a falcon among doves, a shark among herring. Even so, the successful pirate knew when to fight and when to run. With her light, swift galleys, manned with as many as 100 men, of whom all could bear arms, and based in waters virtually impossible to attack from the sea, O'Malley was indeed a predator among largely defenseless prey.

In many ways, the galley was ideal for coastal Irish waters. Although unsuited for heavy seas, the galley didn't need to bother with the wind; it could be rowed from place to place. With its shallow draft, it could hug the coastline during transits, and if necessary, draw itself into the many small coves and inlets along the coast. From accounts of various galley attacks on merchant shipping both in the Mediterranean and the Northern seas, we have a good idea of what it might have been like when an O'Malley galley attacked a passing merchant vessel.

Just south of the Aran Islands lay a 200-ton (181 metric ton) merchant ship, becalmed. It was a "round ship," as the French called them, and was built with a big belly for cargo. This one was larger than many trading vessels, but by no means was it the largest of its sort. From France, in its hold was cargo of wine intended for trade at Galway not far to the northeast. These ships carried a variety of cargo—potential plunder—to the west coast of Ireland: wine, oil, salt, spices, and iron, among other commodities. On their return route they most often carried wool, hides, fish, and timber. At least some gold and silver coin was aboard these ships as well.

A lookout aboard the Irish galley, perhaps with O'Malley herself in command, spotted the ship. The captain gave the orders: the rudder was put to starboard and the oarsmen took up their oars to give chase. These fighting mariners lit matches with which to fire their muskets. If they carried firepots, they used the match to light them as well. They loaded their firearms and strung their bows.

Conditions were perfect for the galley at sea: the wind was calm or light, and the current was not strong. The prey could go nowhere. Even better, the water was too deep for an anchorage, so the ship could let go an anchor and create a "spring," which it could use to turn the ship and bring its broadside to bear. Most likely, the merchantman would surrender immediately, knowing it could neither run nor fight.

The Irish galley approached from the stern, out of the way of the ship's broadside of small cannon, for there were enough of them to wreak havoc on the galley's unprotected oarsmen. The crew brandished swords and other glinting

weapons at the merchantman, trying to intimidate its crew into surrendering. When in range, the galley's captain hailed the ship and called upon its captain to surrender without bloodshed. She ordered her crew to fire a few muskets into the ship's limp sails, effectively punctuating her request. And for a moment the merchant captain intended to comply.

But suddenly the wind rose, a light breeze, enough that if it freshened, the merchantman might make a few knots and escape, providing it could keep the nearby galley at bay. The merchant captain ordered two cannon to be fired astern, and a luckily placed round shot tore fore and aft through the galley, killing a few oarsmen and men-at-arms, but leaving the galley's seaworthiness intact. Immediately, the Irish replied with a volley directed at the gunports, hoping "their small-shot [would] soon beat the gunners from their ports with little danger to themselves, for no great number of small-shot can play upon them out of the narrowness of the poop." The fight was on!

The merchantman, hoping fortune would favor him this day, chose to run. The ship could have turned suddenly upon the galley and fired a broadside, but the wind was light and the turn would have been slow, giving the galley time to change its course and avoid the iron hail. The galley's musketeers fired at the stern ports each time one opened, forcing the gunners to close the ports and take cover. Anyone else who appeared was likewise targeted. The galley came close aboard, the oarsmen drawing its prow toward the quarter where they would board. In a last act of courageous desperation, the stern gunners made two shots at the galley. One of them "hulled" the oared vessel just below the waterline on the starboard side. Quickly, the galley began to take on water.

But the galley's captain knew well how to handle this emergency. Immediately, she ordered the starboard oarsmen to the opposite side. The weight caused the galley to list, or lean, and the hole was raised above the waterline. The carpenter

Early matchlock musket or arquebus. In general, the difference between the two was in caliber and weight: the musket was larger and required a forked rest to prop up its barrel, while the arquebus, or hackbut as it was often called, was smaller and did not require a rest. However, the term *arquebus* sometimes refers to both firearms. The musket and arquebus had the same firing mechanism, consisting of a lock that applied a burning slow match to a small pan primed with gunpowder, which, when ignited, fired the charge in the barrel. Early versions had a lever for a trigger, while later versions were installed with the conventional trigger we are all familiar with. The matchlock ignition system had some drawbacks: its match gave off smoke and, at night, a light, both of which could warn an enemy.
INTERFOTO/Alamy

Muk H.

Inishmurray

Sligo Bay

Downpatrick H.

Killala Bay

Stags of Broadhaven

Benwee H.

Broad Haven

Easky

Ballysadare B.

Coney I.

Erris H.

Glenamoy

Ballycastle

Easky R.

Dromore

SLI

Betraille

Mullet Pen.a

Carrowmore L.

Killala

Easky L.

Inishkea Is.

Crossmolina

Ballina

Ardnaree

Achonry

Slieve Car 2363

Lough Conn

St. Connell Mts.

Tobercurry

Blacksod Bay

Tulaghan

Nephin Beg 3368 Mts.

R. Moy

Foxford

Achill H.

L. Cullen

Swineford

Ballaghaderr

Achill I.

M Castlebar A

Y O R

Achill Sound

Newport

Kilkelly

Clare I.

Clew Bay

Westport

Balla

Ballyhaunis R.

Emlagh Pt.

Ballyglass

C

Croagh Patrick O

Clare A

Inishturk

Louisburgh

N N

Bally

Inishbofin

Killary Harb.

Mulrea Mt. 2685

L. Carra

Robe

Hollymount

Dunmore

Inishark

Lough Mask

Ballinrobe

Glen

Ballynakill Har.

High I.

Joyce's Country

Kilmaine

Cong

Tuam

Twelve Pins 2396

L. Inagh

Clifden

Mamturk Mts.

Shrule

Mannin B.

Ballynahinch

Oughterard

Headford

Mt. Bell

Slyne Head

Connemara

Lough Corrib

G A L W A

Roundstone Bay

Birterbury

Iarconnaught

R. Clare

Moniva

St. Johns (Newfoundland) 2165 Miles

New York 2700 Miles

Killkieran B.

Galway

Athenry

Oranmore

Garomna I.

Cashla B.

Galway Bay

Inishmore

Black H.

Kinvarra

Aran Is.

Inishmaan

Inisheer

Ballyvaghan

Stieve P.

Gort

and a boy quickly plugged the hole. The merchantman had gained some distance and began to ply its stern guns, now that it was out of effective range of the galley.

Hope may spring eternal in man's breast, as poet Alexander Pope wrote, but the Irish galley quickly closed again on the merchantman. Fortune failed to favor the prey this time. The wind died, the merchantman was again becalmed. This time the merchant captain "struck," as surrender was known at sea, hoping to avoid reprisals from an annoyed Irish captain and her crew. Depending on its cargo, the ship's captain might pay tribute to the O'Malleys in the form of coin or cargo and be released, or might find itself plundered and its crew imprisoned and ransomed— or even murdered, according to accusations leveled against the O'Malleys.

Of course, the battle could have gone differently, had the wind and sea favored the merchantman, or had the prey not been a merchantman but a man-of-war. Under sail in a good wind, a ship could outpace a galley, or outmaneuver it and bring its broadside to bear, slaughtering its oarsmen. If it were a man-of-war, its large crew, in conjunction with the dominating height of a ship's decks over that of a galley, would usually have been able to fend off an attack by a single galley.

Years later, one of Grace O'Malley's galleys was attacked by an English man-of-war, the *Tramontana*, between Teelin and Killybegs. The oarsmen pulled furiously on their oars and ran the galley close inshore, where they hoped to escape the ship's great guns and the slaughter they could make. The captain of the *Tramontana* sent a boat in after the galley to capture it or burn it. The galley did not cooperate, but instead, according to the English captain, "entertained a skirmish with my boat for most of an hour and had put her to the worst." But the *Tramontana* came to the rescue, and with "great shot made an end to the fray." A galley full of musketeers could do little against the great guns of a well-armed, well-manned warship, except run away or die gallantly. Pirates typically preferred the former, although many were quite capable of the latter. At close range, even a small cannon could wreak "horrible carnage and havoc" on oarsmen, its shock stunning those nearby and blowing them from their benches, and "mashing to pieces" those in the line of fire.

O'Malley's galleys without doubt escaped many times from English men-of-war by slipping into coves or inlets, or among the shallow waters and cover of the many small islands off the west coast of Ireland. Her home base in Clew Bay was a nightmare of navigation to those who did not know its secrets, and any pursuer who ran aground there was vulnerable to her galleys. Should an enemy penetrate the bay, it still had to breach her castle walls—the tower at Clare Island early on, and later the castle at

Clew Bay and environs, from which Grace O'Malley ran her piracy, blackmail, and mercenary transport operations. The west coast of Ireland is rugged and tortuous, ideal for piracy and other forms of sea roving. Local Irish pirates such as the O'Malleys knew where the rocks, shallows, safe havens, and ambush sites were, and used them to their best advantage. Clew Bay itself was deep and filled with small islands, making it treacherous to attack without detailed knowledge of its maritime geography.

Rockfleet. Her sea-roving tactics were guerrilla-like: hit and run, attack the vulnerable, flee from the strong, and "go to ground" where none dare follow but at great risk to their lives. It was a wise strategy of profit and of living to plunder another day.

Grace O'Malley and her Irish pirates did not attack ships only at sea. They also attacked them at anchor in port. Slipping in at first light, or even at night if they knew the route well enough to be safe from running aground, a galley could grapple a ship and board before anyone knew what was happening, then sail it out of harbor and carry it to an inlet no one would dare enter.

Sometimes such subtlety was unnecessary. In 1538, for example, weather drove four Portuguese ships with cargoes of wine to the Irish coast. A local pirate agreed to pilot one of the ships into harbor for three tons (2.7 metric tons) of wine. "The ship anchored before the chief island, called Inyshyrcan, in front of the strong fortress called Downighlong. When the gentlemen and pirates of those parts had drunk the said wine, they desired more, and invited some of the said merchants to dinner in the said castle, and detained them there in irons. They then manned their Irish galleys, took the said ship, and distributed 72 tuns of the wines that were in her." Doubtless, O'Malley and her pirates engaged in similar productive deceptions.

The effect of the Pirate Queen's attacks on shipping is proved by the complaint of Galway merchants: "The continuing roads used by the Malleys and Flaherties with their galleys along our coasts, where they have taken sundry ships and barks bound for this poor town, which they have not only rifled to the utter overthrow of the owners and merchants, but also have most wickedly murdered divers of our young men, to the great terror of such as would willingly traffic, the let [delay] and hindrance of our trade, and no small weakening of Her Majesty's service." The merchants asked for 200 soldiers to be used "as well by sea to suppress" their piratical insolence. Surely it must have galled them even more that the leader abusing their shipping and their profits was a woman!

By 1577 Grace O'Malley was known by her English enemies as the most successful and most famous of these "roving rebels"—as the "great spoiler and chief commander and director of thieves and murderers at sea."

"MAINTENANCE BY LAND"

The fact that pirates preferred to take their prey by the easiest means available should not suggest that they in any way lacked courage, although doubtless there have been plenty over the ages who did. In the case of Grace and her O'Malleys,

O'Flahertys, Conroys, MacAnallys, and other clan members, courage was expected and was probably displayed most often ashore during plundering raids or attacks on neighboring clans. As at sea, Grace O'Malley led the way ashore, commanding from the front, always ready to do battle, always using her courage as an example to the men who followed her.

Legend tells us that during an assault on Kinturk Castle in County Mayo, young Toby of the Ships grew fearful and hesitated while under fire, perhaps seeking cover when he should have been moving forward as musket ball and arrow shaft buzzed nearby. "Are you trying to hide behind my backside, the place you came from?" his mother reportedly admonished him. In 1583, Theobald Dillon, an English government official, led forces onto the estate of O'Malley's second husband, Richard-in-Iron Bourke, now known as "The MacWilliam," given that he had become the successor to the chiefdom known as "the MacWilliam of Mayo," to collect rents owed to the English crown. In a letter he recorded the result for posterity: "I went ther hence towards the plas wher McWilliam was, who met me and his wife Grayn Ny Vayle with all ther force, and did swer they wolde hav my lyfe for comyng so furr into ther contrie, and specialie his wife wold fyght with me before she was half a myle nier me." At sea or ashore, O'Malley was as willing as any to come to blows.

In many ways, attacks ashore were more lucrative for O'Malley and her pirates. Not only was there plunder in the form of money, goods, and livestock, but there were also people to hold for ransom. Further, attacks on competing clans helped keep them weak and the O'Malleys strong. Ireland was a country of competing clans engaged in plundering, and often barbaric warfare, complicated by an English invasion and the threat of a Spanish invasion as a means of a backdoor attack on England. Such chaos was fertile ground for piracies on land or sea.

In a typical attack ashore, one of O'Malley's galleys would have slipped by night along the coast. Near dawn, as the horizon began to lighten, almost imperceptibly at first, behind the victim village, the galley would make its run toward shore. It could have landed some distance away and its pirates could have marched in the darkness to the town, but by rowing directly to the town there was less chance of discovery. Perhaps a dog would begin to bark when it heard the sound of oars rubbing on timbers and dipping into the sea; perhaps a fisherman would notice the dog and turn his attention toward the Atlantic. Perhaps he would then notice the tiny glow of a lighted match not hidden below the gunwale, or recognize the creak and splash of oar, or

Illustrated circa 1800, this image is of the meeting between pirate queen Grace O'Malley and Queen Elizabeth I of England in July 1593. Although there is no transcript of the conversation itself, Queen Elizabeth did write of the meeting, noting that Grace O'Malley "hath at times lived out of order"—a very polite way of saying she had been a pirate. The pirate queen came off well in the meeting, and was rewarded with the return of "her maintenance by land and sea"—another polite term for being a pirate. That Grace O'Malley was received before the queen of England proves how powerful and well regarded she had become.

even spot a dark form on the water that stood out from the darkness behind it. And perhaps he would even give the alarm.

But it would be too late. With the galley now ashore, and, with but a small number left behind to guard the vessel, most of its 100 men would leap over its sides and rush toward the village. Part would attack the small castle, charging its gate and scaling its walls, while the other part would secure the village itself, cutting down anyone who stood in the way. Villagers who could, fled with what they could. The rest would be rounded up, and some made prisoner and forced to go aboard the galley. Those in the castle had no place to flee. Some would be taken prisoner for ransom, others perhaps as hostages for cattle or other goods to be paid to the O'Malleys later. Others might be killed in reprisal for raids against the O'Malleys, for Irish warfare of the period was brutal and bloodthirsty.

Their dirty deed done, galley and crew would slip away to sea before a counterattack could be organized. Back in their element, none dared attack them, and, barring storm or English man-of-war, they would soon be home again.

Against sworn enemies, Grace O'Malley could combine cold-blooded focus with the cunning of a fox. Around 1565, for example, seeking revenge against the clan MacMahon of Doona Castle after they murdered her lover, Hugh de Lacy, she waited until they made a pilgrimage to Caher Island. Quickly her galleys rowed across the water, cut off the MacMahon boats from escape, and captured them.

Leading her men ashore, she routed and captured the MacMahons, put several to death, then commanded her galleys across the water to Doona Castle and captured it. Fear typically expands beyond its bounds, and O'Malley had shown she could be merciless. Who would not surrender on land or sea when faced by the Pirate Queen, sword or musket in hand, and a hundred or two of her warriors at her side?

A LEGEND IN AND BEYOND HER TIME

Even beyond her piracies on land and sea, the life of Grace O'Malley, compiled largely by historian Anne Chambers, reads as a romantic adventure, as the escapades of a swashbuckling *picara*. She became a pirate after the death of her first husband. She rescued Hugh de Lacy, the shipwrecked son of a wealthy merchant, became his lover, then brutally avenged his death after he was murdered by the clan MacMahon. She married her second husband, Richard-in-Iron Bourke, probably to take advantage of his strong castle, divorced him, gave birth to their son Tibbet-ne-Long, then strategically remarried him, all in furtherance of her clan and piracies. In 1577 she was captured while plundering Desmond and spent nearly two years in prison.

When Richard-in-Iron Bourke led his forces in rebellion against the English, she was released on a promise to bring his activities to a halt. Instead, she renewed her piracies. In 1584 she raised forces against the English governor of Ireland. Two years later she was captured and a gallows erected to make an end of her, but she was released upon an exchange of hostages. She soon supported the attempted Spanish invasion, and in 1589 was accused of treason.

By 1591 she was left largely impotent by superior English naval forces and unable to practice her trade, so in 1593 she made a direct appeal to Queen Elizabeth of England, blaming her piracies on the need to maintain her clan. She was granted an audience of which we unfortunately have no account, but surely it was a fascinating meeting between two brilliant women who wielded a man's power in a man's world. Soon after, Grace O'Malley was granted the authority to "employ all her power to offend and prosecute any offender against us [England]." Once more, Gráinne Ní Mháille commanded galleys on the Irish waters and practiced her sea-roving trade. She died in 1603, a brilliant leader, tactician, and warrior, and one of the great sea rovers of history.

CHAPTER 3

☠

FRANCIS DRAKE

1540?-1596

SINGEING THE SPANISH BEARD WITH DARING, COURAGE, AND SURPRISE TACTICS

For an hour the well-armed men had lain in ambush in the long grass, 50 feet (15 m) from the narrow Spanish road that led from Panama City to Nombre de Dios, before they heard the deep sounding bells of the approaching mule train. Half of the armed men lay on one side of the road, and farther down the road lay the other half so that they might not shoot each other by accident at night. An hour was only a short time to lay in ambush, yet moments still seemed like minutes and minutes like hours as the attackers lay there waiting, sweating in the heat of day, hearing nothing but the sounds of their own breathing and the insects buzzing around them. But soon, as the eighteen English pirates among them hoped, they would have what they had marched nine days through the jungle and across the savanna for.

With these pirates were thirty *Cimarrón* warriors, whom the English referred to as "Cimaroons" and "Maroons." Descendants of African slaves who had escaped from the Spanish and founded their own independent nations in the jungles of Honduras, the *Cimarrónes* had led the pirates to this spot, two leagues from the small town of Venta de Cruces that lay between Nombre de Dios on the Atlantic Coast and Panama City on the Pacific. These piratical seamen and rebel warriors had moved without discovery, though they had passed many times within sight of the great city of Panama itself. Four warriors had led the way a mile (1.6 km) in advance, quietly breaking branches to mark the trail. A dozen more had marched as the vanguard, or "forlorn," as the English often called it, and another dozen as the rearguard. In the center the pirates and their captain had trekked, along with the two *Cimarrón* chiefs. All had moved with the greatest silence and secrecy, for upon this not only the success of their venture depended, but their lives as well.

And now they waited in the tall grass, their arms at the ready. "To conquer by patience" was their unwritten motto, and in less than an hour it would pay off when the time came to leap up from their hiding places and violently seize the moment. It was January 1573.

Commanding these weary yet sharply alert raiders was Francis Drake. Perhaps thirty years old or so, he was short but "of strong limbs" and "broad breasted." His hair was brown, his beard full, and "his eyes rounde, large and clear." Admirers said he was "well favored, fair, and of cheerful countenance," although detractors, and even some less biased observers, noted that he was often haughty and vainglorious, and wanted to "rule fortune." In speech he was gifted: he loved to speak, he knew of what he spoke, he was eloquent, and his words were bold. Although Drake would listen to any man's counsel, he would invariably follow his own. Most important, though, he bore well the weight of command, even in the direst of circumstances.

This was Drake's third voyage as commander of an expedition, and to say that all had not gone as planned was a gross understatement. Little more than eight months before, in May 1572, they had set sail from Plymouth, England, seventy-three men and boys in two small vessels, the *Pascha* of seventy tons (63.5 metric tons) and the *Swan* of twenty-five (22.6 metric tons). Arriving at Puerto Faisán on the Isthmus of Darien, Colombia, Drake discovered that the supplies he had hidden on his previous voyage of reconnaissance had been stolen. Refusing to permit the circumstance to take him aback even in the slightest, he ordered his men to assemble the large, swift boats called pinnaces they carried in the hold. Transferring from their ships to their pinnaces, Drake and his pirates—for indeed they were pirates, having no written commission from their queen—rowed as quietly as they could until they reached Nombre de Dios, the destination of Spanish silver carried overland from Panama to be picked up by the treasure ships. Here, Drake told his men, was a weak, unwalled, rich town, which, if they prevailed, could make them rich and also "recompense" the wrongs the Spaniards had committed against him.

Armed with large matchlock muskets as well as smaller ones called calivers, small shields called targets, longbows, crossbows, partisans, pikes, and fire-pikes, they attacked one night in July 1572, easily capturing the small battery of cannon and dismounting them.

Quickly, though, alarm spread through the town, for having often born the brunt of *Cimarrón* attacks, it was always on guard. Drake ordered a dozen men to stay behind and protect the boats, their only means of escape. With the remainder he charged into Nombre de Dios at their head. The fire-pikes, which were nothing more than pikes topped with a jar of burning combustibles at the end, frightened many of the inhabitants and, more important, lighted the pirates' way, casting long, flickering shadows upon the streets and walls of the colonial town.

The pirates advanced toward the marketplace, and soon received a volley of musket shot from a hastily assembled line of *mosqueteros*. But many of their shots fell short, the lead projectiles burrowing harmlessly into the sand. Drake's men heartily returned the compliment, firing a volley of musket and caliver. Drake now ordered his bowmen into action, and quickly their "fine roving" arrows flew at the Spaniards. As soon as the deadly arrows had left their bows, Drake ordered a charge. Doubtless the sudden assault at close quarters took the Spaniards by surprise. Breathing heavily from excitement, fear, and exertion, the men on the two sides soon came to deadly blows. The pirates hacked and thrust with good English swords, they shoved fire-pikes into the faces of defenders and half pikes into their bellies, they turned their muskets about and clubbed anything that stood in their way. The line broke, and the Spanish retreated. Several of the attackers were injured as they tripped over the sharp arms the defenders had abandoned.

By the English account, Nombre de Dios should by now have belonged to Drake's pirates. Their captain at their head, they broke into the Casa Real, or the king's treasure house, where they claimed to have found an incredible booty: "a pile of bars of silver of … seventy feet in length, of ten feet in breadth, and twelve feet in height, piled up against the wall, each bar was between thirty-five and forty pounds in weight [approximately 21 by 3.6 m, each bar between 16 and 18 kg]."

But as Drake had already learned, fortune is fickle and will have no master— and he who thinks he has mastered her is a fool. Word came that their boats were in danger of being lost to a Spanish counterattack, and that the town was far better defended than they had realized.

Suddenly, a strong thunderstorm broke upon the Englishmen. The downpour wetted powder and bowstrings, leaving the pirates vulnerable to an attack by the superior number of Spaniards armed with pikes and swords. Although the darkness of the night attack had given the attackers the upper hand, it also denied them the ability to judge their situation accurately. Worse, Drake himself

Twentieth-century lithograph by Jean-Leon Huens, of one of Drake's attacks (probably his successful second attack) on the *recuas*, or mule trains, that traveled across the Isthmus of Darien. In particular, the mule trains ferried silver in the form of bars and pieces of eight from Panama. Originating in the mines of Potosí (in modern Bolivia), the silver was carried overland to Arica, then north by sea to Lima, then Guayaquil, then finally to Panama to be carried across the Isthmus of Darien to Nombre de Dios where it would be loaded aboard the treasure fleet.

National Geographic Image Collection / The Bridgeman Art Library International

Mid-eighteenth-century engraving of the battle between the Spanish treasure fleet and the piratical trading fleet of Sir John Hawkins. The English ships are on the right, attempting to escape from a trap they had unintentionally made for themselves. Ships require "sea room" for effective fighting, and Hawkins's decision to remain at anchor and hold San Juan de Ulloa hostage sealed his fate. Trapped, the English fleet was terribly mauled, and most of the English seamen were killed or captured. Hawkins and Drake escaped, however. The ships in the illustration are fanciful, a combination of sixteenth-, seventeenth-, and eighteenth-century characteristics.

Getty Images

fell weak, having been struck by a Spanish musket ball in the leg. The wound, of which he had told no one at first, eventually bled so profusely that his blood filled some of the footprints of his men. Soon he was unable to lead. His men, dismayed and fearing a strong counterattack, retreated from the city, bearing their captain away against his will. They had but one man slain, the trumpeter, although many were wounded.

Of course, Spanish accounts differ. In one, fourteen or fifteen defenders fired upon the English, killing the trumpeter and wounding Drake, forcing the English to immediately retreat in fear of their lives. Meanwhile, the pirates left behind at the fort sounded their trumpet. Hearing no reply, they too retreated, and when the wounded Drake and his men arrived at the fort, "not finding his men which he left there, he and his [men] were in so great feare" that they left their arms and armor "behind them, and putting off their hose, they swamme, and waded all to their pinneses, and so went with their ships again out of port." Only one Spaniard, a man looking out of a window, was killed. That the pirates retreated in the face of a strong defense is no surprise: pirates were after plunder, and plunder was worthless if they did not live to spend it.

But Drake was no stranger to hardship and even disaster at sea and ashore. He invariably had a ready answer of compelling speech that translated immediately into action—with Drake and his unquenchable ambition at its head. Francis Drake would not permit the defeat at Nombre de Dios, or the tactical retreat from the treasure town, however one might choose to call it, to hold him back.

AMBITION, GREED, AND VENGEANCE

Such was Drake's ambition that not even his modest, some would say humble, origins had ever stood in his way. The oldest of the twelve children of a poor farmer in Crowndale, England, Drake was determined to advance himself, both for his own sake and for his family's. By the time he was fourteen he was both an expert seaman and the apprentice master of a small coasting merchant vessel that was often enough a smuggler as well. When her master died, Drake inherited both the vessel and its command. Quickly he had to learn not only the virtues taught by the hazards of the sea (if they do not kill the student first), but also those taught by the hazards of dealing dangerously with dangerous men, namely: preparation, calculation, perseverance, and adaptability, not to mention courage and quick wits, and the use of arms.

In Devon, Drake entered the service of his kinsmen, the famous seagoing Hawkins family, whose members were determined to profit from Spain's New World wealth, one way or another. In November 1566, he sailed on his first Hawkins expedition, this one commanded by experienced trader John Lovell. In Africa they took on slaves—most likely by force of arms—and sailed thence to the Spanish Main to trade slaves for goods and pieces of eight. At Borburata on the Venezuelan coast, the Spanish refused to trade, so the English forced it upon them, but they came away with only 1,500 pieces of eight. The lever used was made of cold sharp steel.

Things went awry at Rio de la Hacha (in modern day Colombia), where Lovell brought his remaining—and now sickly—slaves to the port to sell. According to Spanish accounts, the inhabitants opened fire on the English, who then withdrew. Perhaps the Spanish papists refused outright to trade with the English heretics, whose captain may not have been forceful enough in trying to push a free market on the proud hidalgos and merchants. Perhaps the local merchants refused to pay for unacceptable "merchandise," for the slaves were at death's door after their long inhuman confinement. Or perhaps the Spanish merchants simply cheated the English out of their profits, for, after all, it was

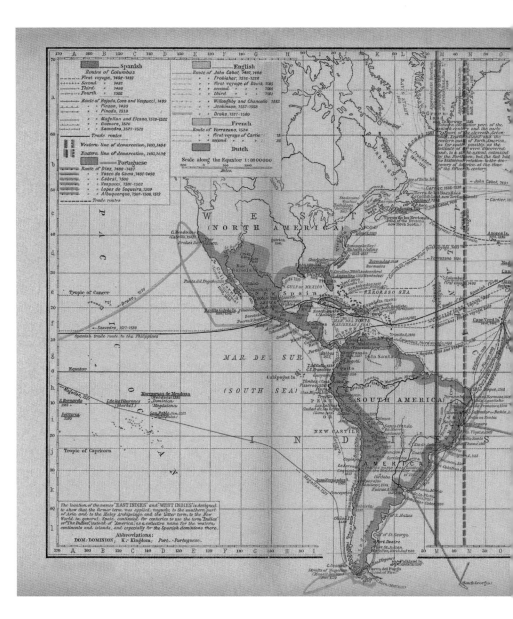

Early twentieth-century map by William R. Shepherd depicting Drake's circumnavigation (in blue), 1577 to 1580. The world-encompassing voyage began as a plundering raid on the Spanish Main, in which Drake and his *Golden Hinde* passed into the South Sea, as the Pacific was then known. Drake attacked along the coast of South and Central America, taking the Spanish by surprise. Too long accustomed to feeling safe along the shores of its Pacific possessions, Spain was caught off guard.

illegal for the English even to trade there in the first place. To Spanish eyes, the English were thieving interlopers, not to mention "Luteranos," as they often called Protestants.

In the end, Lovell abandoned almost a hundred sick slaves ashore and sailed home with ship and crew, first stopping at Hispaniola to raid several small settlements. But the unprofitable voyage surely had a positive effect on the young Francis Drake, for he now realized how rich one might become along the Spanish Main, had he even a small ship and a minimum of arms and men—and provided he was also equipped with courage and tactical wit in abundance.

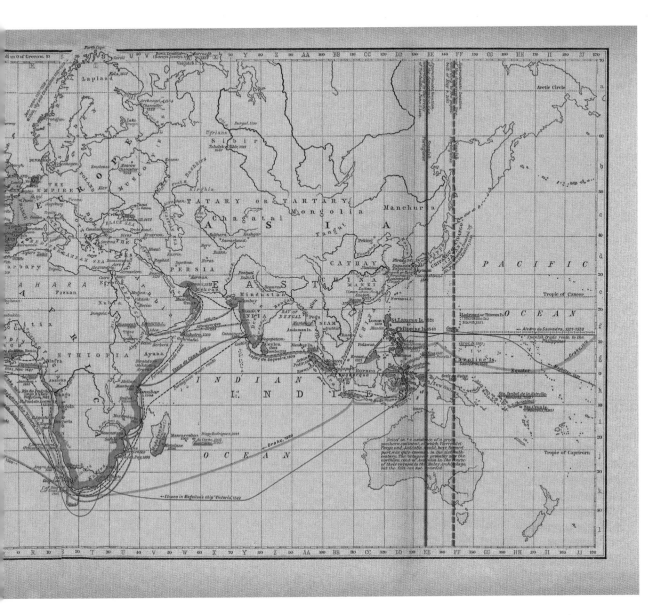

Soon he was at sea again in the same year of his return, 1567. This time, though, he commanded a small, fifty-ton (45 metric tons) vessel, the *Judith*, as part of John Hawkins's third voyage of slave raiding, smuggling, and slave trading. Queen Elizabeth herself invested in the voyage. For Drake, it was doubtless a dream come true to have a command on such a great enterprise of six vessels, ranging from the 700-ton (635 metric ton) *Jesus of Lubeck* to the tiny, forty-ton (36 metric ton) *Angel*.

But again, to say that things did not go well during the adventure is an understatement. Twice the slave raiders were rebuffed on the western coast of Africa. The English landed 150 men on the coast of Senegal, but the Africans sent swarms of arrows into the slave raiders' ranks. A number of Hawkins's men died from poisoned arrows: "Yet there hardly escaped any that had blood drawn of them, but died in a strange sort, with their mouths shut some ten days before they died, and after their wounds were whole."

Eventually, by early February the flotilla had filled its holds with captured slaves, a trade that Drake was learning well. The crossing to the Spanish Main was more difficult than usual, taking seven and a half weeks. Hawkins successfully forced his slave trade at Borburata, Rio de la Hacha, and Santa Marta, but at Cartagena in July his flotilla of slavers was beaten off by Spanish cannon and tactical deception. Heading north, a storm drove Hawkins's ships into the Gulf of Mexico. The vessels then headed south to the Campeche coast of Mexico and in September anchored at the fort of San Juan de Ulloa, where Francis Drake would, some say, forever earn the enmity of John Hawkins.

The locals at first took the English vessels for the expected treasure fleet, which annually called upon the Mexican port of Veracruz and anchored between it and the nearby island fort of San Juan de Ulloa. This mistake eased their entrance considerably. When city officials came out to greet the "Spanish" flagship, Hawkins seized them, according to the Spanish, then demanded control of the island fort. Still, desiring to keep up appearances, Hawkins dispatched a letter to Mexico City, noting that he was there only by force of weather. But the Spaniards believed he was there to seize the rich mule trains coming from Mexico City to meet the fleet. Hawkins, of course, denied he was there for any reason but to seek provisions after the storm.

Unfortunately, whatever Hawkins's intentions were, they were thwarted by the sudden arrival of the Spanish treasure fleet. Hawkins refused it admission until certain conditions were met, ostensibly for the protection of all. In fact, the English were trapped. After negotiations and hostage exchanges, the city, harbor, and fleets stood quietly under a tense, tenuous—and fleeting—truce. How Drake viewed the situation is unknown. He was but a very junior commander in the scheme of things, yet even the smallest of vessels and most junior of commanders can play a crucial role. And so Drake would.

The Spaniards were going to have no part of this standoff—no interloper, and for certain not an English one, was going to tell them what to do in their own great port. Quickly and quietly the Spaniards reinforced their ships and the island by night. Mid-morning the next day the battle began.

The onslaught was furious. The two sides were nearly equal, but the Spaniards quickly recaptured the island fort and turned its guns on the English. It was a battle of anchored ship brutally battering anchored ship. The Spanish lost their admiral, vice admiral, and a stout ship, and Hawkins's *Jesus of Lubeck* was so badly shattered that it was useless, a sitting duck for two Spanish fireships, had they managed to grapple it. Only the *Minion* and Drake's *Judith* survived the battle, the *Minion* by anchoring in the lee of the great ship *Jesus*, where it was screened from the Spanish cannonade. Those who could retreated to the *Minion*. Those who could not, or for whom there was not enough room aboard, were abandoned to the Spanish. Drake did what little he could with his small vessel. According to Job Hortop, one of the gunners aboard the *Jesus of Lubeck*, Drake even laid "the Minion aboord, to take in men and other things needefull, and to goe out ..."

The next morning the *Minion* slipped away to an island a mile (1.6 km) off. But the *Judith* was already gone. Drake's bark, Hawkins wrote, "forsook us in our great misery." Yet according to another witness, Hawkins had commanded Drake to go out. Drake returned to England, leaving no written note of his adventures. His reputation was by no means sullied, and soon he was away to sea again, this time as expedition commander.

By now Drake had a belly full of experience, much of it bad, which is, of course, in a manner of speaking the best—a recipe for wisdom, in other words. He knew much of the geography of the Main and the waters along it. He had learned the ways of Spanish ships, Spanish merchants, Spanish fighting. He knew how to lie in wait and surprise a common merchant ship as it plodded by, forcing it to surrender to his superior number and armament. He knew how to chase a powerful merchantman, pummeling it with chase guns as it ran, pounding it with broadsides when he caught up with it, and then boarding it after battering its crew and rigging until the ship was too weak to fight back or escape. And he knew how to take a town by surprise at night or at dawn when it was most vulnerable.

More important, experience had taught him how to handle a crisis at sea or upon a distant hostile shore, and how to persevere in the face of crisis, hazard, and setback. And he knew where and how he could get rich, and so revenge himself upon the Spaniards who had so far thwarted his adventures.

Two voyages later—the first commanding his *Dragon* and her consort the *Swan* in 1570, to the Chagres River at the Isthmus of Darien, Panama, where he is said to have captured two ships (and, some suggest, been briefly imprisoned at

Rio de la Hacha), and the second a year later in the *Swan* to make a reconnaissance at Darien, cache supplies at Puerto Faisán, and make contact with the *Cimarrónes*—Drake was ready for his third and grand voyage to plunder the Spanish Main.

He set sail in May 1572, and as we have already seen, was defeated at Nombre de Dios. Drake and his injured men recovered from their wounds at Puerto Faisán on the Isthmus of Darien while waiting for the rainy season to end. Roughly two dozen of the English pirates died during this time, most of yellow fever, including his brother, Joseph Drake, commander of the *Swan*. His other brother, John, died of a belly wound received in action during one of several attacks the pirates made on Spanish shipping in the area.

And so we find Drake, his men, and his *Cimarrón* allies a few months later, in January 1573, lying in wait for the great mule trains of Spanish silver and goods that traveled between Panama and Nombre de Dios. Perhaps the Spanish lead that remained beneath the scar of Drake's leg wound reminded him that today would make all the pain and effort worthwhile.

OF *RECUAS* AND REQUIEMS

As the deep sound of the mule bells coming from Venta de Cruces grew nearer, the pirates huddled down in their "ambuscade" positions. Like cowbells, the mule bells could be heard at great distances, and the time that passed from the first sound of the bells to the point at which the beasts of burden and their handlers were abreast of the ambushers must have seemed like an eternity. But Drake's men were under orders to let the *recuas*, or mule trains, from Venta de Cruces pass, for they carried only merchandise. Drake was after silver and gold.

As the *recua* drew near, Robert Pike, drunk on brandy, slipped forward to the edge of the path, along with a *Cimarrón*, to catch sight of the mules. A mounted scout passed by, a page or slave running at his stirrup—and the drunken fool stood up to get a better look. Immediately his *Cimarrón* companion hurled him to the ground and covered him, but it was too late. The Spaniard had spotted Pike's white shirt, for all of Drake's men were wearing their shirts over their jerkins and other apparel so that they would know each other in battle at night, a practice known in Spanish as *camisado*.

The rider galloped toward Panama and gave warning; the *recua* of silver and gold was held back, and Drake captured only those loaded with victuals. Now that the country was alarmed, Drake retreated, defeated this time by the mere

This musketeer, of the time of James I of England, is armed with a caliver. The musketeer's dress and armament is almost identical to that of the late sixteenth century, and doubtless the appearance of some of Francis Drake's men was very similar. The caliver was a light musket, of caliber between that of a true musket and the lighter arquebus or hackbut, and did not require a rest as the heavier matchlock musket did. The musketeer carries a match lighted on both ends in his hand. For safety, only after he has loaded and primed his caliver will he attach the match. At his left side hangs a sword, at his right a powder flask and priming flask.

Getty Images

bungling circumstance of a single man. As he and his pirates retreated through the savanna and thickets, they soon smelled the burning matches of muskets, and so knew the Spanish were near.

Closer they came, and when challenged *"¿Que gente?"* Drake replied, "Englishmen!" and stoutly refused a request to surrender. He told the Spanish officer that he must, for the honor of his mistress the queen, pass—and then fired his pistol into the Spanish troops. The Spaniards, all at the ready, returned fire with a volley of hail shot and quarter shot, which spread out in a broad pattern perfect for fighting at close range in places thick with vegetation. But the pirates gave it right back with musket and bow, then advanced, intending to come to "handy strokes," as they called close quarters.

The Spanish quickly retired, doubtless seeking better ground, and the pirates surged forward to cut them off. Seeing this, the *Cimarrónes* sped ahead of the pirates, bows at the ready, war cries flung into the air, and attacked the Spaniards from both sides. So violent was the assault that one of the *Cimarrónes*, mortally impaled on a Spanish pike, still managed to kill his killer. The Spaniards fled to Venta de Cruces six miles (9.6 km) away, and on their heels surged the pirates and their *Cimarrón* allies. Soon the town belonged to Drake and his men. But again, it was to little avail, for there was nothing of value in the town but food and other supplies. The pirates withdrew to their vessels. Drake was enraged, and doubtless vented his spleen on the deserving Robert Pike.

But Drake would not be put off from his quest for riches. For pirates and privateers, one good haul was the equivalent of a great victory. Although it could not bring back the dead—including Drake's brothers—it would go a long way to satisfy, at least briefly, greed, vengeance, and patriotism. Back at sea, the pirates soon gave chase to a vessel that turned out to be a French rover commanded by Guillaume le Testu, a Huguenot. The captains exchanged gifts: the Frenchman gave Drake a brace of pistols and a valuable scimitar, to which Drake responded with a gold chain and a small notebook he commonly wore.

In short order, need overcame any potential mistrust. The men had common purpose, and a common political and religious enemy in Spain. Further, Drake was now shorthanded, and an alliance would boost his chances of success. Drake and le Testu agreed to articles: the English and French would share equally, for although Drake's men were far fewer in number and their vessels smaller, he pointed out that they knew the territory, had *Cimarrón* allies, and "were to be the principal actors herein." Soon the party advanced into the jungles, thickets, and savannas of Darien, Drake and the *Cimarrónes* in front, to seek the Spanish mule trains.

This time, though, Drake dared to take advantage of the Spanish sense of security by doing the unexpected. The Spanish treasure ships had arrived at Nombre de Dios, which meant that rich *recuas* would be sent daily from Panama. Drake led twenty Frenchmen, fifteen Englishmen, and the *Cimarrónes* ashore. Carefully they worked their way for seven leagues though the jungle until they lay but a mile (1.6 km) away from the road—and on the outskirts of Nombre de Dios itself. So close were they that they could hear the carpenters at work on the ships that lay in the port, not to mention the mule trains that lay but a half hour's careful march away. No Spaniard would have suspected that any pirate would have had the temerity to come so close to the now well-guarded city in such small numbers.

But Drake would not be put off from his quest for riches. For pirates and privateers, one good haul was the equivalent of a great victory. Although it could not bring back the dead—including Drake's brothers—it would go a long way to satisfy, at least briefly, greed, vengeance, and patriotism.

When alerted by their *Cimarrón* scouts, Drake's party moved close to the road. This time there was no drunken pirate to spoil the affair. Three *recuas*, one of fifty mules and two of seventy, came abreast. Quickly the English and French leaped up and grabbed the mules at the head and tail of each *recua*. The mules, trained to lie down when arrested, did so. However, the fifteen Spanish soldiers guarding each did not. A firefight of bullets and arrows at close range immediately broke out, and Drake led the combined force in a brief but hot skirmish. The air was filled with the sounds of musket crack and arrow flight, of braying mules and shouting men, of steel on steel and steel on bone, all punctuated by the occasional ringing of a *recua* bell. The smells of mule sweat, gunpowder, and blood mixed with the humid air. A *Cimarrón* warrior was killed, and the French captain caught a load of hail shot in the belly. Soon, though, the pirates gained the upper hand and the surviving Spaniards retreated to bring reinforcements from Nombre de Dios. But they would be too late by a day. Drake and his pirates escaped with a New World plunder as yet unmatched by that of any English raider.

So great was the haul as to be almost unimaginable: 190 mules, all but four loaded with 300 pounds (136 kg) of silver each, and the remainder with gold. The pirates gathered up as much of the brilliant yellow metal as each man could bear, along with a small number of silver bars. The rest of the treasure they buried or hid in the brush, hoping to return for it, and quite possibly inspiring the subsequent pirate myths of buried treasure. The Spanish, of course, quickly recovered most if not all of it. Drake was now a wealthy man, one who could afford to outfit another great plundering adventure to the New World—and beyond.

SINGEING THE SPANISH BEARD

Francis Drake's daring raid did more than make him wealthy: it made him an enemy of Spain, and it brought him to the close attention of Queen Elizabeth of England. With but a small treasury to sustain her island nation, and with a great enemy—Spain—just south across the water, a sea-roving strategy suited England's interests. Drake had proved that Spain's wealth could be plundered by a small force of men and a few small vessels. With Elizabeth's tacit approval he outfitted a new expedition. For centuries kings and queens had often ignored or even winked at the piracies of their subjects when directed at an enemy, even in peacetime. Queen Elizabeth, however, was entirely complicit in Drake's new voyage.

In 1577 he set sail with a far greater force than he had ever had at his disposal: five ships and barks, including his flagship the *Pelican*, and 164 men. Yet still this was a relatively small expedition for so great an intention. Drake led his flotilla first to the Cape Verde islands, taking aboard en route a Portuguese pilot. He rechristened the *Pelican* the *Golden Hinde* in honor of his patron, Christopher Hatton, whose crest was the golden hind (a hind is a female red deer).

Drake then headed not west, but south. He intended to combine two fundamental tactical principles on this voyage, principles he had by now learned well: attack where you are not expected, and attack where the enemy is unprepared. The exact location of the Strait of Magellan was unknown to the English, but Drake soon found it and sailed through into the Pacific Ocean,

Famous illustrator Howard Pyle's image of Drake's attack on Santo Domingo on New Year's Day in 1586. Pyle accurately, if romantically, depicts the carnage of a fight from barricades in the streets of the Spanish town. Some men lay dead and dying, while smoke obscures the aim of those still fighting. Drake's forces captured the town and extracted a ransom of 25,000 ducats (a ducat was a type of gold coin). Contrary to the common perception of chests filled with large gold coins, the ducats, escudos, and doubloons inside were in fact small coins, roughly the size of a nickel.

Private Collection/The Stapleton Collection / The Bridgeman Art Library International

also known as the South Sea. His appearance was unexpected, and the Spanish possessions unprotected. Over the next two centuries, numerous other pirates, privateers, and naval expeditions would follow in his wake.

Only the *Golden Hinde* made it into the Pacific. Drake immediately went to work plundering the unprotected west coast of South America, in particular the merchant shipping ferrying silver bars, pieces of eight, gold bars, and jewelry, and even emeralds and emerald-encrusted gold jewelry. The inland city of Potosí, in modern-day Bolivia, produced much of Spain's silver, and from nearby Arica on the coast the silver was transported north to Panama aboard ships whose captains and crews were certain they had nothing to fear. It was like shooting fish in a barrel.

In February 1578, the *Golden Hinde* sailed into Lima and found a dozen ships at anchor. Drake plundered them all. Having word of a treasure ship called the *Nuestra Señora de la Concepción*, known by her crew as the *Cacafuego*, or "shitfire," he set out in pursuit. En route he captured a vessel carrying rigging and other cordage, but also eighty pounds (36 kg) of gold. His lookouts were keen to sight the treasure ship, for Drake had promised that he who first sighted her would receive a gold chain he wore around his neck. Eyes strained toward the horizon, looking for the slight dirty spot that would indicate a sail. And soon enough, there she was! The *Golden Hinde* gave chase for three hours, "shotte at her three peeces of ordnance," and captured her. The *Cacafuego*, in spite of her nickname, had no ordnance aboard, and thus no fire to pass rudely at her pirate attackers.

Spain wanted Drake's head; however, Queen Elizabeth not only let him keep it but knighted him as well.

Aboard were riches indeed. Jewels and precious stones, thirteen chests of pieces of eight, eighty pounds (36 kg) of gold, and twenty-six tons (23.5 metric tons)of silver bars or plate, *plata* as the Spanish called it, not to mention other valuable cargo. Drake's men plundered the *Cacafuego*, and Drake ordered her pilot and his boy aboard to assist in navigating the unknown coast. When Drake finally released them, the boy quipped that "our ship shall be called no more the *Cacafuego*, but the *Cacaplata*, and your ship shall be called the *Cacafuego*," to the great amusement of the English rovers.

After pillaging the coast for a while more, Drake sailed north to California on a voyage of exploration, then across the Pacific to the Indies, south around the Cape of Good Hope, and finally north to England to a hero's welcome in 1580. He and his crew were only the second to circumnavigate the world, and many English claimed he was the first captain to have done so, for Magellan had died in the Philippines in 1521 and never made it back to Portugal. Of course, they had conveniently forgotten Juan Sebastián Elcano, Magellan's Spanish second-in-command, who completed the voyage in 1522.

Spain wanted Drake's head; however, Queen Elizabeth not only let him keep it but knighted him as well, perhaps in retaliation for Spanish troops sent to Ireland. Sir Francis Drake was no more a pirate or secret privateer for England. By virtue of his deeds and renown he was now a naval officer, and it was duty first for the navy, profit second—a reversal of the natural order Drake had come to know.

ADMIRAL SIR FRANCIS DRAKE

In 1585, Queen Elizabeth gave Drake permission to lead 2,500 men on an expedition against Spain and her Spanish possessions. He sacked Santo Domingo (in the modern-day Dominican Republic), but lost everything when the ships transporting the great booty were captured. The expedition was a financial loss.

By early 1587, England and Spain were effectively at war. In April, Drake, now one of England's admirals, attacked vessels at anchor in Cadiz harbor, in southern Spain, destroying many. On the way home he captured a rich Spanish galleon—perhaps duty could pay as well as piracy after all. The defeat of the Spanish Armada the following year is too well known to require repeating, save for a single incident in which a Spanish warship filled with treasure managed to fall into Drake's hands. The man who had scourged the Spanish Main claimed he came upon it by accident. In fact, Drake apparently disobeyed orders and broke from the fleet to chase it. Worse, much of the treasure disappeared, angering Queen Elizabeth. Old habits die hard; Drake was still a pirate at heart.

His last great venture came in 1595. John Hawkins, whom Drake had deserted in the *Judith* at San Juan de Ulloa so many years before, was appointed co-commander of the expedition. With an enormous fleet they set sail again for the Americas, but, forewarned, the Spanish in the Caribbean and on the Main were prepared. Where Drake in the past had surprise on his side, he now had only raw but not overwhelming open force. Where once a few dozen men sufficed, many hundreds now could not. At San Juan de Puerto Rico, the English sea dogs sought a treasure ship in harbor; a Spanish round shot shattered the steerage of Drake's ship, the *Defyance*, killing seven men, but leaving not a scratch on Drake. John Hawkins, meanwhile, died of a fever. Now in sole command, Drake made brief attacks at Rio de la Hacha and Santa Marta on the north coast of present-day Colombia. But Panama was his real goal.

On the same day almost twenty-five years before that Robert Pike had dashed any immediate hopes Drake had had of capturing the silver-laden mule trains, Drake managed to get a clear view of the great city of Panama, discerning even "the large street which lieth directly from the sea into the land, south and north." There can be little doubt that on that day he set his mind's eye on one day capturing Spain's principal American port on the Pacific Ocean.

But it was not to be. The attack failed, and the English retreated. Soon afterward, Sir Francis Drake, now fifty-five, was stricken with dysentery and died. He was buried in a lead coffin in the waters just off Portobello. Elated, the Spanish claimed he died of grief over his recent failures. Spain had lost an enemy, England a hero.

THE DRAGON'S LEGACY

Whatever Drake's shortcomings—arrogance, high-handedness, and greed, among others—he also had many virtues. He typically treated his prisoners well, and, in spite of the religious propaganda one occasionally finds in his accounts, he was not on a crusade for anything but "honorable" plunder first and England second, albeit a close second. His national service notwithstanding, Francis Drake was foremost a sea rover, whether he sailed as a pirate, a privateer, or a naval officer. He loved action and adventure, he loved fame and notoriety, he loved word and deed. Especially, he loved the wealth he gained via plundering. In sea roving, Drake was complete. Here, and perhaps only here, all of his qualities and passions worked together to ensure both his success and his renown.

Above all, though, Drake loved himself. Ego does have its purpose, and it would have taken enormous self-confidence for Francis Drake to have looked at the might of Spain and the "compass" of the New World—and indeed of the world itself—and decide that he, along with a few small vessels and few dozen men, was the mere mortal who could steal part of the riches that lay at its heart.

To the English, Drake was and is a national hero, a sea dog who helped lay the foundation of the British Empire, who helped check Spain's imperialist ambitions, and who helped keep England Protestant and free. To the Spanish, though, he was a snarling English dog in need of a few inches of Spanish steel through his throat or a bit of hemp tightened around his neck. Many Spanish historians downplay his role even while respecting it, noting that many of his raids and even his expeditions were little more than nuisances to the great Spanish Empire. Notwithstanding this, Lope de Vega, the greatest of Spanish playwrights, wrote an epic in verse and named it *Dragontea* after Drake. In it he cast many angry, lyrical darts at Drake the Dragon. The epic remains a lasting testament to the hatred and fear Drake inspired along the Spanish Main, and at times even along the coast of Spain.

His national service notwithstanding, Francis Drake was foremost a sea rover, whether he sailed as a pirate, a privateer, or a naval officer.

But no matter how we might view Sir Francis Drake, sea rover extraordinaire, his life still has lessons to teach, particularly in the keys to success. To name a single attribute that ensured Drake's success is a difficult task, for he had many means that worked together. However, we can name one of them as the master, one that often fails because it is too seldom used: Francis Drake knew how to persevere. He refused to quit. If he failed, he learned from his failure and tried again, and again as necessary, until he succeeded. Ultimately, he knew that life's rewards, whatever they were, were not to be had without perseverance and struggle. That Drake proved this over and over on a grand scale is in itself sufficient to make him a hero, humble origins and great piracies notwithstanding.

CHAPTER 4

☠

DIEGO THE MULATTO

unknown-1673

HONOR, VENGEANCE, AND DECEPTION ON THE SPANISH MAIN

On the northeast trade winds they approached, thirteen of them, on the 10th of August, 1633. Three were large ships, seven of medium tonnage. They included frigates and also hookers, which the Spanish called *urcas*, a form of round-bellied, shallow-drafted merchant craft, versatile for both trade and raiding. Two or three were small fore-and-aft-rigged vessels called *balandras*. It was morning, and a crowd had quickly gathered at the port of San Francisco de Campeche, a small but important town on the western shore of the Yucatán Peninsula of Mexico, to observe the small fleet.

Some of the observers noted the quiet beauty of the vessels in the offing, the early sun shining on sails and timbers. Several local merchant vessels—*fragatas del puerto*—were expected, and such arrivals were always a time for celebration, for with them came goods, money, and news. But not all on shore assumed that glad tidings were in order. Instead, they scanned the cut of the sails in view, and then the hulls of the vessels themselves when they finally rose above the horizon. It was soon apparent that only one of the vessels appeared to be Spanish built. The rest appeared to be Dutch—and the Dutch were pirates.

Immediately, the church bells were rung to sound the warning, and soon after the drummers began beating their drums, calling all men to arms. The grand melody of bronze bells dedicated to the service of God both variously clashed and harmonized with the staccato beat of the drums. The fleet approached slowly, but there is no such thing as too much time to prepare for battle. Soldiers and militia quickly armed themselves, including Native Americans and slaves, with weapons ranging from muskets and harquebuses to bows and spears.

Most of the fleet, or *flota* as the townspeople called it, anchored within cannon shot of the town's small battery, but shooting at them with a few small cannon would have been a waste of powder. The three large ships came to anchor four to five miles (6.4 to 8 km) away, for the water closer to town was much too shallow for ships whose draft was ten feet (16 km) or more.

For long hours nothing happened, neither on land nor at sea, other than the obvious preparations for battle. No one fired a shot. In Campeche everyone waited expectantly, feeling for certain that an attack was to come. The only question was when. Waiting while the pirates did nothing created anxiety, and even doubled or trebled fear among the defenders. Perhaps this was what the pirates intended. Doubtless they could hear the bells ringing and the drums beating, doubtless they could see the armed men on shore. Maybe, some of the townspeople hoped, the pirates would leave, knowing that the town was alarmed and thus defended. Although Campeche's entire population was only two or three hundred families, the city was not weak, and its first line of defense was commanded by Captain Domingo Galván Romero, a redoubtable officer.

The sun eventually set behind the small fleet, casting sails and hulls in a more ominous light. Soldiers and militias ashore waited tensely for something to happen. Almost certainly there was tension aboard the vessels of the anchored fleet, but of what sort no one ashore knew. Ashore, the waiting Spaniards wondered what the pirates were up to, whether the sea thieves were debating about where to attack, or better yet, about whether to attack at all, for pirates preferred not to attack well-armed towns except by surprise.

Unfortunately for the townspeople, pirates invariably had a plan, and these pirates were no doubt simply waiting for the depths of night when no one would see them come ashore, when everyone would be exhausted from the tension, when all would be fighting off sleep, when alertness and reaction time were at the their ebb. From midnight until dawn it is usually the attacker who has the physical and psychological advantage, for the attacker chooses the time of attack and feels in control, while the defender must sit and wait.

But Captain Galván was no fool. He ordered his men to expect an attack at night or dawn, and he used all of his energy to keep them awake, alert, and at the ready. He made sure that matches for harquebuses were kept lighted, he made sure his men were not asleep but quiet and ready, he made sure his sentries were alert and watchful.

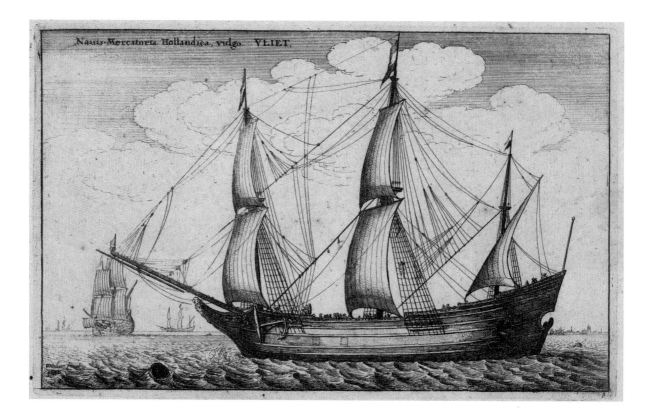

Near midnight the pirates came ashore, first the advance guard, or "forlorn hope" as the Dutch and English called it, and then the main body itself, of 500 men, pirates all—Dutch, English, French, Portuguese, and even some Spaniards, not to mention mulattos and former slaves of various islands and shores of the Spanish Main, and perhaps even some Moskito Indians, as they were known. Strictly speaking, though, these attackers were privateers, for Spain and the Netherlands were at war. But many had been pirates. The Dutch and English, being Spain's Protestant enemies, were seen as always pirates, their commissions notwithstanding.

Midnight passed, and it was now the day of the Feast of Santa Clara de Assisi. The moon had begun to wane but was still bright, like a night sun, just a day past full. The pirates could easily see where they were going, and the moonlight at first cast short shadows, then, as the night grew longer and the sun rose near the horizon, longer ones.

The invaders rowed their boats, quietly at first, along the shore, paralleling the advance already on foot toward the town. The forlorn moved in good order through the neighborhood of San Román, named for the church of Santo Cristo de San Román at the south end of town, then past the undefended first trench near the edge of the town. They passed next near the first row of houses of the town proper at dawn, and advanced toward the second trench—and here flame and smoke exploded from fifty harquebuses in the trench and three cannon in *la torrecilla*, a small stone turret or blockhouse known as Fort San Benito, filling the air with flying lead and iron. Each harquebus was probably loaded with two or three musket balls, and each of the three cannon probably with a murderous mix of musket balls and iron scrap. The ragged, slaughtering volley killed or wounded twenty-five pirates, and shocked the rest into believing they had run into several companies of veterans. They were here for plunder, after all, not heroic suicide. Immediately, many of the pirates turned and ran.

The overall commander of the expedition—Cornelis Corneliszoon Jol, better known as Pie de Palo, or Wooden Leg, for his peg leg—ordered a retreat, and in confusion his men obeyed, to the dismay of the commander of the forlorn. He had a good teacher, he knew how Spaniards fought, and he had been picked to lead the forlorn not only for his valor and knowledge of Campeche but also for his ability to inspire his men. But it was to no avail, for the pirates were retreating quickly out of range.

Seeing the attackers flee from Spanish wrath, Captain Galván led a charge after them, into the open beyond the city itself. But many of the pirates of the forlorn, retreating but still under command of their captain, kept their wits and opened fire on their pursuers. The Spanish counterattack was both valiant and foolish, very much an example of Spanish bravado. Fifty against 500 are poor odds, and fewer against 500 is foolhardy in the extreme, especially on open ground. Still, in the past a handful of men have more than once put a large retreating force into full flight. But not this time. The pirates' fire was even deadlier, and soon Captain Galván and a dozen of his men bled their lives away in the Campeche outskirts.

The pirates regrouped and advanced again toward the town, the forlorn and its commander leading the way. The survivors among the fifty Spaniards of the second trench had retreated to the plaza at the center of Campeche. Here, in the third trench, overlooked by the church of the Virgen de la Inmaculada Concepción, was where the defenders would make their stand.

As he led his pirates toward the *plaza de armas*, the commander of the forlorn paused at the body of Captain Domingo Galván Romero. Briefly he paid his respects, but he had no time for anything more, not to say a prayer, not to speak more than a word or two. He passed on, regretfully, not merely because a gallant soldier had lost his life, but also because the body was that of his godfather, mentor, and old friend.

A Dutch fluyt or flute of the 1640s, by Wenceslas Hollar, first published in 1647, was a common form of Dutch trading vessel, and was often used by pirates and privateers as well. It was shallow-drafted, had a "pinked" or pointed stern, and its hull typically had much tumblehome (that is, the hull curved sharply inward from the waterline to the gunwales). Although three-masted, the flute did not usually carry topgallant sails, making it easier to manage with a small crew. In the first half of the seventeenth century, flutes and vessels with similar hulls were often referred to as hookers. The Spanish fluyt was called an *urca*, a word that derives from hooker.

The godson moved forward to engage the awaiting Spanish defenders. His name was Diego, but he was known over his life by several names, including Diego the Mulatto, Diego de los Reyes, Captain Diego Martín, Diego de la Cruz, Diego Díaz, Diego le Métis, and, many years later, Diego Grillo. But he was known by another name as well: Diego Lucifer. And Diego Lucifer had not only plunder on his mind as he led his pirates into Campeche. He had once lived here, and his mind was also on revenge.

THE DEVIL'S SPAWN

Tradition has it that Diego was an escaped slave from Havana, but he has been confused with another man named both Diego the Mulatto and Diego de los Reyes of some forty years past, a Havana oarsman and escaped slave who helped guide William Parker, an English privateer. Were he this man, Diego would have been seventy-five when he attacked Campeche, and with a mother still living at least four years later, not to mention that his godfather would have been more than ninety years old when he defended Campeche from his godson. There is no indication that Diego was anywhere near this old at this time, and no reason to believe he was.

Diego the pirate and privateer was in fact likely born a free man, a Spanish *criollo*, or Creole, in Havana, probably during the first decade of the century. His mother was African, his father Spanish. He later moved to Campeche, quite likely in the company of his godfather and quite possibly at his behest. That his godfather, or *padrino de bautismo*, was an officer and thus a gentleman or hidalgo indicates that Diego's social class was not humble. He almost certainly had access to formal education, including languages, and formal training in arms as well.

And it was in Campeche that something went awry. Diego was either whipped or received a slap or blow he could not have satisfaction for. What his supposed offense was we do not know. Although a free man, Diego was still a mulatto. White Spaniards, both native born and Creole, typically looked down upon all but their own. Diego's mixed race also barred him from holding certain offices, and may have prevented him from seeking satisfaction either by way of the law, or, for a brave, strong-willed man, by way of the sword for the offense against him. Although mulatto Spaniards often carried swords and used them in duels (which were, strictly speaking, unlawful), Diego's social status nonetheless limited his options. Surely it was here, in the socially and racially stratified society of the Spanish Main, that Diego was compelled to take to sea and inspired to seek revenge.

A *boucanier*, or hunter of cattle and pigs on Hispaniola, from the Dutch edition of Alexandre Exquemelin's *The Buccaneers of America*, 1678. The illustration gives a general sense of the *boucanier*, from whose name the term buccaneer would soon derive. *Boucaniers* were active during Diego's reign, and it's likely that some even sailed with him. In the illustration the *boucanier* is holding a *fusil boucanier*, or "buccaneer musket." These muskets were often six feet (2 m) long or longer, with barrels more than four and a half feet (1.4 m) and a large "club butt." The smaller illustrations show a *boucan de cochon* or pig roast, a *boucanier* duel with muskets, and the common fashion of hunting wild pigs and cattle from the safety of trees.

© Lebrecht Music and Arts Photo Library/Alamy

pag. 84

And he did so with a vengeance. But novices do not go to sea alone and without experience, not if they hope to live long. Diego doubtless knew how to sail and fight. The former he would have learned during trading voyages along the coast, perhaps as far as Veracruz, Havana, and Honduras, perhaps even as a captain. The latter he would have learned at his godfather's side.

Most likely in a small vessel, perhaps even in an open boat or canoe with a mast and sail, and probably with a few men who shared his thirst for vengeance or adventure, Diego put to sea. His supplies would have been few: some arms and powder; a few navigational instruments; several jars of water and bottles of wine, brandy, or perhaps even *pulque* made from the agave; and victuals such as "Indian corn," dried pork, cacao beans, and plantains. Dutch privateers and pirates were common from the Campeche coast into the Gulf of Honduras, and Diego would not have been long in finding them. Quite possibly he sought them in the Bay of Honduras, perhaps even at Blewfield's Bay, named for Albertus or Willem Blauveldt, Dutch traders and sea rovers.

Diego's crews were predominantly Dutch, but doubtless included the usual mix of English, French, Portuguese, Africans, mulattos, mestizos, and Native Americans, yet they took orders from him and were proud to serve under him.

Given his nickname Lucifer, Diego at some point probably sailed under Dutch privateer Hendrick Jacobszoon, popularly known as Lucifer, not to mention as "the worst shark in the sea." A Dutch captain must have taken Diego under his wing, for there is no other way that within a few years that Diego, a Spaniard, no matter how great his abilities, would have advanced so quickly to command Dutch pirates and privateers. Some historians even believe Diego was Jacobszoon's son, and that his real name was Jacob, which, like Diego, means James, although this conflicts with Spanish accounts. It is quite likely that Diego's use of Lucifer was as much in honor of his Dutch pirate mentor as it was for the fear he generated as a renegade among his Spanish Main brethren. It may also, as we shall later see, have been invented by Diego as part of his sly sense of humor.

Diego's crews were predominantly Dutch, but doubtless included the usual mix of English, French, Portuguese, Africans, mulattos, mestizos, and Native Americans, yet they took orders from him and were proud to serve under him. Pirates had an often hypocritical way of looking at race. They would accept some Africans into their crews, for example, yet sell other Africans as slaves. But above all, they valued the courage and ability that led to plunder. And Diego knew how to lead his crews there.

He doubtless first proved his value as a pilot along the coast, but his qualities as leader and warrior soon showed through. Some authorities believe he took command of Jacobszoon's ship *Ter Veere* after the Dutch commander died in 1627. By 1633 Diego commanded not one, but two ships, each manned with largely Dutch crews, and was considered both capable and notorious enough that Wooden Leg Cornelis Jol was willing to sail in consort with him. We do not know much about his early adventures, although he was most likely present at an unprofitable Dutch attack on Trujillo, on the coast of Honduras, just prior to the assault on Campeche. Almost certainly he was with the Dutch on a number of their earlier adventures, had probably already visited the Puritan colony at Providence Island in the Caribbean, a base for privateers, and assuredly had combed the Spanish Main from Veracruz to Trinidad and from Trinidad to Cuba. It was on one such cruise that Diego proved he was more than just a common sea rover bent on plunder and revenge.

THE LADY AND THE PIRATE

In 1636, Fernando Centeno Maldonado, until recently the interim governor of the Yucatán, including the region of Campeche, set out with his wife and retinue from Mérida for Mexico City via Campeche, intending to plead his case before the viceroy. He believed he had been unjustly relieved of his office, that the charges against him were false, and that the viceroy should relieve his successor instead and reappoint Maldonado as governor. Maldonado, it seems, did not get along well with the powerful Franciscan monks in the Yucatán, and they had complained of him to the viceroy.

But Maldonado was no sheep among men, and his meeting with the viceroy might have made for some interesting drama had he lived long enough to make his protest explicit among the many florid courtesies and polite salutations that Spanish honor demanded. Unfortunately, Maldonado died of unknown cause en route in the village of Hecelchakán, and the viceroy was destined never to be confronted by the outraged former governor.

However, his widow, Isabel de Caraveo, was determined to continue the trip to Mexico City, if only to restore some sense of her husband's honor. From Hecelchakán she traveled by road to Campeche, and from there took passage to Veracruz aboard a local vessel. From Veracruz she could make the short trip to the city. But Isabel's journey on the *barco del puerto* would not be a long one.

Hardly had the *barco* stood to sea before it was discovered, chased, and ordered to strike by several pirate vessels. The Spanish vessel quickly lowered its topsails and lay by in the lee of her attackers. The pirates, commanded by Diego, plundered the vessel. But when Diego learned that a lady was aboard, he immediately gave her freedom, ordered that all of her goods and property be restored to her, and took her aboard his own ship. There, to ensure her security—so that she would not be harassed, molested, or raped, in other words—he posted a guard at her door.

Hollywood's screenwriters could not have written a better script. What transpired between Diego and Isabel is unknown, and was probably no more than is written here. Even so, the vengeance-seeking devil pirate had proved himself also a gentleman. He ordered his flotilla to sail to Campeche, and on a nearby beach he put Doña Isabel de Caraveo and her retinue safely ashore. The fame of his courtesy soon spread. Spaniards knew that although Diego was a fearsome pirate, he could be merciful and his word was good. They knew he was an honorable man, and an honorable man would honor good quarter and the terms of surrender—and thus it might be better at times to surrender to him than to fight him.

> *Spaniards knew that although Diego was a fearsome pirate, he could be merciful and his word was good.*

Already Diego combined the knowledge of his enemy and his enemy's lands and seas with a devilish ferocity in battle and the quick mind of a successful tactician. He knew how to collect and use intelligence, how to attack by surprise, and how to use distraction as a tactic in support of surprise—his attack on Campeche was a perfect example. His enemy had learned that in spite of his reputation, he did not make war on women, and that he treated his prisoners well. By the time he reached

Campeche, Diego was ready to make a grand name for himself among the famous leaders of the pirates and privateers of the Caribbean. Here he might profit trebly: in plunder, in name, and, in what originally fed the flame of his roving, in vengeance.

REVENGE!

In Campeche, now the morning of the 11th of August, 1633, Diego carefully led the second advance quickly over the abandoned second trench. He and his forlorn marched one block into the city and down a street parallel to the coast. Along the shore, two boats well manned with armed pirates rowed slowly along, helping to protect the flank.

Diego knew well where he was going. The city was shaped like a rectangle, with the small Fort San Benito and its trench on the south end. Near the center on the west side, along the sea, was the town square and its churches, and on the far north end were the church and convent of San Francisco de Campechuelo. The streets were laid out in a careful grid, as many Spanish New World cities were, making it easy to find one's way around.

Carefully the pirates watched for ambushes as they marched. The air smelled of burned powder and burning match, and thinning wisps of powder smoke from the previous skirmish drifted occasionally by, perhaps suggesting the ghosts of fighting men.

Soon the moon had set and the sun had risen. As they advanced within sight of the plaza, it was plain that 300 men, perhaps more, were packed into a trench, or were ready behind the hastily constructed barricades, and in windows of the nearby buildings. They were men not only from Campeche itself but also from the rancheros and farms nearby. Their harquebuses were at the ready, and the trench bristled with the naked points and edges of pikes and spears.

Quickly assessing the situation, the pirates attacked. Normally, these unconventional sea-roving warriors would open fire on their enemy, attacking them much as they would a ship, firing at them constantly, trying to force them to keep their heads down so that the attackers could either charge the trench and fortification or get close enough to hurl firepots and grenades among the defenders, and perhaps force them from their defenses. Diego may have first ordered a volley or two to test the Spaniards' mettle and see whether they would break and run.

But the defenders stood resolutely wedged in their defensive positions. For several hours the fight raged, each side firing almost constantly at the other.

The pirates knew they must capture the town soon, before reinforcements could arrive. If the pirates gained the city, they might be able to drive them away. Diego and his companion captains had to come up with a plan, and they did.

The pirates increased their fire and moved forward as if to charge the trench, and the defenders in turn placed everyone they could on the line to repulse the attack. Meanwhile, with Diego at their head, a squadron of pirates retreated unobserved from the main body and quickly swept around the flank. Down weakly defended streets they charged, with lead and steel clearing any light barricades in their path. At close quarters the pirates, firing muskets and pistols, swinging musket butts and sharp-edged swords, engaged any defenders who stood their ground.

Now the main body of pirates charged too, sweeping violently over the trench and onto the edge of the plaza. Some Spaniards remained in the trench, while others abandoned it, their officers forming them into a square in the plaza where they loaded and fired volleys while the pirates discharged their own arms into the mass of armed men.

The *alcalde*, or mayor, soon fell dead, and his nephew also, and three other officers. The defenders began to waver, and seeing this, Diego and his rovers desperately pressed the attack. Thirty-seven Spaniards soon lay dead in the plaza, and as the pirates reloaded, aimed, and fired as quickly as they could, six more were struck down by the heavy lead balls of pirate harquebuses. There was no need here for hand-to-hand combat against an enemy standing in the open—the pirates simply cut them down with musket fire.

The defenders now had no choice. They sounded the retreat and withdrew under fire from the city, fleeing to San Francisco de Campechuelo on the northern outskirts. Of the women and children, those who could flee inland did so. A few Spaniards still stood and fought, and at least one of them, named Cornejo, refused to surrender and from the trench continued to try to kill the enemy even after the city was obviously lost. A pirate shot him dead.

In the mayhem that followed, the pirates, as ever is the case, began plundering the city while their captains did their best to keep them under arms and ready for a counterattack. Diego strongly advised Captain Jol that they should pursue the retreating Spaniards and drive them from Campechuelo. Otherwise, there would be an enemy on their flank that might attack at anytime. But Wooden Leg would not agree. He believed that the convent and church were too well defended, and too many men would lose their lives attacking it. More vitally, it would take too much time. Diego, who had borne the brunt of the leadership during the attack, and, with his men, the dangers of the vanguard, resigned himself to Captain Jol's decision. Diego, after all, commanded but two ships in the squadron of thirteen.

For two days the pirates, drunk on Spanish wine, plundered Campeche. Uncooperative or even unlucky prisoners were not treated well. Under the eyes of Diego and Wooden Leg, the pirates murdered a wounded prisoner, Captain Losada, because he could not keep up with them. They left his body, still twitching, behind them. They had intended to use him in the search for plunder, but doubtless there were others who would serve just as well.

A Spanish counterattack could have succeeded while the pirates were drunk, but Campeche's remaining captains and government could not agree on a strategy beyond a timid greedy one. It was even rumored that had the mayor and wealthy men of the city followed the advice of one of their captains, the city might not have fallen. They chose instead to devise their own plan, rather than let the credit for a successful defense fall to him. As it was, this officer, a wealthy captain now wounded in the hip, refused to negotiate at all with the Dutch sea rovers, and swayed the rest of the city fathers to his side. He told the Spanish prisoners paroled to negotiate for the release of the city that he was one of the few who stood to lose the most, and so would pay nothing. To Diego he sent this message: "Do whatever you wish with Campeche."

There would be no ransom for the city, once home to 35,000 Mayans and now home to several hundred Old Spaniards, Creole Spaniards, African slaves, Native Americans, mestizos, and mulattos. The captain, and the rest of the wealthy, would see the city burn rather than ransom it.

And it was this officer, Captain Domingo Rodríguez Calvo, upon whom Diego intended his revenge—for Rodríguez was the man who had given the blow that launched Diego on his piratical rampage. Diego searched everywhere for him, swearing to all he met that he would "cut Rodríguez's ears and nose, but not kill him," proving he was the better man. Eventually, Diego realized that not only had Rodríguez escaped, but also the city fathers were not going to not pay a single piece of eight of the 40,000 demanded. Learning as well that a relief force was on its way from nearby Mérida, the pirates stripped the city of all they found, including a large quantity of the city's most valuable plunder, logwood, that was stacked on the beach. Soon they set sail, leaving the city in flames.

Twelve miles (19 km) from Campeche they released their prisoners and hostages safely ashore. Diego was now a bit richer, and had revenge in part on Campeche, and

thus on Rodríguez. Perhaps a half-revenge was better than none. Still, Rodríguez's nose and ears were intact, and, perhaps what mattered far more to the wealthy, overbearing captain, he still had his riches, the loss of which would doubtless have "cut him" far more. But Diego might still have the last laugh. He was a free man upon the billows of the sea, and might go where he pleased. Rodríguez, however, was bound to Campeche—and Campeche could be attacked again.

LONGEVITY AND A SENSE OF HUMOR

Diego continued his cruises along the Spanish Main, focusing especially on the Bay of Campeche, the Gulf of Honduras, the waters from the Mosquito Coast to

Curaçao, off the coast of Venezuela, and the Cuban coast. He may have even used the Dry Tortugas near the Florida Keys as a base, as Captain Jol did at times.

A year after Campeche, in 1634, he accompanied Dutch privateer Johannes van Walbeeck and Huguenot soldier Pierre le Grand, perhaps the same who will one day be regarded as the first of the great French filibusters, during their capture of Curaçao and Aruba. The islands then became Dutch colonies as well as bases for Dutch privateering and piracy. Two years later he sailed in consort with English privateer Thomas Newman, who commanded the *Happy Return* out of Providence Island, which lay halfway between Costa Rica and Jamaica. They captured a rich Spanish prize that Diego carried to Holland, leaving the English to sue for their share. These and Diego's many other pirate attacks were proof of his ability not only as a tactician but also as a leader. Only a man who knew his business well would have been so sought after.

In 1641 he sacked Sisal, on the Yucatán coast, and Trujillo, and did so again the following year, probably using Guanaja Island in the Bay of Honduras as a base. He sacked Salamanca de Bacalar on the east coast of the Yucatán Peninsula in 1643, and soon served as pilot to William Jackson, an intrepid adventurer and pirate who was busy revitalizing English piracy in the Caribbean, during Jackson's raid on Trujillo. Chances are, he also sailed with, or at least crossed paths with, pirate and privateer Willem Blauveldt and his ship *La Garce*. Reportedly, Diego once even kidnapped one of the wealthiest residents of Havana, held him for a rich ransom, then promised to return within three years as the new Dutch governor of Cuba.

We know little about Diego's appearance, other than his skin color. We do know he wore a rapier and dagger, probably Spanish. We know a bit more about the person he was. He would serenade his crew with his guitar. At some point he married a Dutch woman, probably in Curaçao. From one of Diego's prisoners, English Catholic priest Thomas Gage, we know that his mother was still living in 1637. Indeed, Diego invited

The region popularly known as the Spanish Main, taken from an early twentieth-century map by William R. Shepherd. Strictly speaking, the Spanish Main was any of the American mainland occupied or claimed by Spain, although in practice the term was often extended to include the entire region, including the Caribbean Sea and environs. Diego the Mulatto's pirate voyages ranged from the Gulf of Campeche to the Gulf of Honduras, to Cuba and the Straits of Florida.

his prisoner to "a stately dinner" and, knowing that Gage was traveling to Havana, drank a toast to his mother and asked the priest to "remember him to her, and how that for her sake he had used well and courteously in what he did."

In particular, though, he appears to have had an extraordinary sense of humor, which historian Jean-Pierre Moreau has astutely pointed out. In 1634, while sailing in the company of Dutch privateer Adrian Clas, Diego cast aside his usual clothing and arms, pretended to be a Spanish prisoner, and made friends with a real Spanish prisoner, Domingo de Tartas Salazar, until recently the captain of the *San Francisco y San Benito* and now a prisoner of Captain Clas. Claiming to be "Diego de los Reyes" from Seville and speaking with an accent that sounded more Portuguese than Castilian, Diego convinced the Spanish captain with his false identity, only to leave him astounded to later discover that he had been duped by the notorious pirate. Diego may well have been using the humorous deception—he appears to have been quite the actor—to gather intelligence for his and Captain Clas's use. Be that as it may, Captain de Tartas had no idea that the Diego whom he had befriended was also the "Diego de la Cruz" who had recently raided Honduras.

Diego's ability to mislead people was also a necessary characteristic of his tactical sense. Deception is, after all, a critical component of warfare, whether of single combat in the form of a duel or of an attack on a ship or town. But no matter its purpose, Diego was always ready to add humor and panache to his deceptions. In 1638, he wrote a letter to the governor of Cuba, identifying himself as Diego Martín, the mulatto privateer who had been ravaging the Spanish Main. He was ready, he wrote, to serve Spain. And Spain was ready to have him. It was not at all uncommon for nations to grant commissions to renegades of other nations, as well as to restore their own renegades to service. After all, this was less expensive than trying to track them across the seas, and they could be put to good use attacking the enemy with whom they had served. The Spanish crown was willing to grant Diego a pardon, make him an admiral, and pay him eighty *escudos* (160 pieces of eight) a month.

Diego's ruse worked. While the governor of Cuba was waiting for him to abandon the Dutch and join the Spanish at Havana, he was actually raiding the Yucatán coast. By the 1640s, Spain had had quite enough of Diego, and issued a royal edict to use "every possible remedy to be taken to capture the mulatto pirate." Diego, however, by whatever name he was known at the time, remained free.

Indeed, it is quite likely that Diego himself coined many of the names he was known by, simply out of his sense of humor. At Yucatán he called himself Diego de

Twentieth-century illustration of murderous filibuster Jean David Nau, better known as l'Ollonois, from Frank Stockton's *Buccaneers and Pirates of Our Coasts* (1913). Diego the Mulatto sailed with l'Ollonois circa 1668, just prior to the famed pirate's death. L'Ollonois was both intrepid and successful, but also a ruthless butcher of men. He met his end on the Isthmus of Darien at the hands of Native Americans, who tore him limb from limb while he was alive, then burned the pieces and scattered their ashes to the wind.

la Cruz. To Captain de Tartas he was Diego de los Reyes. And to the governor of Havana he was Diego Martín, which may have been his real name, given that his mother still lived in Havana and this was doubtless known to many. The fact that he consistently used the name Diego strongly suggests his sense of humor. If he had been changing his name solely to create confusion, he could have used any variety of names. But he always used Diego, a name common enough not to make the joke too obvious. We can imagine his laughter at the consternation he surely created among Spanish governors, coastal inhabitants, and pirate hunters. In fact, part of his modern legacy is the confusion among many historians as to how many Diego the Mulatto pirates there really were. Quite likely Diego, best known as "Captain Diego" among those with whom he sailed, would be laughing just as hard now.

VENGEANCE FINALLY FINDS DIEGO

The unanswered question, of course, is whether Diego ever got his revenge on his nemesis Captain Rodríguez Calvo. And the answer is, unfortunately, that we do not know. Perhaps Rodríguez continued to keep his pieces of eight to himself, not to mention his nose and ears. Probably, though, he lost some of his wealth to Diego's repeated attacks on Campeche shipping. Diego sacked Campeche again in 1642, and perhaps he finally had his revenge. But if Rodríguez knew what was good for him, he fled to the hills as soon as the town was lost to the famous pirate a second time.

There is little word of Diego in the 1650s, and many historians assume he retired or died. Yet in the 1660s a Diego the Mulatto appeared again, first sailing with the French pirate and butcher of men Jean David Nau, known as François l'Ollonois. Diego was almost certainly the "Pirate of Campeche" who joined Henry Morgan's raid on Portobello in 1668, lending strength to the argument that there was only one Diego the Mulatto. Two years later he commanded the *St. Jean* of eighty tons (72.5 metric tons), ten guns, and eighty men, part of buccaneer Henry Morgan's expedition to Panama. At times, Diego cruised with Dutch freebooter Jan Lucas. To those who say he would be much too old—he might have been in his sixties—or much too lucky to still be a-roving, we need only note that it was not unknown for buccaneers to practice their trade for three or more decades. One thirty-year veteran was in his eighties when he died, and Willem Blauveldt, the Dutch privateer noted earlier, was still cruising for plunder in 1663. These were tough, experienced, lucky, and above all, smart men.

By 1673, Diego had not only the Spanish after him but also, because they had made peace with Spain after Morgan sacked Panama, the English. But the grand old renegade pirate refused to retire. The French pirate base at Tortuga was now his home. The Dutch were too busy trading with the Spanish, and the English were looking to do the same. Diego continued to attack the Spanish.

However, Diego, who now called himself Diego Grillo, soon lived up to his original nickname, Lucifer. In June 1673, he captured a Spanish merchant ship sailing from Havana to Campeche. Three Spanish ships crewed with 150 men sailed from Havana in pursuit and soon found Diego. The old pirate engaged them with his fifteen-gun frigate. The details of the fight are lacking, but almost certainly Diego attacked at close range, 100 yards (91.5 km) or less, using his great guns to shatter timbers, shred rigging, and slaughter men, while his musketeers blazed away, forcing Spanish gunners and *arcabuseros* to keep their heads down. Diego captured at least one of the vessels, and some say all three—and hanged the twenty Spaniards aboard who were born in Spain. The rest he set free.

Perhaps Diego still nursed his ancient grudge, and now blamed all "Old Spain men" for the dishonor done him. It is hard to avoid the possibility that Diego was in some way making a social or political statement, even if he hanged the Spaniards because he knew they intended to hang him immediately from the yardarm. Pirates were known to sometimes hang those who came to hang them.

But Spain soon had her revenge. Roughly two months later, Diego's consort, Jan Lucas, was captured on the Campeche coast, carried to Veracruz, and hanged or strangled. And likewise soon after, Diego himself was captured and hanged, or so several secondary accounts say, without providing any details.

If we believe these accounts, then Diego the Mulatto, "Christian Creole, privateer and admiral of Holland," not to mention freebooter, filibuster, and pirate, was finally no more. Vengeance, after all, has a way of coming home to roost, and if it does not, time sooner or later will. Diego's noteworthy sense of humor may seem somewhat paradoxical for a man who sought revenge and for whom revenge was his original motivation. Yet the two are not incompatible. Diego's quotation of a Spanish proverb to his prisoner Thomas Gage may well have reflected his general attitude: *"Hoy por me, mañana for ti."* That is, "Today for me, tomorrow for you."

Whatever his end, tomorrow did finally come for the noble and "much esteemed" Captain Diego, cutthroat pirate and gentleman privateer.

CHAPTER 5

☠

HENRY MORGAN

1635-1688

THE FEARLESS TACTICAL GENIUS WHO SACKED
THE SPANISH MAIN

On the ninth day the ragtag army emerged from the jungle. Exhausted, starving, and wild-eyed, they fell violently upon a herd of cattle and horses on the plain. With their long-barreled buccaneer guns they shot the beasts, then with hunting knives, bayonets, and cutlasses they slaughtered them where they lay, leaving the carcasses to be treated as carrion, not to mention as a likely foreshadowing of what was to come, one way or another.

After days without food, days in which some had resorted to boiling and eating the leather of their belts and cartridge boxes, their stomachs would not let them wait for the meat to roast. They ate until they were gorged, then they quietly prepared their arms. Before them lay the city of Panama, one of the greatest pearls on the Spanish Main, just waiting to be prized from its shell by men with audacity, fortitude, and skill at arms. Men seeking such great booty required a great leader. Theirs was Henry Morgan.

At sunrise on January 28, 1671, this army of 1,200 buccaneers, filibusters, and volunteers arrayed themselves for battle. Most were veterans of fights at sea and ashore, of ship boardings, pillaging raids, and sackings of cities. Before them across the plain as many as 2,000 armed men stood ready. A few of these defenders were grizzled veterans of wars against pirates and Native Americans, but most were new to the fearful practice of warfare. Many were local merchants and landowners, some brave, some tepid, some plainly fearful in spite of trying to hide behind their hidalgo pride.

Far more, however, were people of color: Africans, and also mulattos, mestizos, and others of mixed race, both slave and free, armed with lances and machetes with which some could skillfully open a man's chest or flay him to the bone. Amerindians, allied with the Spanish and armed with bow and arrow, stood at the ready. Some of the infantry were armed appropriately with heavy matchlock muskets, but most who had firearms carried light muskets called harquebuses, which the buccaneers called "hackbuts," as well as other firearms more suitable to hunting than to the battle at hand. Panamanian governor Pérez de Guzman would later complain of his army's poor armament.

Perhaps a fifth of the Spanish were mounted. Their horses pawed and snorted in the distracted idleness of waiting, bored yet knowing something was about to happen—this was no training day or parade. Some defenders, boastful or silent, believed victory might come easily, given Spanish courage and especially that their cause was right. Surely God would not grant victory to heretics! Had they not prayed to the blessed Lady of the Pure and Immaculate Conception? Yet God also said that men must help themselves, and thus soon the defenders of Panama must cease praying and begin fighting, calling upon Saint James—"Santiago!"—to aid them in their quest for victory. All knew what was at stake: their homes, their families, the honor of their women, and, for some of them, most important of all, their riches.

THE CALL OF THE BUCCANEERS

On this small plain the Spanish force now faced an army, many of whose men had long scourged the Spanish Main, and whose leader had proved his worth many times over. Once more he had done so by leading them for nine days across the treacherous jungle waterways of the Isthmus of Panama, through ambushes by Spaniards and allied Amerindians, and he intended today to lead them to victory. Defeat meant death or enslavement. It was not an option.

Henry Morgan had risen from relatively humble origins to his place as the greatest leader of the Caribbean sea rovers. Little, though, is known of his early years. Even his appearance is somewhat conjectural. A woodcut made two decades later suggests he was a sturdy young man with intense eyes, a dominant nose, and a small mouth. His hair was probably shoulder length, although most certainly tied in a queue at sea, and very likely he already sported the small mustache he wore in his later years.

By 1658 or 1659, the young Welshman Henry Morgan was in Port Royal, the capital of Jamaica, and one of the greatest pirate ports of the age. When or how he came in the Caribbean is still debated; he may have arrived as an indentured

An 1880 illustration, artist unknown, of Henry Morgan's surprise attack on the ships of the pirate hunting Armada de Barlovento at Maracaibo in 1669. The ship at the center is Morgan's fire ship flying the Spanish colors as a means of deceiving the Spanish fleet long enough to bring the fire ship alongside. The Armada de Barlovento, long intended as a fleet to protect the Spanish Main against pirates, had only recently been brought into existence. In its first significant engagement against pirates, Henry Morgan destroyed the larger part of the fleet.

servant. Whatever his origins, Morgan quickly joined the buccaneers feasting on the Main. The call of plundering adventure and the rewards it could bring—riches, women, and renown—were impossible to resist.

Soon Morgan signed aboard a privateer, quite possibly Richard Guy's *Hopewell Adventure* in 1659. Privateers brought goods and many thousands of the silver pieces of eight into the colony, and also helped keep the greedy inquisitorial Spaniard at bay while the enterprising Englishman intruded both quietly and violently upon the Spanish Main.

Once at sea, Morgan quickly distinguished himself during the capture of a Spanish vessel, and the riches aboard inspired him to keep to the trade. Because Morgan was not yet a commander, he would have made his reputation in close action. Buccaneers' tactics at sea were simple, but even simple tactics require preparation, timing, and aggressive execution. Drawing from the many accounts of buccaneer fights against Spanish vessels, we see a small vessel of a few great guns and several swivel guns called *patereroes*—or even no artillery at all—lying in wait for a small Spanish ship.

Quickly the chase is on! The buccaneer vessel, its hull built for speed and probably "payed" with tallow and chalk to help it slip through the water more easily, rapidly

gains on its prey. The Spaniard hopes to keep its distance until nightfall, when escape is more likely. It would run itself aground, but cannot, for the buccaneer has slipped between it and the shore. Soon there is no choice but to fight.

Coming within range of Spanish guns, the buccaneers lie along the bulwarks on deck, under cover, until they are within musket range, at which point they open fire aggressively, keeping up a constant, well-aimed fusillade. At first they fire from the forecastle and, if the buccaneer vessel is square rigged, from the foreyard as well. Then, as they range broadside to broadside, they fire from all points, aiming at anyone who exposes himself, but they try especially to kill the officers and helmsman. Spanish defenders wisely duck under cover but some unwisely remain there.

Every time a Spanish gun crew tries to open a gunport, it is met with musket balls. Their number dwindles, and some defenders fear to put a musket over the rail and shoot back. Their officers threaten to run them through. Finally, realizing they must defend themselves or be taken, the crew musters its best effort. But it will not be enough.

Alongside the buccaneer vessel comes, its bow ranging board and board with the Spaniard's main shrouds. The rovers themselves are massed on the forecastle, eager, their adrenaline up, their hearts pounding. They hurl grappling hooks into the Spaniard's shrouds.

A few Spaniards hurl grenades and firepots onto the buccaneer deck, but most have already retreated behind barricaded bulkheads. Just before they board, the buccaneers likewise hurl grenades and firepots onto Spanish decks to clear them of mines and men, then leap aboard, the thick smoke helping to conceal them. If any Spaniard remains on deck, he is quickly dispatched with pistol, cutlass, or boarding ax, for the number ranged against him is overwhelming. No man, as the proverb goes, however strong and brave, can be a Hercules against a multitude.

To flush the barricaded Spaniards from behind bulkheads and below decks, the buccaneers chop and hack holes into the deck, and the defenders in turn shoot wherever light suddenly appears, killing some of their attackers. Other defenders snipe and toss grenades from loopholes. When the holes in the deck are large enough, the buccaneers shove grenades and firepots through them. None can withstand the burns and suffocation of incendiaries in a confined space, and men start choking, screaming, and begging for quarter. Sooner or later, the fight is over. The Spaniard strikes its colors, the buccaneers pillage and plunder.

During battle, the scene on deck resembles a glorious hell to buccaneers: thick smoke coiling on decks and around masts and yards, the smell of blood and burned powder on the air, the flash and sharp crack of musket and pistol, the glint and crash of cutlass in ear and eye, and the cries and shouts of men frightened, emboldened, and enraged—of men living, dying, and about to die, some in defense of property, some in quest of it, and all in defense of their lives at the expense of others'. Black powder has a peculiarly rich, acrid smell when burned on or around seawater, and almost certainly some buccaneers come to associate this odor with the chests of Spanish silver they haul out onto decks darkened with blood and burned powder.

In this hell Morgan learned his first lessons in leadership under fire. Buccaneers all considered themselves leaders, and buccaneer leaders were expected to lead from the front in battle. They had to display both courage and intelligence, and above all, they had to be successful or the crew would turn them out. Men who aspired to lead their buccaneer brethren had to prove themselves in the same way, and it was here in the ugly, violent world of the close fight that Morgan doubtless first made his name. But it was attacks on Spanish cities that he would become known for. Here were the riches of Spain. The buccaneer need not lie in wait for them or chase them. He had but to land, attack, sack, and then escape to sea.

After three or four cruises, Morgan's reputation was assured—and reputation was a critical part of becoming a captain. According to buccaneer-surgeon Alexandre Exquemelin, he now "passed among the buccaneers as a very good soldier. He was intrepid and determined." Just as important, he had not only saved most of his shares of plunder but had also increased them by successful gambling. Most buccaneers were avid gamblers, and one of their favorite dice

A Correct Map of Jamaica, originally printed in the *Royal Magazine*, 1760. The island, captured as a consolation prize after the failed English attack on Hispaniola in 1655, was ideally situated for English buccaneering adventures—for piracy and privateering, that is. Port Royal, the famous port of the buccaneers from 1655 until the late 1680s, is located on the southeastern portion of the island at the end of a long spit of land. In 1692, an earthquake destroyed much of Port Royal, leaving an underwater city rediscovered by archaeologists in the twentieth century.

The Buccaneers in the West Indies in the XVII Century, 1910

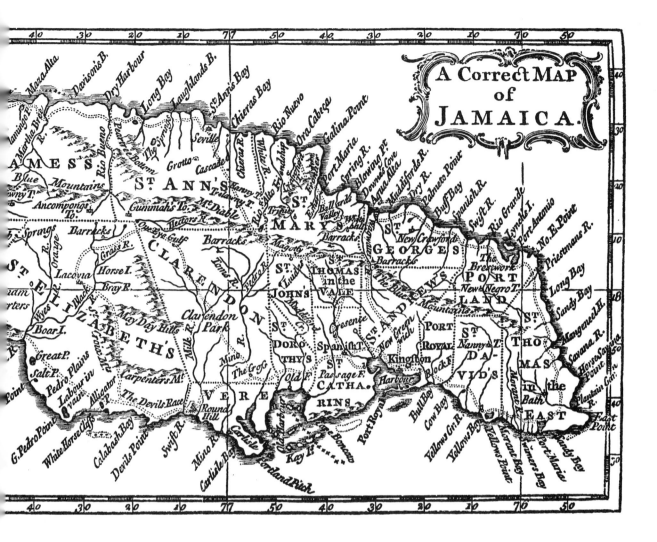

games was called passage. It was an old and simple enough game based on even odds, and it would seem impossible to consistently win at it, but there were many ways to cheat, and side bets on almost any aspect or outcome were common.

PLUNDERING INLAND

Henry Morgan also learned that the real money in piracy was in leadership and ownership. The owner of the vessel received payment in shares, a dozen or so to a small ship, perhaps half to a brigantine or sloop, and thirty or more to a large ship.

Morgan and several of his companions pooled their funds, bought a small vessel, and recruited a crew. The journals of buccaneers and of those who witnessed them all note that buccaneers chose their captains democratically, each man having a single vote. The crew immediately and unanimously voted Henry Morgan as their captain.

His first cruise in command began in 1663 under a false commission, and such was his reputation that he was accompanied by the famous buccaneer captains Morrice and Jackman. They raided the Campeche coast of Mexico and captured several vessels, most of them probably carrying the valuable dyewood called logwood. At the Río Tabasco, they marched 300 miles (483 km) inland and sacked Villa de Mosa, only to find on their return that Spaniards had captured their ships. Morgan took the setback in stride, for he had learned that everything will not always go according to plan, and that obstacles must be turned to one's advantage whenever possible. The buccaneers fended off a Spanish attack, then, with only two barks and four canoes, sailed south and sacked Río Lagartos and Trujillo, in Honduras.

It was attacks on Spanish cities that Henry Morgan would become known for. Here were the riches of Spain. The buccaneer need not lie in wait for them or chase them. He had but to land, attack, sack, and then escape to sea.

By now, he also understood that effective tactics required good intelligence, and the buccaneers were highly proficient in its collection and use. He knew they also required a well-thought-out plan, one that anticipated obstacles and other surprises. Effective tactics also required able leaders and able men willing to follow them. But tactics were often at their best when a bit of unexpected, near-reckless daring was thrown in for good measure.

Putting the principle to use, they sailed south, marched inland again, and sacked Granada, Nicaragua. These deep inland expeditions taught Morgan not only how to attack Spanish cities and towns but also how to lead men long distances across rough terrain. Buccaneers by their very origins were amphibious. Many had been present at the English conquest of Jamaica in 1655, and soon cut their teeth on early raids along the Spanish Main. Quickly they had learned to fight and survive in two elements. They knew how to read the sea and live off the land, and they knew how to kill men in both.

Yet inland expeditions are far more complicated than attacks on coastal towns, and men who undertake armed incursions deep into enemy country require strong yet often subtle leadership. Morale fractures when men begin to wonder whether their leader can salvage an expedition in trouble, or whether they will eat today or maybe only tomorrow, or whether they are on some fruitless venture whose only reward will be to die on an unregarded patch of foreign territory.

Given the daring scope and substantial booty of their twenty-two-month cruise, Morgan and company were received triumphantly in Port Royal. Here the old veteran buccaneer Edward Mansfield, "admiral" of the buccaneers, recruited Morgan to join him as his vice admiral. Unfortunately, the political situation had grown complicated. England was now at peace with Spain and at war with the Netherlands, and Mansfield, along with Morgan and other captains, was commissioned to attack Dutch ships and settlements in the Leeward Islands. Happily, Mansfield and Morgan ignored the commission, and in 1666 attacked the Spanish Main instead. England did not punish the buccaneers. To tell them they could not rob the Spanish Main would be to send them over to the French, or even turn them loose upon the sea as pirates beholden to none.

Upon his next return to Port Royal, Morgan found he had gone from a noted and notorious buccaneer to a famous and infamous one. The old buccaneer Mansfield soon died, of natural causes in some accounts, at the hands of Spaniards in others. Buccaneers and their captains now clamored to serve under Morgan. According to Jamaica surgeon Richard Browne, the men who volunteered to sail with Morgan were such that they knew "every creek, and the Spaniard's mode of fighting, and be a town never so well fortified, and the numbers never so unequal, if money or good plunder be in the case, they will either win it manfully or die courageously." That Morgan was now their admiral showed the caliber and character of man he was. And he yearned for even greater, more profitable victories.

EXTRACTING WEALTH FROM CUBA

Outfitting a ship in 1668, thirty-three-year-old Henry Morgan called for a rendezvous at the south Cuba cays to plan his next expedition. He may have been sent to Cuba by the Jamaica governor to gather intelligence about an impending attack on Jamaica, or perhaps to free English seamen imprisoned by the Spanish. Whatever the inspiration, with a small fleet and 700 buccaneers Morgan set sail for Santa Maria, a small port south of Puerto del Principe, the intended target.

Secrecy was paramount, but not everything could be kept from Spanish prisoners. One of them, an English speaker, overheard buccaneers talking about

Morgan's plans, and leaped overboard near shore. Manning several canoes, buccaneers rowed in quick pursuit, but a lone man hiding among the mangrove is hard to find. Having no time for a lengthy search, the buccaneers gave up. The prisoner had escaped. The alarm was given.

England was now at peace with Spain and at war with the Netherlands, and Mansfield, along with Morgan and other captains, was commissioned to attack Dutch ships and settlements in the Leeward Islands. Happily, Mansfield and Morgan ignored the commission, and in 1666 attacked the Spanish Main instead.

Knowing he might have lost the most critical of tactical elements, surprise, Morgan quickly landed his men and led them in battle order along the main road. Just ahead was a barricade, proof that the defenders of Puerto del Principe lay in wait. Rather than lead his men in a long dirty fight from barricade to barricade and ambush to ambush, Morgan again took his men through the hinterland and caught the defenders off guard. Still, the Spaniards bravely stood their ground when the buccaneers advanced on them "with drums beating and banners flying." Spanish cavalry charged the buccaneer rear, but Morgan's men held firm and used their famed shooting skill to slaughter the horsemen. In pairs they worked, one buccaneer aiming and firing while his partner reloaded. Musket balls flew ceaselessly and with deadly accuracy. Simultaneously, Morgan ordered his buccaneers to form their ranks into a half-moon formation and assault the Spanish infantry in front of them. At first the defenders resisted fiercely, but their conventional martial skills and lack of combat experience were no match for the buccaneers' expert shooting and rash courage.

The piratical onslaught forced the inhabitants to retreat in chaotic disorder to the town. There they shut themselves up in their houses and sniped at the 600 or more advancing buccaneers. Morgan had to put a stop to this, so he threatened to burn the town to ashes and tear women and children to pieces in front of the faces of the valiant defenders. Fear was yet another weapon in Morgan's arsenal. The town surrendered. The pillaging began.

Given that buccaneering was a "for profit" enterprise, the victors did everything in their power, including torture, to force prisoners to reveal their money and goods. They might "wold" a man by tying a tourniquet around his forehead and tightening it, a practice that long predated the buccaneers. They might burn a prisoner with slow matches. They might hoist another by his testicles. Another they might stab with their cutlasses, or rub his feet with grease and light it afire, or strappado—that is, hoist him by his arms tied behind the back, then drop him, causing his shoulders to pop from their sockets. Even the poorest of men were tortured, and some were even murdered though they had nothing. The cruelty of Morgan's buccaneers was not limited to men. The greedy invaders left women and children locked in churches for several days, starving. Many perished.

Torture was commonplace among buccaneers, just as it was among Spanish pirates and *guardas costas*. Some historians have tried to downplay torture by buccaneers, claiming Spanish sources do not much mention it so it must not have happened. But torture is in fact described in a number of Spanish accounts, and given the circumstances and human nature, it would be unrealistic to doubt that torture occurred.

Brutality comes easily to men on a battlefield, especially to those on a violent quest for money. Buccaneers typically used torture to force prisoners to reveal their wealth, or to get intelligence about a city or town's defenses. We do not know whether Morgan drew personal gratification from torture as some buccaneers did. L'Ollonois, for example, personally hacked a prisoner to pieces as an example to other prisoners to reveal their wealth, and even cut the heart out of one prisoner while he still lived, then chewed on it raw.

Eyewitness accounts do not describe Morgan personally abusing prisoners in this manner. Even so, in one lurid and quite possibly exaggerated or even false account he was accused of having a female prisoner stripped and starved because she would not yield her body to him. Most likely, Morgan simply considered torture a practical tactic against an enemy who deserved it. To the Spanish it gave him the reputation of a butcher of the innocent, although some Spaniards themselves had a reputation for torture. After all, did Spain think England had forgotten her old enemy? Did Spain not hope to set the Spanish Inquisition upon English Protestants?

Yet in spite of their great brutality in extracting Spanish wealth at Puerto del Principe, the buccaneers managed to loot only 50,000 pieces of eight, far too little to pay the debts incurred outfitting the expedition. The inhabitants, forewarned, had hidden much of their wealth, or had escaped with it. The cruel victory was also

a hollow one. Henry Morgan had failed, and many of his French followers deserted him when they could not agree on articles for the next cruise. He needed another raid, a profitable one, and soon, if he were to keep his reputation and command.

"I CAN MAKE YOU RICH"

One of the keys to great leadership is the immeasurable ability to persuade, and Henry Morgan had it. According to Exquemelin, after Puerto del Principe he charmed his crew by appealing to their greed and his record. He told his buccaneers he could make them rich, but only if they followed him. He told the anxious, eager men to trust him and soon he would divulge his plans. And his men believed him.

Quickly he gathered them together, adding a vessel recently arrived from cruising off Campeche. Now Morgan had nine vessels, a commission authorizing him to make reprisals at sea, and 460 men sustained only by the hope of the great riches he had promised to deliver. South they sailed, but only his captains knew his intention: to sack the rich trading town of Portobello on the Caribbean side of the Isthmus of Panama. When he finally revealed his plans, some buccaneers objected that the town was too strong. Portobello, though small, was wealthy and in theory well fortified, for from here were the silver and goods of the South Sea ferried to Havana and thence to Spain aboard the great Spanish galleons.

Morgan replied that they would attack by surprise, at night, that the Spaniards did not know they were nearby and would not be expecting an attack. Indeed, Morgan and his captains had apparently abandoned the idea of attacking Havana because surprise would be difficult and the town was now too well fortified. Others objected that they were too few to attack such a strong place. But Morgan had yet another answer: because they were so few, each man's share would be all the greater. "If our number is small, our hearts are great," he told them.

The buccaneers' arrival on the coast was not kept secret for long. Fortune aided him by providing a canoe filled with several escaped English prisoners from Portobello, who confirmed that the city was largely unprepared for attack. At Boca del Toro the small fleet came to anchor. Leaving a small number of men behind to handle the vessels, 422 buccaneers boarded twenty-eight canoes.

They slipped along the coast for three nights, eighteen to twenty men per canoe, coming ashore to sleep and conceal themselves during the day. On the fourth night they pulled their oars as silently as they could until midnight, and went ashore, having rowed more than 100 miles (161 km). They prepared their arms, then marched in

Buccaneers torturing prisoners at Panama, in a print made from a contemporary copper engraving. Torture was common among buccaneers, and was used primarily in the search for plunder. Prisoners were subjected to a variety of cruelties—none of them original among the pirates, however—to get them to reveal their valuables. Some prisoners who had nothing left to reveal were tortured to death, the buccaneers refusing to believe them. Buccaneers also used torture to extract intelligence about a town or city's defenses.

ragged order toward Portobello, some twelve miles (19 km) distant. In complete darkness they made their way, doubtless stumbling and cursing under their breaths, for the new moon was only two days past. They moved quickly, fearing that a Spanish canoe they had earlier surprised but could not capture was bringing the alarm.

Morgan needed another raid, a profitable one, and soon, if he were to keep his reputation and command.

To reduce the chance of getting lost or being surprised, they were guided by one of the escaped English prisoners. Even so, except under a bright moon the movement of armed men at night is difficult, and almost certainly some of the 400 buccaneers straggled or stepped off of the trail or made too much noise. The thought of ambush was ever in their minds, even knowing they likely had surprise on their sides. But they saw no glow of slow match that would signal an ambush, nor did they smell its acrid odor, and never were they surprised by sudden bright flashes followed by the loud ragged cracks that would prove to be a volley of musketry.

At the city's first outpost they surprised the sentry and severely questioned him. To intimidate him they pretended to doubt his every word, telling him repeatedly that he lied and so they must kill him. Eventually, satisfied—perhaps—that Portobello remained unprepared for the attack, they forced the sentry to march in the vanguard, making it plain to him that he would be one of the first to die if he led them into a trap—or for that matter, if they were ambushed or discovered at all. This has been a common tactic for centuries, and is used in some military operations with guides of uncertain reliability even today.

A couple of miles (kilometers) from town they demanded the surrender of a small redoubt, unable to pass it without being discovered, and unable to capture it without firing on it. But the defenders stoutly refused, opened fire, and were quickly defeated. The brief fight reportedly alarmed the town, although at that distance the sound of muskets does not travel well.

The buccaneers moved forward as fast as they could in the darkness, and, fortune smiling upon them, found the town alarmed but its defenses in disarray. According to some Spanish sources, Morgan hesitated when he saw the great central fort, Santiago de la Gloria, commonly called "the Glory" by the buccaneers, fearing he was advancing into a trap. Reportedly reassured by his guide, he ordered his men to attack. We cannot know for certain whether the story is true, for the defeated often invent such stories, just as the victorious invariably try to cover up such truths.

The half-built fort San Geronimo at the far end of town fell quickly as inhabitants meanwhile tried to hide their valuables by dumping them down wells or into cisterns, or by hiding or burying them elsewhere. Some had managed to escape with valuables into the Glory.

And it was the strongly built Glory that was Morgan's greatest challenge. Without its capture he could secure neither the town nor the port. Morgan's buccaneers, many of them located on the nearby hill called La Gloria, opened fire on the fort's great guns, and harassed, wounded, and even killed musketeers and men serving the cannon. Again, the buccaneers were lucky: the cannon were poorly mounted and their powder poor as well, a not uncommon circumstance among the defenses along the Spanish Main.

A 1678 copper engraving of Henry Morgan's attack on Portobello. The illustration shows Morgan's men climbing the walls of the great central fort, Santiago de la Gloria, as described in Alexandre Exquemelin's famous book, *The Buccaneers of America*. According to Exquemelin, the buccaneers built the ladders wide enough so that two or more men could scale them side-by-side. However, according to Spanish records, the buccaneers found Spanish ladders and appropriated them for their own use. The buccaneers who scaled the walls braved a fiery rain of firepots and other incendiaries. © INTERFOTO/Alamy

But the defenders had other weapons besides cannon and muskets. As some of the attackers fired at the fort's musketeers and cannon, Morgan ordered others forward, armed with grenades and boarding axes. Through a gauntlet of musket lead and cannon shot they ran until they reached the walls, leaving Spanish musketeers unable to shoot at them without exposing themselves. Here, protected by the smoke of the battlefield and the covering fire of their fellows, some buccaneers tried to hurl grenades over the ramparts while others tried to blow or chop open the gate and sally port.

But the battlefield could be even deadlier here, for Spanish defenders hurled explosives and "fireworks" down upon buccaneer heads. Iron grenades exploded

Morgan at Porto Bello by Howard Pyle. Although romanticized, as was Pyle's style, the 1887 illustration conveys the helplessness of Spanish prisoners after the sack of the town. The old gentleman on his knees suggests the threat of torture, while the bound woman prisoner hints at rape and other debauchery. Henry Morgan is clearly in charge, although just how much control he actually had over his buccaneers as they looted is debatable.

among the attackers, sending ragged chunks of shrapnel flying among them. Firepots and powder barrels, filled with gunpowder and wrapped with burning slow match, hit the ground, shattered, and ignited among the buccaneers. The great white-hot flashes of gunpowder choked and blinded them. The explosions could burn flesh to the bone, and ignite cartridge boxes and powder chargers slung from belts and straps. The buccaneers, busy aiming, shooting, and reloading, leaped away or dove for cover when they saw the deadly munitions coming their way, and simultaneously shouted warnings to their comrades-in-arms, much as fighting men do today. The buccaneers, held at bay by Spanish incendiaries, retreated.

Henry Morgan knew he had to do something. Quickly he ordered his men to round up the mayor, some nuns and other women, a few old men, and a couple of priests or friars, many still in their nightclothes, and forced them to advance as human shields, in front of his buccaneers, against the castle gate. But the proud Spaniards, hoping they would not have to fire upon their own, realized they must, and did.

This time, though, the buccaneers were undaunted. "One troop managed to set the fort gate on fire" while others used ladders to scale the walls. With grenades and firepots they furiously attacked the Spaniards, forcing them from their protected positions. Now the fight came to "handy grips." Buccaneers fired pistols at close range, and followed up with their cutlasses. Some defenders refused quarter. These the buccaneers overwhelmed, and with ball and blade ended their lives. More than half of the eighty or more defenders died. The town now belonged to Morgan and his sea fighters. He had lost only eighteen men.

THE PIRATE HUNTERS

When he returned to Port Royal, Morgan was hailed as a hero. He planned next to attack the Spanish treasure fleet, but his flagship exploded during a drunken celebration. Morgan was one of the few to survive. The *flota* plan was abandoned for an attack on Maracaibo, Venezuela. With fifteen small vessels and 1,000 men, Morgan made the voyage to the Venezuelan coast in 1669 but only half of his men and vessels arrived at the rendevous. Easily they passed the bottleneck of the great lake of Maracaibo and found its fort largely abandoned. They plundered the town and for a few weeks afterward the hinterland and surrounding coast, including Gibraltar, torturing inhabitants "in the usual manner."

Having wrought what they could from the region, Morgan ordered a return to Port Royal. Forewarned that Spanish warships of the pirate-hunting Armada de Barlovento awaited him outside the lake, the buccaneer admiral sent a scout sloop to the bottleneck, and indeed Morgan's fleet was trapped. His small vessels stood little chance against the well-armed and well-manned frigates in a conventional engagement. He knew he had to quickly devise a ruse that would gain him surprise, and thus advantage. He rallied his men in this desperate situation, and ordered them to build a fireship. They filled a captured Spanish merchant ship with pitch, tar, brimstone, and gunpowder, then disguised it as Morgan's flagship by adding fake great guns as well as wooden props that looked like men. As an added touch, they hoisted Morgan's colors.

In the darkness, Morgan's fleet approached the Spanish men-of-war anchored in the bottleneck. Led by the fireship, the small vessels engaged the Spaniards, but their light cannon did little damage and served only to mask the approach of the fireship. The crew of the Spanish flagship watched as what appeared to be Morgan's own flagship approached. Quickly they recognized that the buccaneers intended to board, and for this the Spaniards were ready. Did not the Spanish sailor and sea soldier fight his fiercest in boarding actions?

Alongside the Spanish flagship came the fireship, and grappled. But instead of the flash and crack of musketry and great guns, the Spaniards were met with smoke and flame. They tried desperately to cut free of the burning ship, but its deck exploded, sending burning debris aboard the Spaniard. In moments the flagship was on fire, and all those who could abandoned her. Meanwhile, the second Spanish man-of-war deliberately ran itself aground near the fort, and the buccaneers captured the third in its haste to escape. In short order Morgan had destroyed the cream

In typical fashion, buccaneers are shown storming castle walls, although in fact the battle for Panama was fought on a savanna, largely in the open, with buccaneer musketry—a constant, accurate fire of individual shots, as opposed to volleys—carrying the day. The cannon in the foreground is anachronistic. Nonetheless, the illustration by Alan Tupper True, published in the December 1906 issue of *Outing* magazine, conveys a good sense of the action surrounding the storming of a fortification, an act repeated in many Spanish cities—just not Panama.

of Spain's New World maritime defenses. More than 130 of the Spanish crewmen were lost. Now the buccaneers had but to run past the fort and sail into the open sea. Yet as they came abreast, its cannon opened fire with a devastating barrage. Morgan ordered a retreat.

Yet again, Henry Morgan was not cowed. Here was an opportunity for tactics in their purest form: victory via deception! He had to work quickly, for other Spanish men-of-war were surely on their way. He ordered his men to build scaling ladders, then sent boat after boat of them ashore in a mangrove swamp near the fort. Immediately the defenders knew what the perfidious buccaneers were up to: an attack from the landward, weakly defended side of the fort. As fast as they could the defenders moved the fort's cannon to face the direction of the forthcoming attack.

Yet none came, for none had actually landed at all! Instead, they had lain down in the boats on the return, leading the Spanish to believe the boats were empty. That night Morgan's fleet sailed safely through the bottleneck before the Spaniards could move their cannon back to the seaward side. The cruel joke was on the battered, tortured, and now fully humiliated Spaniards.

Morgan the hero returned to Port Royal, where his men engaged themselves as usual after a successful cruise. In this "dunghill of the Universe" populated by a "most ungodly debauched people," they first hit the taverns, gorging themselves on food and drinking rum until they were drunk, hurling their glasses against the floor or the wall after each shot. Next they bought new clothes and dressed extravagantly, then gambled and whored. Some bought new arms, and some even invested in plantations, leaving nearly all of them as broke as they were before

Maracaibo. Before long, hundreds of buccaneers were clamoring to cruise with Morgan again. For this reason he always had men willing to undertake the rover's trade of "no purchase no pay." Without them, he could have done nothing.

THE GREATEST BUCCANEER

Thus we find Henry Morgan in 1671 with his men on the savanna before the city of Panama. Victory is swift for the unconventional sea warrior-thieves. The Spanish cavalry charge, but are put to flight by 200 French *boucaniers*, whose extraordinary accuracy and constant fire are devastating. The Spanish infantry attacks, and fails. Meanwhile, some of the defenders stampede a herd of 2,000 oxen at the buccaneers' rear, but this trick cannot work against men who know how to handle and kill livestock. The stampede fails too, and the oxen trample more defenders than attackers. Many of the infantry break ranks and run away. In no time the city belongs to Henry Morgan.

Henry Morgan returned to Port Royal a rich man. Many of his buccaneers, though, were shipwrecked on the Spanish Main and lost their lives. Others felt he had cheated them of their just shares. In Spain and England, the resounding victory made such a noise that the English king resolved to suppress the buccaneers. Henry Morgan, being the greatest of them, was brought to England under arrest in 1672, yet two years later he was made Sir Henry Morgan and sent to Jamaica as lieutenant governor.

In his final years he was rich, owned several plantations, drank heavily with former buccaneers and "privateers," made enemies of a few simpering politicians, cursed much, and was accused of consorting with pirates. He sued the publishers of the first English editions of buccaneer-surgeon Alexandre Exquemelin's *The Buccaneers of America* for libel and won. It was not the book's accusations of his brutality, greed, and mercilessness that angered Morgan, but those of piracy. No more would he be referred to as a pirate, but the descriptions of how his buccaneers tortured, raped, and burned remained.

Morgan did not last long as lieutenant governor before politics did him in. He managed to capture a few pirates, in spite of his obvious affection for some of them. He died in 1688, almost certainly of cirrhosis of the liver brought on by drinking far too much far too often. He received a state funeral with the extraordinary compliment of a twenty-two-gun salute, and was mourned by many. His grave disappeared with much of Port Royal in the 1692 earthquake, and his bones now lie protected somewhere among the shallow ruins of the underwater city.

CHAPTER 6

JUAN CORSO

unknown-1685

BARBARIC AMBUSHES IN SHALLOW WATERS

The captains and crews of the three English sloops at anchor in April 1681 at the Laguna de Términos, an inland lagoon more than forty miles (64 km) wide on the Campeche coast of Mexico, were always on their guard, and today was no exception. The sloops were there to load logwood cut by the loggers ashore, most of them English, who were interloping on Spanish territory.

The threat their lookouts searched horizon and coast for was Spanish pirates, or more correctly, Spanish *guardas costas*, or coast guards. *Guardas costas* were usually privateers authorized to patrol and protect Spanish coastline, and their captains were typically referred to as *capitáns de corso*, or "privateer captains." They were ruthless men, and it paid to be prepared for them.

Today, though, it was not Spanish sails the sloop crews sighted on the horizon, but canoes along the coast, which could have been anything: local Spanish traders, logwood cutters, Native Americans, or even buccaneers. The answer was provided soon enough. They were English seamen, and they recounted how they had come to trade and buy logwood, also known as Campeche wood, from which a valuable dye was made. Several weeks earlier Spanish *guardas costas*, whose armed ships the English often referred to as *armadillos*, had attacked them and captured the *Susan,* a ketch out of London, and three others as well.

The captain of the captured ketch had protested, telling his captors that he had a pass from the Earl of Carlisle, governor of Jamaica, but the Spaniards ignored it, knowing full well that such passes were often mere excuses for piracy. The prisoners were carried to a Spanish jail in Campeche, and their vessels seized as prizes. Those few who had escaped ashore lived as they could on monkeys, iguanas, "and other loathsome reptiles" until they found canoes, sailed to Trist Island, which along with Port Royal Island separated the lagoon from the sea, and discovered the three sloops that would be their salvation.

Or so they thought. In early May, the Spanish entered the lagoon in force. Their *armadillos* and piraguas, or "half-galleys," quickly captured two of the sloops, but the third, trapped between sea and shore, ran itself aground at the south edge of the lagoon on Beef Island. Its crew made its way ashore to the large coastal island and joined up with other survivors and logwood cutters, some eighty men in all. Soon, they

This eighteenth-century pen and ink and watercolor Spanish map depicts the Laguna de Términos on the Campeche coast of Mexico. Note that the map is oriented with south at the top. Port Royal Island is at the center at the north end of the lagoon, and Trist Island (Isla de Tris) is next to it on the right. To the right of Trist Island is the entrance channel. Beef Island is the section of land on the right, and the small island in the lagoon is either One Bush Key or Searles Isaland, often noted in the journals of English buccaneers such as William Dampier.

Library of Congress

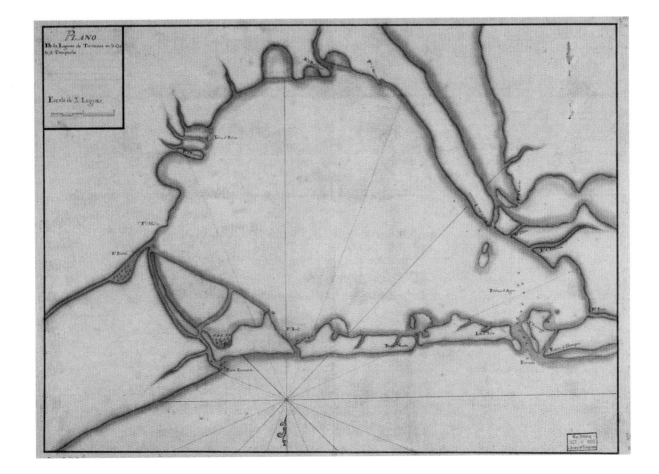

knew, the Spaniards would depart, and the marooned men would live off the land—they were a hardy lot—until more logwood sloops and ketches arrived. They would simply retreat to their rude village of tents and small primitive buildings.

When not chased by Spaniards, loggers, often working in water up to their knees, chopped down logwood trees inland and on the coastal islands, cut them into manageable lengths, and stacked them to await the arrival of the sloops and ketches that brought pieces of eight, not to mention rum and sugar for making punch, which the loggers would get drunk on for days in celebration. When sober, the logwood cutters and hunters would load their logwood and cattle hides aboard the waiting vessel, whose captain would then sail to Jamaica and sell the cargo.

On Beef Island there was plenty of fresh water to drink if the rum ran out, and plenty of cattle for food. There were the usual hazards, of course, of alligators and aggressive feral cattle, but they knew how to deal with those threats. The capture of the sloops would change nothing.

But not this time. The Spanish commander sent soldiers ashore to Beef Island, where they engaged the logwood cutters and quickly routed them. Most fled and hid among the mangrove and other dense vegetation of the island; a few were killed or wounded. The Spaniards were diligent in their work, finding and destroying all the loggers' canoes but one, and burning their small buildings, tents, and supplies. The *armadillos* and piraguas remained on station for a month, well into May 1680, and captured two more vessels. A third, the *Laurel* of Boston, commanded by Robert Oxe, stoutly fought off her attackers and escaped.

The heavily manned flotilla was commanded by Captain Don Felipe de la Barrera y Villegas, a noted pirate hunter who would defend the town, shores, and waters of Campeche against pirates until his death in the early eighteenth century. He did his best to defend San Francisco de Campeche when buccaneers George Spurre and Edward Neville led the sack of the city in 1678, and this raid on Laguna de Términos was in part a reprisal. Serving under him, probably as captains of the piraguas, were Pedro de Castro and Juan Corso. De Castro was the senior of the two, but Corso would soon prove himself far busier and better at robbing the English and French.

They were more than mere interlopers, these English, French, Dutch, and others who trespassed on the Spanish Main and cut down logwood trees, loaded them onto ships, and sold them in Jamaica. Often these men were smugglers at times as well, trading goods by stealth in Spanish ports. Worse, most were *Luteranos* or *Calvinistas*, as the Spanish called Protestants. They were heretics, in other words, not to mention "sons of whores, cuckolds, and drunkards."

But worst of all, most had been, still were, and would probably always be pirates. In their small barks, sloops, brigantines, and *barcalongas*, these trespassers took breaks from cutting logwood, and cruised along the Campeche coast, capturing small vessels, and sometimes even large ones. They raided small rancheros and villages, and left them destitute. These logwood cutters were thieves, as were the men who supplied them with rum and bought their cargo, the smugglers who came to trade on the Spanish Main, and the "sloop men" who came to Spanish islands to capture turtles and gather, or "rake," salt, both of which were valuable commodities in the Caribbean. Obviously, the pirates themselves were thieves. And thieves had to be dealt with, or, like rats, their infestation would grow until it overtook everything.

The fact was, Spain considered any trespassing vessel to be prey, and any vessel carrying *frutas de las Indias*—Spanish goods from the Americas—was also prey. Of course, Spanish privateer and pirate captains loosely interpreted what Spanish goods were. If something in a cargo might have originated on the Spanish Main, whether or not it could also have originated in English, French, or Dutch colonies, it was considered Spanish nonetheless. It was a simple enough pretense, and it was how Spanish *guardas costas* and privateers became pirates. Like their English, French, and Dutch brethren who pretended to be "privateers," so the Spanish pirate in the Caribbean pretended to be protecting the Spanish realm. And often he actually was. But just as often he was a pirate.

Barrera, doubtless with de Castro and Corso in his company, went ashore in June on Beef Island to parlay with the loggers, hunters, and seamen. He promised them security for their "lives, persons, and wearing apparel," which meant he would not kill, abuse, or strip them. He promised also that within two months of their arrival at San Francisco de Campeche he would provide them with a vessel to carry them to Cayenne (in modern-day French Guiana), South America, or Jamaica. The marooned men agreed with his terms, and surrendered. By June, the siege of the logwood camps was over.

Yet Barrera had lied. He packed his prisoners—eighty or ninety had surrendered to him, and as many more had been captured already—into the small holds of two *armadillos* and sailed to Campeche, where they were brutally confined and starved in a "dark dungeon," then sold into slavery. At Veracruz they were

confined in a "close and stinking tan-house," and soon were transported to Mexico City, where they were paraded through the streets before being put to work as slaves. They were fed little and found themselves overwhelmed with lice. One prisoner died in Mexico City, and his body was dragged naked through the streets, mutilated on order of the clergy, then cut to pieces and left as food for dogs and vultures. Many of these men were actually innocent seamen, who had only been doing what they believed they had a license to do. Only a few ever escaped.

Perhaps deliberately, perhaps by mere example, Barrera had given Juan Corso the brutal strategy he would put to notorious use for the next five years. Barrera, however, was soon captured by the English and imprisoned in London.

TO BE A SPANISH PIRATE

Little is known about Juan Corso, also known as Corzo, Costa, and de Costa, other than as a sea rover. We don't know what he looked like, or when he was born, or his nationality for certain. His name may have been an assumed one. Corso was a fairly common Spanish and Italian surname, but it also meant "privateering," and so could have been a nickname. Other Spanish rovers—Blas Miguel Corso, for example—appended the word to their names.

There is a good chance that Corso was a Spaniard, but he could also have been Italian, Portuguese, Corsican, Sicilian, Slavic, Greek, or even a "Levanter," one of the many peoples of the eastern Mediterranean, all of whom the English referred to as "Greeks." His first mate, for example, was Giorgio Niccola from Venetia, which is either Venice or the region surrounding it. Doubtless his crews were multinational and multiethnic. Spanish *guardas costas*, privateers, and pirates were, like the English, French, and Dutch pirates, men of many nations and races, and many Spanish "pirate" crews were composed largely of "Greeks," mulattos, mestizos, and Africans. An English buccaneer called them "barbarous and cruel," Governor Sir Thomas Lynch of Jamaica called them "a mongrel parcel of thieves and rogues," and Lieutenant Governor Hender Molesworth of Jamaica called them "rogues culled out for the villanies that they commit."

We don't know for certain what motivated Corso as a privateer and pirate, but as with many of his sort, plunder and adventure were probably sufficient. Revenge in response to piratical insults to national honor, though, is a possibility. It was time to pay back the English and French for their century and a half of piracy on the Spanish Main.

This fanciful nineteenth-century lithography by Paul Hardy is entitled "Repelling Pirates with a Blast of the Swivel Gun." Swivel guns, also referred to as patereroes, were highly effective against boarders in open vessels, whether small boats as in the illustration, or larger canoes, piraguas, and half galleys. They were also used against boarders on ships as they prepared to come alongside and board. The swivel gun was typically loaded with a small bag of musket balls or scrap metal. At sixty yards its shot pattern might be six feet (2 m) across, but at this range and beyond its effectiveness diminished quickly.

Peter Newark Pictures/ Bridgeman Art Library International

A month later, in July 1680, Corso and de Castro put back to sea in large piraguas that the English referred to as periagers or periagoes. The Spanish in the Caribbean used two sorts of rowing vessels for pirate hunting. The typical piragua carried forty-five to seventy men, from two to six small cannon called swivels or *patereroes*, thirty to forty oars, and usually a single mast and sail, while the typical half-galley carried anywhere from sixty-five to 120 men, four to six swivels in the stern and a great gun in the bow, fifty oars, and two masts and sails. These vessels, often jokingly referred to by the Spanish as "trading galleys" because they usually returned with "goods," were light and swift and drew only a foot and a half (0.5 m) of water, making them ideal for sneaking up on unsuspecting vessels or from launching quickly from ashore when they came by. They were no match for a well-armed, well-manned pirate ship or man-of-war frigate, but they were perfect for capturing trading vessels and making raids.

Corso and de Castro cruised from Campeche south into the Gulf of Honduras searching along coasts and among keys for any vessel that was not Spanish. At the Cochinos Isles near Trujillo, Honduras, they discovered an English ship at anchor. Almost certainly they had intelligence of this intruder via local fishing boats and other local vessels, and knew where to find it. The frigate was filling its water casks, and most likely was in the region for logwood and trade. Had it been there for piracy, it would have had a large crew and the attackers might have "caught a Tartar," as the expression went, and had a battle on their hands they did not want.

Immediately, Corso and de Castro prepared to attack. Surely they scouted the anchored ship, and, learning that most of its crew were ashore, struck with great surprise at night. We don't know what tactics Corso and de Castro actually used to attack the ship at anchor, but there were only a few practical ones. Almost without doubt, using the islands to help screen their approach, the piraguas advanced at night quietly under oar, their masts lowered and stowed on "gallows" on deck so that their profiles would be even smaller. With their shallow draft, they had little to fear from shoals.

Assuming Corso and de Castro had surprise on their side, their boarders, probably seventy or more, swarmed into the waist of each ship like lightening as the piraguas came alongside, every Spaniard screaming "*Mata! Mata!*" ("Kill! Kill!"), all armed with cutlass, machete, or rapier, many armed as well with miquelet-lock pistols that they fired at point-blank range, sometimes shoving the barrel into the enemy's belly before pulling the trigger. Anyone who stood in their way was bound to be cut down. The fight was brief. The attackers killed two English seamen before quarter was granted. It was impossible for fewer than a dozen men to stand against such an onslaught.

The ship was the *Laurel*, whose captain, Robert Oxe, had fought off the *armadillos* of Campeche the previous May, waging a fight that lasted more than two hours, or, as Oxe himself described it, for "four or five glasses." This time he had no such luck. Now a prisoner, he complained of his capture and produced the governor of Jamaica's pass to cut and trade in logwood. According to Captain Oxe, "the Spanish captain slighted Lord Carlisle's pass, flinging it from him and boasting that deponent's was the twenty-second ship he had captured that summer. They said that they would come to Jamaica, too, presently, and that they had taken five hundred English prisoners." It must have been a satisfying moment to capture the ship that not two months ago had confounded them at Laguna de Términos.

Whether out of anger, sheer cruelty, or to send a message, or for all three reasons, the Spanish captain, almost certainly Corso, and crew abused Captain Oxe by "hanging him up at the fore braces several times, beating him with their cutlasses, and striking him in the face after an inhuman cruel manner." Still, Oxe and eight of his men got off relatively easy, for the Spaniards set them free near the Turneffe Islands along the coast of modern-day Belize, in a canoe with two days' worth of provisions. First, though, Corso and his men captured a small frigate nearby, and probably soon after, another ship, doubtless seizing them as they had the *Laurel*.

From the Turneffe Islands Corso and de Castro set sail back north for Campeche, but before they arrived they were informed that a large ship lay at the Laguna de Términos. As fast as they could they pursued their course and soon discovered a thirty-six-gun ship in the lagoon. The draft of their new flagship was too great to pass into the small body of water, and the piraguas were vulnerable to the ship's guns on open water. Corso and de Castro blockaded the lagoon entrance and bargained instead, eventually persuading the captain to surrender. How well the ship's captain and crew were accommodated is unknown, but if Corso treated them as he had treated Captain Oxe and his crew, they did not come off well.

The ship was the *Nuestra Señora del Honhón* of 335 tons (304 metric tons). Elated with their success, they renamed the *Honhón* the *León Coronado* (Crowned Lion) and the large frigate they had captured at Turneffe, the *León*. The names, something of a departure from the usual Spanish practice of naming ships after religious figures, perhaps says something about Corso and de Castro's intentions, and about how they saw themselves as well. De Castro sailed north to Veracruz with the prizes, leaving Corso to return to Campeche with a single piragua. Corso may have put some of his English prisoners to the oars, as he would with the prisoners from of his later prizes.

Upon his arrival at Campeche, Corso found to his chagrin that the local authorities were infuriated to learn that de Castro had carried the prizes to Veracruz. De Castro and Corso had been commissioned in Campeche, not Veracruz. It was a matter not only of local pride, but, more important to the merchants of Campeche, of money. De Castro probably wanted to show off in Veracruz, home of the pirate-hunting flotilla known as the Armada de Barlovento and the destination of the treasure fleet known as the *Flota de Nueva Espagna*—but the glory and profit belonged to Campeche. The *alcalde*, or mayor, ordered Corso arrested, and immediately sent a piragua in haste after de Castro, but it failed to overtake his flotilla. Corso remained under arrest until March 1681, when the viceroy of Mexico finally pronounced his and de Castro's actions legitimate.

With two powerful ships at their disposal—the *León Coronado* and the *León*—Corso and de Castro spent the next year and a half clearing Campeche and the Bay of Honduras of as many interloping English and French traders, loggers, turtle fishermen, and pirates as possible. Any foreign vessel, however innocent its cargo or passage, was also prey, which by definition made the *guardas costas* pirates. Plunder was the object. For Corso and de Castro, it was the best of both worlds: piracy and revenge as duty and obligation.

METHODICAL CRUELTY AND MURDER

In 1682, the *León Coronado* was incorporated into the Armada de Barlovento under her original name, the *Nuestra Señora del Honhón,* leaving the dutiful pirates without their best ship. This was probably a significant part of the reason Juan Corso soon shifted his hunting grounds to the waters surrounding Cuba, Spain's largest island colony in the Caribbean, and apparently parted with de Castro. It was wonderful new territory for Corso. English turtle fishermen called constantly at the nearby Cayman Islands, and buccaneers and filibusters often rendezvoused and provisioned among the myriad Spanish keys on the south side of the island. North of the island was the Old Strait of Bahama, used by many vessels departing the Caribbean for Europe, as well as by those sailing to the Bahamas to "fish" for silver or trade at the English colony at New Providence.

En route to Cuba from Campeche via the Honduran coast in 1682, Corso captured three English ships and also an English sloop with a cargo of sixty slaves, along with some cloth, gold, and silver. With two and sometimes three piraguas at his disposal, Corso established his base at Santiago de Cuba, a town ideally located on the southeastern coast of Cuba and almost five miles (8 km) deep within its bay. From here he had easy access not only to the south Cuban islands and the north Cuban coast, but also to the Windward Passage, between Cuba and Saint-Domingue (modern-day Haiti), and even Jamaica to the south. He quickly set to work, and for the next two years made a name for himself as one of the most notorious pirates of the Caribbean by ambushing English and French trading sloops and often brutally abusing their crews. His first two prizes in these new waters were English ships from Jamaica.

Corso captured his prey, usually trading sloops and ketches, in two ways. If his piraguas were at sea, he would attack from leeward—from downwind, that is—whenever possible. This forced the prey to sail to windward, which was the slowest point of sail, giving the rowing vessels a chance to capture them. If the wind was calm, he could attack from any direction. Privateers and pirates often lay in wait along trade routes and at "choke points" without their sails set, to make it harder for their prey to spot them. Indeed, seeing a vessel underway with no sail set was de facto proof that it was a pirate or privateer. In Corso's case, he would also have lowered his mast, making it very difficult to spot his vessels "in the trough of the sea."

As soon as the prey was close enough, his piraguas would shoot forth under oar, closing as quickly as possible until within 100 yards (91.5 m) or so, at which point his musketeers, probably armed with a variety of matchlock, miquelet-lock, and flintlock muskets, would send forth a slaughtering volume of lead. Two or more swivels would add to the volume. If necessary, and wind and water were accommodating, Corso would have hoisted mast and sail. If he fought under any colors, they were probably a "red ensign"—the flag of no quarter—at the stern and the "Spanish flag," probably the Cross of Burgundy, at the masthead, as at least one Spanish pirate, perhaps Corso himself, did.

If the enemy still resisted, Corso's piraguas would come alongside to board, shoving their bows amidships while their crews hurled grenades and firepots onto the deck, then board screaming and shouting, their adrenaline coursing, the combination of excitement and fear causing them to strike at anything in their path.

If the enemy retreated to closed quarters, Corso and his men dealt with them in the usual fashion. Most small vessels such as sloops and ketches probably surrendered without much of a fight, unless they were well armed and manned.

Corso's most successful tactic, however, was to lie in wait in shallow waters of the islands and shores frequented by turtle fishermen and traders. His piraguas were drawn ashore and hidden, or laid quietly among the mangrove, or rowed slowly along the coast where it was difficult to spot them, then they surged out as fast as their oarsmen could row when an unsuspecting sloop anchored. Typically, Corso's men would either open fire immediately, or, perhaps noting that their quarry was ready to make a fight of it, would "present all their small arms" and threaten to open fire if they did not surrender. If their prey ran itself aground to escape, all the better. But even in such cases, the pirates would often search ashore for the fleeing, hiding crew. He had other tactics as well, and was probably the Spanish pirate who deceptively attacked and murdered Captain Prenar who had come to trade at Cuba. Corso came alongside in a canoe, pretending to desire to trade with the sloop, then attacked.

In August 1683, Corso captured Captain Boucher Clauson and his English sloop *Hereford* among the Cuban islands, after the sloop was driven there by "stress of weather." In Clauson's words: "While I was at anchor there came one Juan de Costa, in a periago of fifty men, who at once opened fire of small arms and dangerously wounded one man. I made no resistance, but they boarded and, in spite of my protests that I had done no trade, forced me into St. Jago, where the governor and Juan Costa detained both sloop and goods, to the value of £4,000, without any examination of me or any legal process."

Corso and the governor seized Clauson's sloop and goods without any legal process at all, or even a pretense of one. Advised to appeal to the court at Santo Domingo on Hispaniola, Clauson did, and received an order for the seizure of the governor's estate to satisfy his claim. Governor Lynch of Jamaica sent an

l. Spanish Guarda

A Spanish *guarda costa* boarding Captain Jenkins's ship and cutting off his ear, an eighteenth-century English engraving of the act that precipitated the War of Jenkins's Ear in 1739. The *guarda costa* is on the left, and the artist has depicted it with the typical high stern of many seventeenth century Spanish ships. Spanish *guarda costas* were notorious for their treatment of prisoners, although the English, French, and Spanish had little to complain about, given the depredations of their pirates and privateers.

...boarding Capt. Jenkins's Ship and Cutting off his Ear.

English man-of-war to escort Clauson to Santiago de Cuba to demand payment, but the governor of the city made excuses, and his friends privately told Captain Clauson that the next time he would be killed.

It was contrary to a treaty between England and Spain for the Spanish to attack English sloops at the Caymans or on the high seas, or to seize *frutas de las Indias* unless they could be proved to be Spanish. But Corso did anyway, and his prizes were "condemned"—formally determined to be now the property of their captors, that is—in Santiago de Cuba. The proceeds were happily shared among captain and crew, not to mention with the governor as well. Bribed by a share of each prize, he was happy to look the other way.

Whenever Corso captured a sloop or ketch, he and his men threatened its crews with death, and told them that they intended to attack all the English they met, and give them no quarter. Corso routinely made murderous declarations, swearing, for example, that he would kill every man in every "turtling" vessel he captured. Given that most of their prisoners survived, this was obvious exaggeration, probably intended by Corso, if not to frighten the English away, then to frighten them into striking their sails and colors on sight of a Spanish piragua or half-galley, merely on the basis of Corso's reputation. On the other hand, Corso's torture of prisoners offered a purpose beyond mere cruelty or a violent message: he would torture them until they confessed that they were indeed trading with the Spanish, whether it was true or not. From there, it was a simple matter of claiming the vessel and its cargo as contraband.

> *Whenever Corso captured a sloop or ketch, he and his men threatened its crew with death, and told them that they intended to attack all the English they met, and give them no quarter.*

But not all of Corso's prisoners survived. Corso is probably the pirate who captured two English sloops, commanded by "one Bodeler and one Wall," in 1683 and murdered the captains and several of their crew. He had earlier captured an English boat with a crew of four, and killed one man—cut his head off, to be specific—because he was sick and could not row strongly.

One of his many prizes was a New England ketch filled with salt "raked" at Salt Tortuga, an island near the coast of Venezuela. It had been captured by French filibusters, and Corso and his pirates seized it, probably in early 1684, while it was en route to Petit Goave, Haiti. They carried the prize into Santiago de Cuba, where its cargo was sold, perhaps this time with a legitimate proceeding. The English crew was imprisoned, but the French filibusters were tried and convicted of piracy. However, as the pirates were being marched to their deaths, the Spanish residents of the town, fearing a reprisal from the French on Saint-Domingue, rose in their defense and prevented their sentences from being carried out.

Corso realized that capturing small fishing and trading sloops, although reasonably lucrative, paled in comparison to the plunder to be had raiding ashore, as the buccaneers and filibusters did. From Santiago de Cuba he set sail with his galleys for the short voyage, perhaps only two days, across the Windward Passage to the north coast of Saint-Domingue. For several years now the filibusters—French pirates, that is—had abandoned their famous haunt at Tortuga Island, just off the coast of Hispaniola, and now resided to the south at Petit Goave. The north coast was largely unprotected but for Port-de-Paix. Corso and his pirates swiftly struck the coast, burning French farms, stealing slaves, and taking other prisoners. Reprisal was but a pretense: this was out-and-out piracy, no different than that practiced by the buccaneers and filibusters who scourged the Spanish Main.

By mid-1683, Corso's depredations had become so notorious that the French governor of Saint-Domingue issued privateering commissions against Spain, and threatened to send his filibusters—there were 1,000 or more based at Petit Goave—to sack Santiago de Cuba in revenge. The English governor of Jamaica was more direct: he threatened war with England if the governor of Havana did not bring Corso to heel. But the attack on Santiago de Cuba never took place. The filibusters, and doubtless the French government secretly as well, had a design on Veracruz instead, a much greater city through which the wealth of Mexico passed to the treasure fleet, and implemented it successfully—and brutally. This in turn inspired more attacks by Spanish pirates, which in turn threatened to create even more buccaneers and filibusters in reprisal for Spanish attacks. It was an ugly, bloody cycle of theft and murder, which pirates like Corso exploited successfully.

Since 1680, Corso had repeatedly threatened to raid Jamaica for slaves, but his great expedition never got underway. He may, however, have been one of the captains who sacked the English-held New Providence, in the Bahamas, in January 1684, partly in reprisal for commissions issued there to pirates against the Spaniards some time before, and probably partly in reprisal for any English pirates who had been at the sack of Veracruz the year before. The expedition's leader, Don Juan de Larco, led a force variously estimated at either 170 or 250 men and at least two piraguas or *barcalongas*. Using three captured "sloopmen" as pilots, the pirates swept ashore at dawn. Most of the residents—some 600 of them, including men who could bear arms—fled to the woods, except for

Pirates boarding a ship from a small boat, from Frank Stockton's late-nineteenth-century *Buccaneers and Pirates of Our Coasts*. The illustration shows Pierre la Grand leading his men aboard an overconfident Spanish galleon, although it could just as easily be of any pirate or privateer sneak attack, including those of Spanish *guarda costas* like Juan Corso. Here, pirates are boarding at the stern along the mizzen shrouds. In fact, pirates usually boarded amidships at the main shrouds, where the freeboard was lower and the main shrouds and chains could be grasped to aid in boarding.

fourteen, probably buccaneers, who held their own against the attackers and retreated safely away, too dangerous to be followed. One inhabitant noted that had there been fifty of these men, the Spanish would never have captured the island. De Larco and his men soon sailed away with a decent haul of booty.

Some accounts, however, write of a second raid on the port soon after, this one led by Corso himself, in which the attackers "burnt all the houses, murdered the governor, and several more in cold blood, stripped the rest of the men naked, and carried away the women, children, and negroes to Havana." Some even claimed that the governor was "roasted on a spit" after he was killed, but according to early-eighteenth-century historian John Oldmixon, this almost certainly was "said to [i]ncrease the terror of the story, and might be better in a poem than in a history." The island was left uninhabited for three or more years afterward.

But the depredations of Corso and his brethren were far more devastating on English and French vessels, including the turtle fishermen, than they were on English towns, coasts, and ports. By 1684, English turtle fishing had all but been shut down, creating something of a crisis, for as many as 2,000 people dined almost daily on turtle in Port Royal, Jamaica, alone. In port, it was the standard fare of the crews of Jamaica vessels, and it was just as popular ashore among both freemen and slaves.

The English governor had to do something to put a stop to the Spanish pirates, of whom Corso was by now the most renowned. Surely Corso also knew that sooner or later a force would be sent against him, even if it wasn't a raid against Santiago de Cuba, or against Trinidad de Cuba, where he appeared to have shifted to, either permanently or for convenience. It was perfectly located for attacking English sloops visiting the cays, given its location immediately to the north of them. Doubtless Corso had a similar arrangement with the governor there as he had at Santiago de Cuba.

The Jamaica governor had often sent a man-of-war against the Spanish pirates in Cuba with some success, but not even man-of-war sloops could pursue piraguas and half-galleys into the very shallow waters they hid in and retreated into when chased. There was only one solution: at Port Royal the English built their own half-galley and beginning in the spring of 1683 sent it periodically into the Cuban cays where, eventually and finally, perhaps in late 1683, Corso was forced into a fight with something more than a weak turtling sloop or merchant ketch.

The English half-galley was armed with several swivels, and almost certainly with a great gun in the bow. Manned with volunteers, many of them surely veteran buccaneers or former buccaneers, plus naval seamen and officers, the galley was not only a formidable force in the shallow waters but also certainly a surprise. With fifty to seventy men in Corso's piragua, or even more if he now commanded a half-galley, he would not have given up without a fight. The renown from such a victory—not to mention the prisoners who could be ransomed—may well have incited him to fight when running would have been a wiser course.

How the battle went we do not know. The English galley's chase gun was a deadly weapon against a piragua, if it could be brought to bear. The fight would have been primarily an exchange of musket fire while maneuvering, the galley trying to hit the piragua with its bow gun, and each side endeavoring to kill the other's musketeers and oarsmen until they could close and board. A fight in November 1684 between an English man-of-war sloop and a Spanish pirate half-galley lasted two hours. Perhaps this fight did also. Eventually, though, Corso had no choice but to escape, probably by running and hiding among the cays or in a creek on the coast, then slipping away to Trinidad de Cuba when he could, relieved at his escape, and furious as well at his defeat. Assuredly, more would suffer at his hands in revenge.

In a small but curious turn of fate, the lieutenant of the galley that almost captured Corso, Captain Derick Cornelison, who was also a buccaneer and hunter of sunken treasure, was later captured in the cays by "Don Juan Balosa" in early 1684. Of course, this was part of the problem of English complaints about Spanish piracy, for many now "upstanding" English citizens of Jamaica had once been pirates, Henry

Morgan included. At any rate, Cornelison's sloop was taken as a prize to Trinidad, his crew imprisoned there, and he barely escaped under threat of death from the governor. He returned aboard the HMS *Bonito*, whose captain had orders to seek the release of Cornelison's crew. But it is not this simple coincidence that is curious: one has to wonder whether Don Juan Balosa, and perhaps some other Spanish pirates with the title and name Don Juan, although it was a very common one, was not actually Corso, perhaps changing his name to confuse the English, much as Diego the Mulatto had done to confuse the Spanish (see chapter 4).

THE SEARCH FOR LASALLE

By 1685, pressure was mounting against the Spanish pirates of Cuba. Several times English men-of-war had attacked, and the French had become just as violently diligent. Pressure from the English and French governments had been brought to bear on Spain, along with the not-so-subtle threat of releasing the scourge of the buccaneers and filibusters onto the Spanish Main. In particular, the English in Jamaica had been doing their reasonable best to suppress their own pirates, although not in all cases successfully. Perhaps Corso realized it was time to go elsewhere, and so he returned to Mexico.

There he learned that the great French explorer René-Robert Cavelier, Sieur de La Salle, had established a settlement somewhere on the Gulf Coast of North America. The Spanish had learned of this through their interrogation of Denis Thomas, a seaman who had deserted the expedition when it visited Petit Goave en route, and soon after joined the French pirates who attacked Campeche. Curiously, some historians now believe that the raid on Veracruz in 1683 was in part cover for La Salle's expedition.

Corso saw this news as an opportunity. He would discover the settlement's location, and destroy it. Not only would he be doing Spain a great service—for any French settlement on the Gulf Coast could threaten the Spanish treasure fleets—but he would profit from it as well. Had not Spain ripped great wealth from the belly of the New World? The Gulf Coast of North America was reportedly rich territory, but few knew much about it. Corso would gain both wealth and renown. And he would teach the French to never set foot on Spanish territory again.

In the spring of 1685, Corso set sail in a half-galley, an ideal vessel for searching among the inlets and barrier islands of the Gulf Coast. In April they stopped at Tuxpan, roughly 130 miles (209 km) north, to pay their respects to the church, and there Corso was joined again by Pedro de Castro. They headed farther north along the coast, first to Tampico, where they took on supplies and intended to recruit a Native American pilot, but could not find one. From there they headed east along the Gulf Coast toward Apalachee, Florida. At one point they passed so close to the French "Grand Camp" on Matagorda Island, Texas, that those ashore could see men aboard the piragua, and prepared their arms in case of attack. But Corso and de Castro went right on by, never knowing they had missed the tiny, starving, failing French village of tents. A storm forced Corso's piragua southeast to the coast of Florida, where it was stranded ashore for two weeks while the crew made repairs.

Corso put back to sea, but foul weather struck again and on May 19 forced the half-galley into an inlet. The half-galley lost its anchor, so Corso put twenty-five men into the shallow water to help fashion a mooring. But when the wind shifted he was forced to leave them behind, lest his vessel be destroyed on rocks and shoals. As soon as he could, he rescued sixteen—the other nine had wandered off for food. He later signaled that the rest should meet him at Apalachee Bay, but he underestimated the distance. The nine were marooned by circumstance.

Corso headed north to search along the coast from east to west, but at Cape San Blas, Florida, another storm attacked and once more wrecked his half-galley—this time permanently. Roughly thirty-five men survived the shipwreck, including Corso and de Castro, but not for long. They had lost their vessel and most of their supplies and arms, and were left practically naked in a hostile wilderness. Starvation and exposure struck with equal force, and many of the stranded men perished, including Corso, who died "of a weakness that he suffered in the breast." The survivors soon turned to cannibalism, carving up corpses and cooking them "without wasting even the heads." Only a handful of Corso's entire crew was ever rescued. De Castro was never seen again.

We'll never know how many English and French vessels Corso captured, either on his own or in consort with de Castro, but fifty or more is a reasonable guess. He caused France to threaten the destruction of Spanish ports and England to threaten war with Spain. He was as successful as many English, French, and Dutch pirates, and was more successful—and far more cruel—than many pirates who are far better known. Importantly, he reminds us of the thin lines between pirate and patriot, between truth and tale, and between courage and outrage.

CHAPTER 7

☠

BARTHOLOMEW SHARP

1650–post 1699

A GAMBLER AT SEA AND ON SHORE
WHO BROKE NEW FRONTIERS

Quietly they rowed up the Río Dulce in the Bay of Amatique, then came quickly ashore near Fort San Felipe de Lara in the early light, these buccaneers who left Jamaica pretending they were going to cut logwood in Honduras. Piracy was their real motive, and their primary targets were the warehouses, or *bodegas* as the Spanish called them, filled with heavy chests of indigo, cochineal, and annatto dyes; fifty- and one-hundred-pound (22.6 and 45.3 kg) hide-wrapped *seróns* of cacao beans; great bundles of cowhides; chests and casks of medicinal sarsaparilla, jalap, and michoacán; and casks of tortoiseshell. Among the property of the rich merchants should be at least a few chests filled with pieces of eight and "plate"—silver ingots called pigs and sows—weighing more than 100 pounds (45.3 kg) apiece, providing they hadn't had time to hide them.

This potential plunder was intended for a great *urca* of 700 tons (635 metric tons) or more and its smaller *patache*, or escort ship, which lay at anchor at some distance. But these pirates had no frigates with which to attack the slow but large, high-sided "hulk" or "Honduras ship," as the English called it, and its *patache* at sea. They had only tiny barks, sloops, *barcalongas*, and canoes that Spanish guns would shiver into splinters, and onto whose decks—if the pirates could even get close enough to the great ship—Spanish crews would hurl firepots and grenades, searing and slaughtering the crews.

And it is for this reason these pirates did not wait to attack the fully laden ships at sea, as they had before, but attacked ashore instead. Doubtless they recalled that only a year ago Captain John Bennet, an old hand among the buccaneers, was battered severely by the great hulk at sea when he tried to capture it with

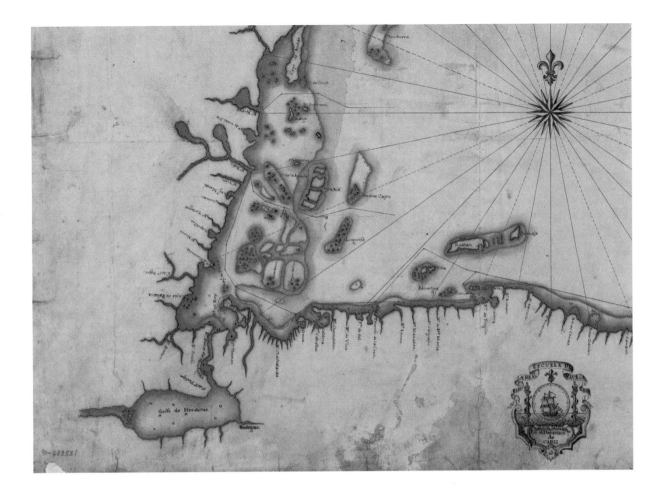

his brigantine and another small vessel. Eighty buccaneers and filibusters were lost that day—including Bennet.

The year was 1679. Having lain in wait at their usual bases in the Gulf of Honduras—at Coxon's Hole on Roatán, or on Guanaja, or among the Sapodilla and other cays that line the western edge of the gulf where the pirates pretended to be going to cut logwood—the buccaneers surged from their lair when the time was right, only a day distant from the Bay of Amatique by sail or a day or two by oar along the coast. From fishermen, Native Americans, and small coastal traders they knew when the *urcas* arrived and when the *bodegas* were full.

This time, the pirates chose to attack as soon as the *bodegas* were filled with goods, but before the ships were well laden. Most likely, the attacking buccaneers had

Eighteenth-century Spanish map of the coast of Honduras. The Bay of Amatique lies just above Lake Izabal (named on the map as the Golfo de Honduras) in the left corner. From the Bay of Amatique, Sharp and Coxon's buccaneers traveled south via the Rio Dulce and attacked the "Castillo de San Phelipe," as the fort is named on the map. The bodegas, or warehouses, were probably located as they are on the map, along a tributary shown on the southeast corner of Lake Izabal. The red lines on the map indicate sailing routes.
Library of Congress

A BARQUE IN THE WEST INDIES
ABOUT 1720

A BRIGANTINE IN THE WEST INDIES ABOUT 1720

Illustrations of a sloop and briganteen originally published in the early eighteenth century by Jacques Gueroult du Pas and Jean-Baptiste Labat. The sloop (referred to as a barque in the illustration) was the workhorse of many pirates, privateers, and pirate hunters from the mid-seventeenth century through the first quarter of the eighteenth century. With its fore-and-aft rig, it could chase or escape quickly to windward. The "Jamaica" or "Bermuda" sloop often had a mast that leaned sharply aft.
The Pirates of the New England Coast, 1923

rowed and sailed their dugout canoes from their tropical base to the Bay of Amatique. If they needed to, they laid up by day under the coastal mangrove, well hidden. Their small vessels followed afterward, ready to carry the successful buccaneers and their plunder home after the raid.

The buccaneers rowed twenty-five miles (40.2 km) up the Rio Dulce, slipped as silently as possible ashore, then attacked the Spanish fort while its sentries slept. If there was any call to arms, the buccaneers fired upon the hastily assembled defenders, suppressing their volleys, while others flanked them and at close range discharged loads of musket ball topped with seven or eight small shot. At this distance these "shotgun" loads, which the buccaneers referred to as "small shot," were devastating. After weakening the enemy defenses, perhaps by grenades as well, the pirates stormed any remaining holdouts, firing their pistols so close that they may have left powder burns on their victims. Cutlasses cleaved through smoke and dust, and large fish-bellied butts of buccaneer muskets cracked skulls as they were brought down upon Spanish heads. The small castle was easily taken.

All in all, there really was not much of a fight—surprise, violence, and the fear they inspired made the pirates' work easy. The warehouses, probably located a dozen or more miles (19.3 km)to the south along a creek that emptied into the lake, and commonly guarded only by a handful of local Native Americans and mulattos, soon belonged to the buccaneers. At the same time, other buccaneers captured the anchored *urca* and its *patache*, at least according to one account, perhaps by slipping alongside in canoes at dawn and quickly boarding.

The principal commander of these buccaneers was John Coxon, a fairly young yet veteran buccaneer, one of the new generation of captains that filled the places left by Henry Morgan and his captains who got rich and retired after the sack of Panama eight years prior, in 1671. With him was Bartholomew Sharp, probably known familiarly as Bat, for his name is given by one English buccaneer as "Batt. Sharpe," by the French often as "Betcharpe," and by the Spanish as "Batharpe." Sharp had been a buccaneer for thirteen years, first taking up the profession of blood and plunder when he was sixteen, perhaps as a legitimate buccaneer-privateer during the Second Anglo-Dutch War. Without doubt he served under Morgan in some capacity, and was almost certainly at Panama in 1671; at Segovia, Nicaragua, in 1675; and at the capture of Santa Marta, in modern-day Colombia, in 1677.

Despite his disdain for authority, the jealousy he created when he repeatedly won at dice against his fellow pirates, and a divisive personality that often led crews to mutiny against him, Sharp's superb seamanship and fearless leadership under fire would ultimately lead him to be known as the pirate who scourged the Pacific coast of the Spanish Main and opened the door for others to follow.

At present he probably commanded about forty men aboard his tiny twenty-five-ton (22.6 metric tons) bark mounted with two cannon, quite possibly mere swivels. If they were carriage-mounted guns, they were no more than three-pounders, puny guns compared to those of a Spanish frigate or merchantman. And a bark? It was but a single-decked vessel with two masts and one or two sails on each mast—mere flotsam, in a manner of speaking, hardly the vessel to strike fear all along the Spanish Main. Yet, as buccaneer-surgeon Alexandre Exquemelin pointed out, with courage and cunning these buccaneers made up for their deficiencies in ships, cannon, and other material.

And it was with these virtues that these buccaneers under Coxon and Sharp captured "the hulk and store-houses at Honduras." But even pirates could be too cunning, as we shall shortly see. They plundered the *bodegas* methodically, even civilly. They captured heavy wooden chests filled with rich blue bricks of indigo dye, as many as 1,000—more than any other plunder, according to one account. Each had a certain mark on it, indicating ownership.

The buccaneers loaded one great stack of chests into their canoes and ferried them to their waiting barks, sloops, and *barcalonga*. They had to choose their plunder carefully, for they could not load it all aboard their small vessels. They did not keep the *urca* and *patache*, perhaps because they were great, slow, lumbering ships that did not sail well to windward—and Port Royal, Jamaica, was well to windward.

Captain Coxon gave the order to load another great pile nearby, but a Spanish gentleman prisoner interrupted him. He pointed out the marks on the chests and told the buccaneers that they belonged to the Spanish ship captains, while those with other marks belonged to merchants. He suggested that it was better to rob merchants than sea captains like themselves. The buccaneers, who had little sympathy for Spanish merchants, agreed, and left the pile of chests alone, instead loading other piles with marks identical to the first chests.

But the Spanish gentleman had the last laugh. The chests he said belonged to sea captains actually belonged to merchants, and were filled with scarlet-colored bricks of annatto, a red dye made from *achiote* seeds, as the pirates later discovered when they opened the few "ship captain" chests they had taken

with them. Whereas indigo sold for three pieces of eight per eight pounds (3.6 kg), annatto sold for four. The buccaneers had inadvertently cut their profit by a quarter. It took more than tactical courage and cunning to be a successful buccaneer. It also took business sense and a suspicious mind, especially when dealing with merchants and government officials.

Coxon and Sharp smuggled some of their plunder ashore among Jamaica's many small, isolated coves. But, after a brief bit of negotiation, the Jamaica governor agreed to look the other way as long as the buccaneers paid customs duties on the indigo. Naturally, he then pretended the plunder made its way into Jamaica via "honest ships." And why shouldn't the governor agree? The customs duties would strengthen Jamaica's anemic treasury. Once again, profit and pragmatism took precedence over pirate hunting. Governor Charles Howard, Earl of Carlisle, even privately agreed to mediate disputes among the pirates over their plunder. Some of Sharp's men had deserted when they saw a pirate-hunting frigate, for example, and Sharp and his crew now refused to pay them their shares. The men appealed to the governor, who promised to do what he could: "If you will be unruly, I know how and have hampered as mad fellows as any of you; but if you will be orderly and governed you will be used like men."

All in all, the raid was profitable, but not nearly enough for men who would quickly squander their pieces of eight in the taverns and stews—whorehouses, that is—of Port Royal. They needed another raid, and another legal pretense so that the Jamaica authorities would not try to hinder their roving. Port Royal, its willingness to accept pirate plunder notwithstanding, had become hostile to buccaneers in the years following Morgan's plundering of Panama. The merchants of Jamaica were growing rich, and trading slaves and merchandise to the Spanish had become more profitable than stealing from them. Now often the buccaneers had to sneak their plunder in or bribe government officials, all while doing their best to avoid pirate-hunting men-of-war. They needed breathing room, and new places to plunder. And soon they would find them. As for Sharp, whether he intended to or not—and probably he did—he was about to take center stage among the pirates of the Caribbean by crossing overland into another ocean.

THE GREAT SOUTH SEA

In late 1679, under the guise of a three-month commission, purchased for ten pieces of eight, to cut logwood in the Bay of Honduras, the buccaneers set sail for the San

Mediterranean pirates playing dice for prisoners, early seventeenth century. Gambling was endemic not only among pirates, but among seamen in general. Many pirates, including Bartholomew Sharp, were rabid gamblers. This is not surprising, given that most pirates were risk-takers. Gambling was often prohibited aboard ship, even among pirates, but was commonly permitted ashore or perhaps even at anchor. Dice was the common gambling instrument, and passage probably the most common game among buccaneers.

Getty Images

Blas Islands along the Darien coast of Panama. First, they sacked nearby Portobello, but the plunder was only 100 pieces of eight per man, far too little.

Soon afterward, seven companies of buccaneers assembled on the Isthmus of Darien, pretending that "Chief Golden Cap," a local Native American chief, had commissioned them to make war on the Spanish. The buccaneer "general" was Captain John Coxon, who commanded two companies, as did Captain Peter Harris. Captains Sharp, Richard Sawkins, and Edmund Cook each commanded a single company. In all, more than 300 men began the march across Darien.

Important to historians and lovers of adventure, the odyssey was blessed with a number of articulate, literate buccaneers, seven of whom wrote journals recounting it, five of them from beginning to end, leaving us with the most detailed written record of any piratical expedition in history.

En route, the buccaneers crept up on Santa Maria and surprised the town. Richard Sawkins led the way, breaching the wooden palisade literally by pulling up several wooden poles, then leading a charge inside to attack the fort with musket and grenade. Expecting riches, they came away with only some church plate, gold dust, wine, brandy, "jerck" (dried) pork, and bread. They continued their rugged, ragged journey across the isthmus, but avoided attacking "New" Panama, built after Morgan reduced Old Panama to ashes, for it was too strong.

Waiting for them in the Bay of Panama were three Spanish men-of-war, called *armadillos*, commanded by Don Jacinto de Barahona. The pirates captured local canoes and barks, checked their arms, and attacked the ships, seeking both plunder and an open door to the South Sea. The buccaneers fired their muskets from their open canoes while the Spaniards shot back from the protection of their ships. Through a thick bank of foglike gunpowder smoke the canoes came alongside the *armadillos*. The buccaneers fired up at the defenders, forcing their heads down, then hurled grenades onto Spanish decks, sending flame and shrapnel among the valiant men of the Main. Pirate and Spaniard each killed and wounded or killed many of the other. Captain Harris was shot through both legs and died two days later of his battle wounds, as buccaneer captains often did. Barahona died in battle as well. In the end, the pirates prevailed, and noted well the courage of the Spanish defenders, two-thirds of whom were Africans and mestizos.

Still, the plunder was not great, but in the harbor they captured a 400-ton (366 metric tons) Spanish treasure ship or galleon, the *Santissima Trinidad*, or *Trinity* as the buccaneers soon called her, Anglicizing her name. They took the

A ship's surgeon treats crewmembers afflicted with scurvy, which Bartholomew Sharp's men suffered from on long voyages. The disease—a seaman grew "scorbutick" in the language of the day— is caused by vitamin C deficiency, although this was not known until the eighteenth century. Even so, seventeenth-century voyagers were well aware that fresh fruit and vegetables were effective against scurvy. Symptoms of scurvy include yellowish, limp skin; severe lethargy; weakness; impaired circulation; leg and joint pain; diminished mental faculties; a susceptibility to infection; and eventually, inflamed, bleeding gums. The disease is fatal if not treated.
© Photri/Topham/The
Image Works

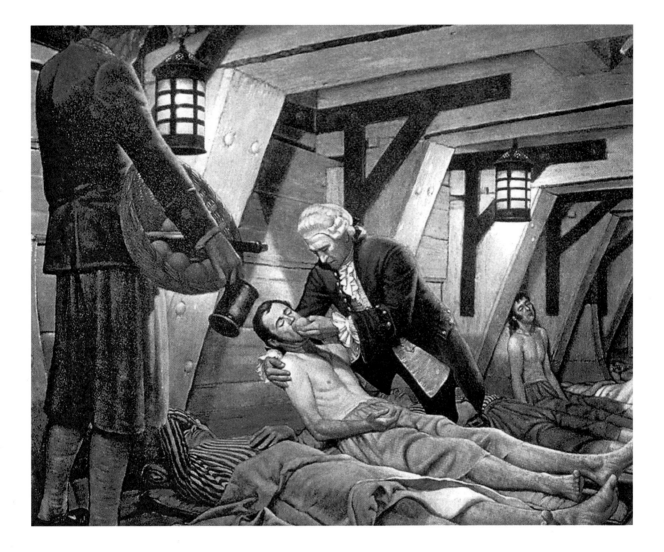

ship without a fight and released her crew. She carried no treasure, and had no great guns mounted, but the buccaneers still made her their flagship, for she was the best sailor in the South Sea.

Immediately, though, the voyage was bedeviled with its first "mutiny." Captain Coxon, accused of cowardice during the Panama battle, abandoned the expedition, along with many of his men. Richard Sawkins was elected "general." Not long afterward, on May 22, 1680, Sawkins led the attack on Puebla Nueva, Panama, charging the stockade. Mulatto and mestizo hunters armed with lances counterattacked, and Sawkins, armed only with a pistol, could shoot only one before the rest lanced him repeatedly, killing him and three other pirates.

A Spanish cup-hilted rapier. Although not all seventeenth-century Spanish rapiers were cup-hilted, many, and perhaps most, were. The design was simple yet provided excellent protection to the hand and wrist. Spanish noblemen and *hildalgos*, not to mention any man who claimed such social stations, however poor he might be, carried the rapier. Spaniards in general used the rapier long after other nations had abandoned it for the smallsword. The example depicted here is highly chiseled and would have been very expensive, carried only by a wealthy gentleman or merchant. Most cup-hilt rapiers, such as those found in the Caribbean, were much simpler. Many were of crude construction, yet still very serviceable.

The loss of Sawkins called for another election, and soon Sharp was in command. Through desertion and death the expedition was soon down to fewer than 150 men. Sharp had to prove himself by making the voyage a profitable one, and he intended to do so. He considered attacking Guayaquil, the main port of Peru, but by now the city was warned of buccaneers in the South Sea.

OF COURAGE AND CUNNING

Instead, in September 1680, Sharp set a course to "fetch" Arica, the Chilean *embarcadero*, or port, from which vast quantities of pieces of eight, mined and minted at nearby Potosí, were shipped. But the course could not be a direct one, for the southeast trade winds blew nearly due north along the coast. Sharp ordered the *Trinity* southwest, out to sea. Two weeks and 1,000 miles (1,609 kg) they sailed before Sharp, an excellent navigator who also relied on local captured pilots and other prisoners, ordered an easterly course.

After two more weeks, food and water grew extremely low, and the symptoms of scurvy began to show: pale, spotted flesh and swollen, bleeding gums. For food the buccaneers were allowed only five ounces (141.8 g) of cornmeal per day. Water was rationed too, and a pint (473 ml) per day—one account says half a pint (237 ml)—was too little to sustain men in any condition for long. Some were willing to pay as much as thirty pieces of eight for a pint (473 ml). Dehydration caused men to become short-tempered, selfish, shortsighted, and sluggish. Buccaneer and writer Basil Ringrose noted that here was a "great disturbance" among the crew, and some, himself included, could not even sleep at night due to the "greatness" of the "drought." Buccaneer minds began to dwell obsessively on thirst-quenching liquids as the body demanded them for survival. They argued, they doubted their leadership, they doubted the conduct of the expedition, they doubted their reason for being where they were at all—yet, so far at sea, they could do nothing except keep to their course.

But Arica could satiate their desire for booty and quench two thirsts, that of water and of wine. After six weeks at sea, the buccaneers heard the cry of "Land! Land!" from the maintop. Sharp set a course to Arica, and north of the town he manned two canoes with thirty men between them, the "striking dory" with eight, and the piragua, or great canoe, with thirty-seven. The surf was too great where they first tried to land, and they were discovered at the second. Spanish horsemen raced to the beach, daring the pirates to come ashore and fight. In the nearby harbor, small Spanish ships fired their swivel guns in "vaporing" defiance. The buccaneers knew that to fire at such range proved that one was either afraid or an amateur—or both. Still, they did not go ashore there, for Arica was large and now alarmed. Such places must only be attacked by surprise.

Sharp now ordered the *Trinity* to Ilo, seventy miles (112.6 km) north. There, on the morning of October 28, he led four canoes and fifty men ashore, eight of whom were left behind to guard the canoes, and who would proceed forward only if they saw a smoke signal. Sharp's company soon discovered that Ilo was protected by only a barricade "thirty paces long, of clay and banks of sand." After a brief skirmish, the defenders and inhabitants retreated into the hills. The buccaneers hoisted English colors at two places, perhaps the Union flag and the English naval ensign, a signal that it was safe for the *Trinity* to approach. They plundered the town of pork, "pitch, tar, oil, wine, and flour," but, unfortunately, of nothing that glittered.

Sharp now ordered as many men as could be spared to come ashore, and led the sixty "fittest to march" to search for hidden plunder. Four miles (6.4 km) they marched, into a rich countryside filled with "fig, olive, orange, lemon and lime-trees." It was a curious scene perhaps, the rude pirates, many of them barefoot, some carrying their muskets casually over their shoulders while others carried them at the ready, many possibly joking while others quietly enjoyed the almost pastoral atmosphere of sunshine, richly scented air, and fields and groves of green.

The Spaniards observed this searching, seeking march, and at one point rolled large rocks down upon the buccaneers. But the pirates were unscathed. They soon discovered a large "sugar-works" where cane juice was turned into loaves of sugar. Sharp sent his "linguister"—his interpreter, that is—with a white flag to the Spaniards, to tell them that the pirates would accept eighty head of cattle as ransom for the sugar-works, which otherwise had little value to them. The Spanish agreed, and the next day sent sixteen and assured Sharp that the rest were on their way. Meanwhile, the buccaneers cut wood for fuel and filled jars and casks with water.

But the next morning there were no more cattle. Again the Spanish provided assurances. "By noon," they said. But at noon there were none. Like the prisoner at the *bodegas* in the Bay of Amatique, these Spaniards knew well the ancient legal maxim, that it was no crime to break a promise made to a pirate: "For they are a sort of men with whom we ought to have neither faith nor oath in common." Of course, it paid to be careful when deceiving pirates, for spiteful armed men could be very dangerous, and by now Sharp knew what his enemy was up to. Without doubt they had raised a force against the pirates and even now it was on its way. Sharp immediately ordered the sugar-works plundered and destroyed. The buccaneers broke the "coppers, cogs, and multitudes of great jars of oil," then burned the sugar-works, including its house and mill, and the cane fields where the Spaniards had hidden much of the sugar.

As the pirates marched back to their canoes, the Spanish well punished for their perfidy, at least as the buccaneers saw it, Sharp and his men spied 300 horsemen headed toward the shore, where only twenty unsuspecting buccaneers were on guard. Quickly Sharp ordered his men into action. As fast as they could they ran toward the shore to join their companions and cut off the horsemen. Each of his buccaneers was armed with a musket and thirty cartridges, plus a pistol or two and a cutlass. But it was the musket that would make the difference.

The buccaneers just barely arrived at the shore before the horsemen. Putting themselves in battle order, they opened fire. The engagement was long and desultory, each side keeping its distance and firing as it could; buccaneer marksmanship kept the Spaniards at bay. According to Sharp, the buccaneers "gave them their bellies full on't." Nonetheless, knowing that reinforcements were on the way, Sharp wisely ordered the buccaneers into the launch and canoes that night. They made their escape, but unfortunately left much of their plunder behind, most of which was provisions they desperately needed, far more important to them right now than Spanish silver.

Still, each man came away with seven and a half pounds (3.4 kg) of sugar, plus some "garden herbs, roots, and most excellent fruit." But the only flesh they found was a mule that quickly became roast meat in buccaneer hands. Still, these few victuals were wonderful "belly timber" after weeks of flour cakes called "dough-boys" dipped in pork lard. It is easy to forget how simple pleasures can boost the spirit. Soon each of the buccaneers had quenched his thirst, filled his belly, and satisfied his sweet tooth. But the provisions were too few, and shortly they would again be left with only bread and water. They had to attack again, and at a place like Arica, where plunder and provisions in quantity might be had.

To sea again they headed, under Sharp's orders, this time to the Chilean port of Coquimbo and the nearby town of La Serena. Again they sailed a month out to sea to avoid the coastal winds, and again provisions grew short. For a while they

The Strait of Magellan, through which Bartholomew Sharp and his remaining crew passed at the end of their South Sea pirating adventure, as depicted in Hack's South Sea atlas. Hack made multiple copies of the atlas, itself a copy of the Spanish *derrotero*, or sailing instructions, captured by Bartholomew Sharp. Intended as intelligence for subsequent English voyages into the region, the Hack atlases may never have actually been used for this purpose. Hack's *derrotero* copies vary in their details. Some, for example, mention the wreck of the Spanish whom Sharp missed at Guayaquil while others do not.

© National Maritime Museum, London / The Image Works

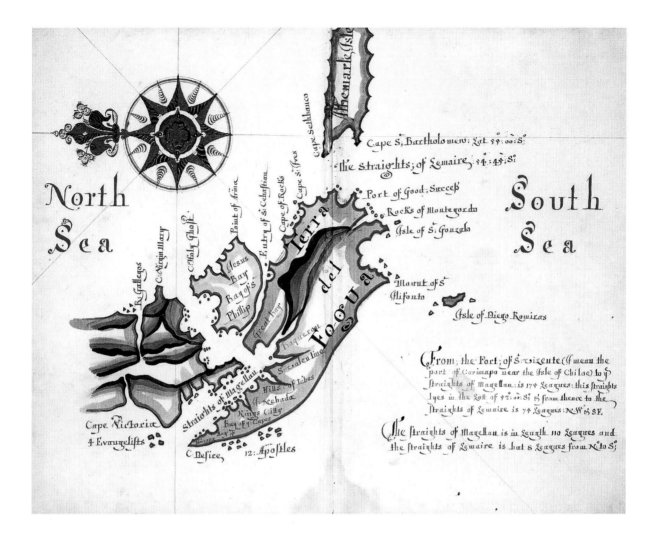

had chocolate, captured at Ilo, to mix with their water. At least it was something. Tempers once more grew short. Sharp wanted to head south this year, through the Strait of Magellan and back to the Caribbean, but many of his crew did not because they wanted more plunder. They grumbled, "saying thay had not voyage enough."

Sharp was part of the problem. He had diced incessantly ashore during the voyage—gambling at sea was apparently prohibited by the articles, for it could be destructive to morale and cohesion, but gambling ashore was not—and he won far more often than he lost. He also had his two shares as captain plus the two shares he inherited from Captain Sawkins when he died. Sharp had more than enough pieces of eight to content him. Of course, he was ready to go home, in spite of promising each man 1,000 pounds' (0.45 metric tons) worth of plunder in English money. The buccaneers who had lost much of their plunder at dice grumbled most. Mutiny was in the air again.

Sharp's navigation continued to prove true, and the buccaneers made landfall near the small port of Coquimbo on December 2, 1680. Here the buccaneers knew they could have the provisions they needed, and if they captured nearby La Serena, a town of seven churches and one chapel—it must therefore be "rich of gold and silver"—they could have fistfuls of coin as well. That night, Sharp ordered the canoes and launch hoisted out, and in them a party of eighty-five or more "stout fellows" set out, Sharp in command. They vowed revenge for the "affronts" the men of Ilo put on them, and all were resolved not to return without plunder. But the launch, heavy and filled to capacity with men, rowed slowly, and the canoes soon left it behind.

It was almost a deadly mistake. Sharp, who as ever was in the vanguard, landed with the men in the canoes and immediately led the buccaneers forward without waiting for the launch. Perhaps he felt they would lose the great advantage of surprise if they waited. Soon, though, he discovered he should have waited, for here, as at Arica and Ilo, they were already discovered. As many as 150 Spanish horsemen suddenly attacked Sharp's small party as it arrived three miles (4.8 km) inland. They were raggedly and variously armed, these Spanish horsemen of Coquimbo and La Serena: "Thay had not all gunns, some launces, other spades," the latter of which were "spados," which derived from *espadas*—rapiers, in other words. But the horsemen refused to permit their poor arms to stop them. Galloping forward, they surrounded and attacked the small party of buccaneers.

Sharp was too experienced a commander not to realize the situation he and his buccaneers were in. Shouting orders, he put his men in groups of five, and told them to fire only one group at a time. This way, the buccaneers kept up a constant fire, one group firing at a time, not in volleys but with each man aiming and firing individually, "to keep the longer from a close fight." Every man would "maintain his ground, or fall upon the spot" he stood on. The buccaneer onslaught was tremendous; its accuracy and sustained fire kept the Spanish horsemen at bay, and killed or wounded those who approached. So quickly did the buccaneers load and fire that in the time of two volleys, men who had fired had already reloaded. Only one pirate was wounded, but the Spanish lost "three of their chiefest men," and four more of their captains were wounded, all of whom they gathered up, then retreated in disorder.

The buccaneers pursued, but at a leisurely pace: Sharp wanted to give the men in the launch time to catch up, assuming they made it ashore. When they did, they followed their fellow buccaneers by "the tracks of our feet and the tops of cartridges" bitten off and spat out when loading. Joined again, the full company pursued the Spanish horse, which would pretend to be ready to give battle, then suddenly ride away. Soon the buccaneers realized they were being led in the opposite direction of La Serena to give time for the residents to escape. Already most of their valuables had been hidden. Once more, Sharp and his buccaneers had been misled by clever Spanish deception.

With Sharp at their head, the buccaneers finally entered La Serena, a town entirely unfortified. Many inhabitants remained, far more than the buccaneers could control, so they told them to hide in the churches because the other buccaneers en route to the town would kill anyone they found in the open. As soon as the churches were filled with prisoners, the pirates "placed at each door a barrel of gunpowder with a train to it and a man standing with a lighted match, who told them that, if they offered to stir out, he would presently give fire." The buccaneers leisurely plundered La Serena of cattle, hogs, wine, and "indifferent good brandy." But of riches there were only church plate and silk hangings.

Again, though, the buccaneers were delighted with the fruit of many sorts, and gorged themselves with fruit described in almost lascivious detail in three buccaneer journals. One journal recounts a "delightsome garden for all sorts of fruite, a[s] cherries, appricocks, peaches, apples, pares, prunellos, strawberries," and the two others are just as wantonly descriptive. The body damaged by thirst demanded these "garden delights," and Sharp's band of cutthroat buccaneers, dehydrated and suffering from scurvy, ravenously devoured it, the juice dripping down chins onto dusty, dirty, tattered, some of them bloody, all of them powder-stained, shirts.

The town secure, Sharp sent a party into the hinterland to search for plunder, but they found only an "old Indian woman and three children." Even the slaves, who were common pirate plunder, were missing, sent far away lest they revolt against their owners when the pirates attacked. One account claims the slaves were murdered to prevent them from rising.

Under a flag of truce the town leaders and buccaneers negotiated a ransom, and agreed on 95,000 pieces of eight. Each side complimented the other and they drank "very friendly together." One Spaniard even asked the pirates to burn his house, whether or not they burned the town. It was the subject of a lawsuit, and he was going to lose it. Doubtless he preferred the victor have no use of it. The Spanish promised to deliver the ransom in the next day or two.

But again the perfidy—or cunning tactics!—of the Spaniard reared its head again. That night an intrepid Native American fisherman, using an inflated horsehide or hog skin, swam out to the *Trinity*. With him he carried a match lighted at each end, plus oakum, brimstone, and other combustible material, all laid on top of the hide. He stuffed the combustibles between the rudderpost and the rudder, then set fire to them, intending to burn the ship. At first the buccaneers believed the fire was set by their prisoners, and so they threatened to kill them. Soon, though, they realized the source of the fire, and quickly put out the flames before they did much damage. It was a brilliant attempt at destroying the pirates. Had it succeeded, the sea thieves would have had no way to escape. Later that night, a minor earthquake shook the city. Perhaps both Spaniard and buccaneer took it as an omen for better or worse.

There was more perfidy to come. Later that night the Spaniards opened sluices and flooded the town ankle deep, perhaps to prevent the pirates from burning it. But it was a useless tactic. Sharp, realizing the Spaniards would pay the buccaneers only in treachery, ordered the town burned. The buccaneers remained as long as they could, ensuring that the town was well aflame. They even locked the doors of the churches to prevent the townspeople from saving church decorations, relics, and the organs, one of which was in every church in La Serena. Only one church survived the flames.

At sea again, Sharp set a course for Juan Fernández Island, off the Chilean coast, which would one day become famous as the home of marooner Alexander Selkirk and the inspiration for *Robinson Crusoe*. Here they cut wood, loaded water, and slaughtered goats for provision—and here they also divided into two factions. The cruise had not been profitable enough, and some buccaneers wanted to sail home while others wanted to seek more plunder. Sharp, they said, had three thousand pieces of eight, while two-thirds of the company had no plunder left. The end result? Sharp was voted out of office.

ON TRIAL FOR PIRACY

In many ways, the rest of the voyage made Sharp's reputation for life. His replacement, John Watling, first engaged in a game of cat and mouse with three Spanish men-of-war. Had the buccaneers been able to separate one from the rest, they might have attacked. As it was, if they boarded one, the rest could come alongside board in support of the attacked Spaniard. Watling wisely chose to stand off, but was condemned by some for being "faint hearted." Desperate for plunder to satisfy his crew, Watling next decided to attack Arica again, in spite of overwhelming evidence that the port was well defended. Sharp vehemently opposed the attack, and "washed his hands" of the plan. He even deplored the murder of a prisoner who claimed the town was well defended, which indeed turned out to be true.

The assault, made on January 30, 1681, was a disaster. Watling was killed in action, and the buccaneers, despite their persistence and courage, were soundly defeated. Amid the battle, the surviving buccaneers beseeched Sharp to command again, and, after briefly pretending to consider the idea, took charge and led his men on an epic retreat under fire. Grouped in a circle with their wounded in the center, the buccaneers fought their way to the shore and escaped, a great credit to Sharp's leadership. The buccaneers knew who could best lead them in a fight.

After another desertion, the buccaneers were now too few to attack any good-sized town. They learned they had missed a ship with 100,000 pieces of eight aboard; it had wrecked on Santa Clara, an island shaped like a corpse in a shroud. They did, however, capture two fairly rich, poorly defended ships, the *San Pedro*, with 37,000 pieces of eight aboard, and the *Santo Rosario*, with even greater prizes aboard. Although the buccaneers foolishly ignored an enormous quantity of "pigs" of tin that turned out to be silver, they did plunder a Spanish chart book covering the known Pacific coast of the Americas. It was extraordinarily valuable intelligence, for until now only Spain knew in detail what was on the far side of the Americas.

Sharp commanded the *Trinity* through the Strait of Magellan and back to the Caribbean, where he was arrested. In June 1682 he was tried for piracy in England and acquitted. No English jury was going to find a scourge of the Spanish Main like Bartholomew Sharp guilty. Of course, there was speculation behind the scenes that the Spanish chart book that he was willing to share with the crown helped his acquittal.

In 1682, Sharp was offered command of the English man-of-war sloop *Bonetta*, which was intended to search for sunken silver. It was a way back to the Caribbean for him, for English ships were otherwise barred from carrying him there. But he never took command. Instead, after squandering most of his plunder "in good fellowship" and discovering that no merchantman would take him as a passenger anywhere out of fear he would seduce the crew into piracy, he purchased a small boat that lay at London Bridge, recruited sixteen men, captured a small French merchantman in the Downs and took it for his own, stole cattle from Romney Marsh to provision his voyage, and set sail for the Caribbean. The Spanish, when they heard Sharp had returned, were outraged.

Sharp, however, knew how the world really worked. In 1684 he accepted a legitimate commission from Sir William Stapleton, governor of the Leeward Islands, to pursue "savage Indians and pirates." Now he could pretend to be legitimate—not the buccaneer or pirate who called himself a "privateer" in hope of preventing his neck from being stretched if he got caught. Sharp knew what could be done with a false commission—what couldn't he do with a real one?

Of course, Sharp was still Sharp. He did capture a pirate, Thomas Henley, but instead of sending Henley's ship, a small frigate stolen from the Spanish, to be declared to the prize court, he instead took it for his own. Renaming it the *Josiah*, he fitted it out with ten great guns, eight swivels, and 100 men. In 1685, he joined French pirates and attacked Campeche, Mexico, with them, later claiming the French "made him do it." The next year, he sailed to Bermuda to sell the slaves still in his possession from the sack of Campeche. Here the colonists were in rebellion against the governor, but only in Hollywood do pirates lead or join popular rebellions against unjust governments. Pirates and unjust governments are one and the same, as St. Augustine pointed out. Only the scale is different. Sharp, soon joined by another buccaneer ship, quickly put down the rebellion.

About the same time, Sharp was accused of piracy by a Captain William Peniston of unknown relationship. Indeed, Peniston also accused him of absconding from debt, stealing cattle, and committing treason, and served writs on him at Bermuda. But the pirate simply "lit his pipe or wiped his breech with them," doubtless with a smile. Unfortunately for Sharp, another adversary, Captain George St. Lo of the Royal Navy, was a different sort, a man not to be trifled with by pirates—and he, unlike Peniston, had the authority to deal with them. Under a warrant from the governor of Nevis, he arrested Sharp and carried him to Nevis for trial. Not surprisingly, on December 30, 1686, a grand jury found insufficient cause to prosecute the slick buccaneer, and on February 12, 1687, he was acquitted by a petty jury on other charges. Captain St. Lo was ordered back to England.

Sharp's career afterward is less well known. In 1688 he was "commander" of Anguilla, but soon had to abandon the island when it was attacked by the French during King William's War. From 1689 to 1690 he led a company of buccaneers and volunteers, probably as privateers, serving under General Christopher Codrington against the French in the Leeward Islands. He most certainly hoped to both serve his king and plunder the French.

SHARP'S VIRTUES AND LEGACY

Sharp succeeded, in spite of himself, for two reasons. Foremost was his exceptional skill at doing what buccaneers did. He was a master mariner, an outstanding navigator, and, above all, a good tactician at sea and ashore, with an extraordinary ability to lead under fire. For this last virtue alone his many flaws may be forgiven. It helped, of course, that his enemy was often inadequately prepared. He even treated his prisoners well, at least the freemen among them, although under his command the buccaneers murdered a friar, the chaplain of a vessel that had come out to fight them. Almost as important as his piratical skill was his ability to convince people that his virtues outweighed his flaws. He convinced buccaneers, juries, and even governors that he belonged on the Spanish Main—armed, in command, and free.

His legacy, however, is far greater than the sum of his parts. It was "Batharpe" the Spanish knew as the commander of the South Sea expedition; it was "Batharpe" who struck fear into their hearts when they heard he had returned to the Caribbean after he was acquitted on charges of piracy. Even the English remembered—and many even praised—Sharp as the commander in the South Sea; some likened him to Henry Morgan. After all, Sharp's voyage, while not particularly profitable, was epic in scope and daring. It was the first buccaneer voyage to the South Sea, and it scared the hell out of the Spanish there, opened the door for two more major buccaneer and filibuster expeditions into the region, and forced Spain to finally defend its thousands of miles (kilometers) of Pacific coastline.

The last we hear of Captain Bartholomew Sharp, age forty-nine, was in 1699 at St. Thomas, where he was under arrest for various "misdemeanors." St. Thomas was well known for its past relations with pirates, not to mention for various other skullduggery. We can only imagine what Sharp, who had "sworn allegiance to the king of Denmark," might have done to incur the governor's ire. Perhaps again it had something to do with accusations, a pipe, and someone's "breech." But misdemeanors are only petty crimes—Sharp had twice survived trials for piracy, a hanging offense. Hopefully, the venerable buccaneer survived long enough to see at least one more adventure through to the end.

CHAPTER 8

EDWARD "BLACKBEARD" TEACH

unknown-1718

"HERE WAS AN END OF THAT COURAGEOUS BRUTE"

The pirate fired the first shot, disturbing the quiet calm of sea and air. It was aimed at a boat taking soundings in the early morning in advance of the two merchant sloops in its wake. Immediately, the king's colors flew aloft on the approaching sloops, first on the *Jane*, the larger of the two, then followed immediately on the *Ranger*. Colors were always hoisted before the first shot was fired aboard a man-of-war, even when the enemy was a pirate. The sloops were hired men-of-war in spite of their merchant appearance, obviously recruited for the specific purpose of hunting this saltwater thief in his lair in Ocracoke Inlet, North Carolina, on the 22 of November 1718.

Quickly the pirate sloop, the *Adventure*, cut its cable, for to remain at anchor would be suicide. A boarding ax would have done the trick, and the anchor would remain marked with a buoy so that it could be retrieved later by the victor, whomever he might be. The pirate probably had another anchor, and even if he did not, losing an anchor was better than having to fight before he was ready. Just as quickly, the pirate sloop hoisted sail as the attackers made their best way toward it under sail and oar, helped along by the incoming tide. The pirate had a few minutes to make ready, but the sloops approaching in the meager breeze were already "made clear for engaging"—they were ready to fight.

Part of being a successful pirate captain was knowing when to fight and when to run. In most cases, a successful pirate would run away from pirate hunters, for there was seldom profit to be had in a fight with a man-of-war. "Hard knocks" followed by a hanging—first by the neck until dead, then in chains—were often the result.

Some pirates, though, were all for fighting a man-of-war, profit be damned, or at least they swore they were. Even so, most pirates of the early eighteenth century either fled, or if they could not, put up only a token resistance, then surrendered, their many boasts and promises to the contrary notwithstanding. "They were prodigiously afraid of meeting with any of His Majesty's ships, nor could they endure to hear any talk of them," wrote one pirate prisoner.

And indeed, this pirate ran at first, to gain some time to make ready to fight, to weigh his options, or simply because he did indeed intend to run. By the time he was well underway, one of the pirate hunters had taken the sounding boat in tow, and both had approached within "gunshot"—point-blank range, in other words—of the cannon, probably three-pounders, mounted on the pirate sloop.

The clash probably began as a running fight. But there are several differing accounts, so we must make educated guesses as to what actually happened. Running fights, which pirates were invariably familiar with—although usually as the pursuer, not the prey or "chase" as it was called—had their own

Blackbeard as depicted in an illustration from Charles Johnson's *The General History of the Robberies and Murders of the Most Notorious Pirates*, and based on Johnson's description of the pirate captain. His beard is braided and tied with ribbons, lighted slow matches protrude from beneath his hat, he wears a pair of bandolier holding braces of pistols, and one hand rests on a short musket, probably a musketoon. Only Johnson mentions the lighted matches, and his description of Blackbeard's appearance may be a bit of poetic license. Regarding Blackbeard's age, his beard would have hidden it well.

special tactics. If the chased vessel had guns astern and the attacker was dead astern, all was well and good. The chased vessel had only to blaze away. But if the attackers were a bit to one side or the other, then the chased vessel had to turn a bit to shoot—and this would slow it down considerably.

The fleeing pirate did his best to keep his sloop beyond the distance of "half musket," roughly 100 yards (91.5 m) or a bit more, from his two pursuers, for

NORTH CAROLINA
COAST LINE.

Showing every Inlet, Sound, & Bay
of special interest from FORTRESS
MONROE to SOUTH CAROLINA.

GEN⁺ BURNSIDE.

this would let him shoot at the enemy astern, but keep him out of the enemy's effective small arms' range. Unfortunately, this strategy failed for the pirate in Ocracoke Inlet: the attacking sloops, using their oars to augment their sails and the tidal current, were closing quickly. Little if any damage had so far been done on either side. Chances are, the pirate only had small cannon called swivels mounted at his stern, and these were only effective at close distance.

Soon coming within range of a speaking trumpet, pirate and pirate hunter hailed each other. The commander of the pirate-hunting sloops was Lieutenant Robert Maynard of the HMS *Pearl*. The pirate opposing him was Captain Edward Teach, best known by his nom de guerre, Blackbeard. He had been up all night drinking "with some of his own men, and the master of a merchantman," but doubtless, given his size and steady practice, could hold his liquor better than most. Still, he may have been hungover, focusing on his adversary through a rum-born haze, his head still spinning a bit as he regarded the man who had obviously come to see him dead.

If Maynard spoke first, his words may have been the traditional "Ahoy!" but more likely were on the order of "Amain for the king of England!"—an order to show submission. But in most accounts, Blackbeard hailed first, and what he said differs a bit in each account.

According to Maynard, Blackbeard called the English seamen "cowardly puppies" and swore "he would neither give nor take quarter." According to a newspaper account, Blackbeard told Maynard "he was for King George, desiring him to hoist out his boat and come aboard." Maynard shouted back that he would come aboard with his sloop, to which Blackbeard replied that if Maynard "would let him alone, he would not meddle with him." Maynard responded that he would have Blackbeard "dead or alive," even at the cost of his own life.

The version of pirate chronicler Captain Charles Johnson was of course the most poetic: "Damn you for villains, who are you? And whence came you?" Blackbeard shouted.

"You may see by our colors we are no pirates," Maynard replied across the water. He may have flown the British naval ensign or the Union flag at his stern, or he may have flown the full suite, so to speak: the king's ensign at the stern, a commission pendant on the single mast, and the Union flag on the bowsprit's jackstaff. Whether Blackbeard yet flew his piratical colors, described in an often inaccurate letter printed in a London newspaper as a "black ensign with a death's head," is not certain. If he did

Civil War–era map of the North Carolina coast, showing "every inlet, sound & bay of special interest." At Ocracoke Inlet, Blackbeard made his common anchorages with Bath Town as his home base. The area was ideal for a pirate's nest: it was located along a critical trade route, yet was difficult to access. To attack a pirate at Ocracoke, a pirate hunter required shallow-draft vessels, a good pilot with knowledge of the area, and surprise.

Library of Congress

so, it was to bid defiance to the men-of-war. Whatever he flew, it was not the "bloody red banner," also known as the flag of defiance, that indicated no quarter.

According to Johnson, Blackbeard then "bid" Maynard to send his boat across, to which the Lieutenant replied, "I cannot spare my boat, but I will come aboard you as soon as I can, with my sloop."

"Damnation seize my soul if I give you quarter or take any from you," Blackbeard replied, tossing down a glass of liquor. Maynard shouted back that he expected no quarter, nor would he give any.

Both men were as good as their word. Blackbeard would turn out to be one of the few pirates of his age who at least once would neither run nor go quietly to the devil. The fight between pirate and pirate hunter was about to get very ugly.

Twentieth-century illustration by Clive Uptton of "Captain" Maynard's "sloop" bearing down upon Blackbeard's "ship." Such illustrations are common but often misleading depictions of Blackbeard's final stand. Shown here are ships, not sloops as was actually the case. The vessels of both Lieutenant Maynard and Blackbeard were single-mast, fore-and-aft rigged, and small. Although some ships did board others perpendicularly, as shown here, the bow crashing amidships, this was a dangerous practice, for the attacked ship could bring all guns to bear. More common—and far more safe—was to board in parallel, bow placed amidships.

A FRIGHTENING APPEARANCE

In one of history's ironies, appearance often outweighs substance. A pirate's image, for example, could cause more fear than his past deeds or ability warranted. One look—a flag hoisted at the maintop, the sight of a mass of cutlass-waving men cursing and threatening from a distance—and the fight is over. This is what Blackbeard counted on. It made his job easy.

The infamous pirate reportedly began his brief but notorious career soon after serving aboard a common Jamaica privateer during Queen Anne's War, which ended in 1713. Many seamen were out of work, including many of the privateers who had fought for plunder during the war. A fair number turned pirate. Blackbeard probably did so in 1715, when many men did, although the first mention of him is in 1716 as the commander of a small sloop mounted with six guns under arch-pirate Benjamin Hornigold. Prior to this he had never commanded a vessel in action or in peace, although according to Charles Johnson he had the reputation of "uncommon boldness and personal courage."

His birth year is unknown, although some have speculated that he was born around 1680, based on popular engravings and woodcuts made after his death, as well as on the idea that he would have to have been older, in his thirties perhaps, to command respect of pirates, most of whom were in their mid- to late twenties. But the images of Blackbeard, made by men who had almost certainly never seen the famous pirate, are misleading and cannot be used to estimate age with any degree of accuracy. Further, it was not age, but ability that made a pirate captain. He had to be a capable, successful commander in battle, and a profitable one, too.

If we look instead at the age of mariners who served aboard privateers, we find boys as young as ten, and volunteers in their teens. Looking from privateers to pirates, it was not uncommon to see pirate captains in their mid-twenties. Using this criterion, Blackbeard could have been born as late as 1690, perhaps even a bit later. He could also have been born before 1680. A good but unsatisfactory guess is that he was between twenty-five and forty years old in 1716.

His birthplace is similarly unknown. Charles Johnson said he was born in Bristol, England. Other historians and authors have claimed he was born in Jamaica, Virginia, and North Carolina. No one really knows for certain, but Johnson's claim is the most likely, given that he had access to living sources.

As for his surname, Teach is what most historians have settled on. It was common in newspapers of the time, and in Johnson's *A General History of the Robberies and Murders of the Most Notorious Pirates*. However, in other documents, Blackbeard's name was spelled a variety of ways, including many variations of Thatch, often in the same document. We might never know his real name, especially if his name was a false one, as some pirates' names were.

Of his character, most of what we know comes from Johnson's book. Curiously, unlike many of his contemporaries, Blackbeard treated most of his prisoners fairly well, although one captain was reportedly "abused." Perhaps the image alone sufficed, and he did not need to beat or torture his prisoners to get his message across. But he did not treat everyone else as well as he apparently did his prisoners. According to Johnson, he once randomly but deliberately cocked a small pair of pistols under the table at which he, his gunner Israel Hands, and a pilot were sitting. "When the pistols were ready, he blew out the candle and crossing his hands, discharged them at his company. Hands, the master, was shot through the knee and lamed for life." Perhaps Blackbeard thought this would keep his men in awe of him. Perhaps he was just cruel, drunk, and bored.

Blackbeard would also, according to Johnson, "prostitute" his teenage wife to five or six of his crew, one after the other, while he watched, after having "lain with her" himself all night, which, if true, is merely a much too polite way of saying he let his crew rape her. Likewise, he and his crew were said to have taken "liberties" with the wives and daughters of the planters—really a term for farmers of most any size—around Bath-Town when he made it his pirate base. Doubtless some gave of themselves freely, but it is likely that others were forced. Perhaps Johnson was engaging in literary license, but the possibility of hardened pirates threateningly taking advantage of a local population is indeed likely. Some

Blackbeard lying dead on the deck of Maynard's sloop, from an illustration in Frank Stockton's *Buccaneers and Pirates of Our Coast*. Artists have commonly taken liberties with the facts in order to evoke a sense of action, and this illustration, showing a ship instead of a sloop, exemplifies the practice. Maynard, left, should be armed with a cutlass instead of a broadsword, and it would be bent or broken. Blackbeard, according to one newspaper at the time, was killed by decapitation. As such, his head should be lying on the deck, or already held by its beard or locks by a jubilant pirate-hunting seaman.

historians have downplayed these stories suggesting rape, considering them to be inventions, exaggerations, or mere gossip; others have not even addressed them.

But above all it is his appearance for which he is remembered. According to Johnson, his "beard was black, which he suffered to grow of an extravagant length; as to breadth, it came up to his eyes. He was accustomed to twist it with ribbons, in small tails, after the manner of our Ramillies wigs, and turn them about his ears. In time of action he wore a sling over his shoulders, with three brace of pistols, hanging in holsters, like bandoliers; and stuck lighted matches under his hat, which appearing on each side of his face, his eyes naturally looking fierce and

wild, made him altogether such a figure that imagination cannot form an idea of a Fury from hell to look more frightful." It should be noted that no eyewitness ever mentioned Blackbeard's burning matches, but it was not unknown for sailors handling grenades in a sea battle to wear burning matches in their hats.

A prisoner of Blackbeard described him as "a tall spare man with a very black beard which he wore very long." A "spare" man was built lean and strong. Blackbeard was not a large, stout man as he is often depicted, but a lean and vigorous one.

His fearsome appearance notwithstanding, it was unlikely to intimidate a merchantman into surrendering—the effect was best up close, not at the 100- to 250-yard (91.5 to 228.6 m) range of a fight at sea, and was thus theatrical, a vanity to draw attention, including from his crew. Surely it served to inspire them, who, like howling imps, were happy to stand by their devil-captain in time of action. But even though Blackbeard's appearance may have been theatrical, its long-term effect was probably profound. Sailors who had been captured by him would later talk of Blackbeard the Pirate, the great-bearded thundering beast decorated with half a dozen or more pistols, who boarded ships with matches burning around his face and smoke swirling around his head.

The fear he generated in this way would serve him well—many merchant crews were surely defeated long before they ever saw the notorious Blackbeard. A seventeenth-century naval captain noted how easily the "false optics" of fear could deceive by exaggeration, even making people see a threat where there was little or none. Most merchant seamen never looked beyond the black flag with skull and bones and the black braided beard fearsomely augmented with matches aglow. They knew what the image meant, and that was enough.

In the spring of 1717, Blackbeard and Hornigold set sail from the port of New Providence, an ungoverned "freeport" in the Bahamas, then home to several pirate vessels and crews. En route to the North American coast, they captured two sloops and a ship, from the latter of which they "got plunder to a considerable value." At some point, Blackbeard took command of a twelve-gun sloop and named her *Revenge*. With two sloops and Hornigold's thirty-gun *Ranger*, Blackbeard could practice ideal pirate tactics. The three vessels could spread themselves out wide across the sea, just in sight of one another, and signal to each other of any ship sighted. The sloops could race down upon the prey, and if it turned out to be too powerful for them, they could hold it at bay until Hornigold's more powerful ship came up.

In this same year, Blackbeard may also have first met the dilettante pirate Stede Bonnet, a bored Barbadian planter who had turned pirate, knowing nothing of the sea. Some accounts put this meeting later. Soon, Blackbeard was on his own, for Hornigold had accepted the king's amnesty, turned himself into a former circumnavigating privateer and now governor Woodes Rogers, who settled at New Providence to suppress the pirates. Blackbeard, however, wanted no part of any amnesty, at least not for now.

Returning to the Caribbean from Virginia later that year, Blackbeard, his "fleet" now down to two sloops, captured a French Guinea-man—a ship trading to the Guinea coast for slaves, and thence to Martinique—named *La Concorde*.

Blackbeard mounted the 200-ton (181.4 metric tons), fourteen- to sixteen-gun ship with forty guns. A large number were swivels, for at 200 tons (181.4 metric tons), the ship could not have carried forty great guns—twenty to twenty-four was the absolute maximum. So Blackboard likely had sixteen to twenty sakers or six-

Late-nineteenth-century illustration of a confrontation between Blackbeard and dilettante pirate Stede Bonnet, from Frank Stockton's *Buccaneers and Pirates of Our Coast*. The date and circumstances of Blackbeard's original alliance with Bonnet are debated, but it is generally accepted that Blackbeard relieved Bonnet of his command, or caused him to be relieved, an unusual act among pirates. Typically, only Bonnet's crew could have removed him from office. That Blackbeard could cause this on his own inspiration illustrates the regard his and other crews had for him, and his command over them.

pounders mounted on the main deck, and the remainder, three- or four-pounders, on the quarterdeck (usually there were no more than four or six there and often none). But by mounting a few swivels on the quarterdeck and forecastle, and one between each of the main-deck guns, we can count forty. Blackbeard may have made her flush-decked by tearing down her quarterdeck and forecastle, but this we have no way of knowing unless the archaeology of the wreck one day provides the answer.

When she was refitted, he named her the *Queen Anne's Revenge* and set sail. She was the equivalent of a small pirate-hunting sixth-rate man-of-war, and would have been shot to pieces by a fourth- or fifth-rate man-of-war. Still, she was a powerful little ship, more than enough to threaten any coast not defended by an English man-of-war. But she was not the great ship with two full decks of cannon Hollywood and fiction have accustomed us to seeing.

Even so, Blackbeard's flotilla of ship and sloops was a substantial force with which to intimidate a merchantman, whose crews were typically small. He needed only to outrun his prey, hoist the intimidating black flag, and have each crewman wave his cutlass in the air. If necessary, Blackbeard might fire a shot "across the forefoot," which was a mariner's term for "across the bow." The black flag was probably intimidating enough for most crews.

The only period description—and it may not be accurate—we have of Blackbeard's pirate colors describes a death's head, which usually indicates only a skull but sometimes refers to both skull and crossed bones, on a black field. Any other flag described as Blackbeard's is probably sheer invention. In general, the black flag with skull or "death's head" and crossed bones, as well as with other images such as hourglasses, full skeletons, and bleeding hearts, began to be used regularly among pirates of Blackbeard's era around 1716.

The infamous "black flag" of Blackbeard and other pirates served its purpose well—it scared the prey into surrendering without a fight. This is how many pirates of Blackbeard's era captured most of their prizes: they frightened them into submission, usually without even firing a shot. Merchant crews were usually too small to fight against seventy, one hundred, or even far more pirates. Their best means of dealing with pirates was to run away. It did not help that there were not enough men-of-war in the New World. For the pirate, it was a field day—free pickings for everyone, at least at sea. The days of pirates sacking rich cities and doing battle with men-of-war filled with treasure were over. The common merchantman was now the sole prey, and they could be quite profitable, slavers especially.

Occasionally, though, some merchant crews did put up a fight, barricading themselves behind closed quarters and giving their pirate attackers hell. Many even got the better of their attackers. But woe be it to the merchant crew that put up a fight and then surrendered! This being said, there is no record of a merchant vessel trying to fight Blackbeard.

According to Charles Johnson and, a century later, historian Thomas Southey, Blackbeard was soon after, in late 1717, chased by the British fifth-rate man-of-war *Scarborough* and fought her to a standstill. The *Scarborough* was reportedly "very short of hands, and very sickly." However, the ship's log does not mention the fight, and there are no other records of the engagement. In other words, it never happened, and if it had and the *Scarborough* had her full complement of men, it most certainly would have ended badly for the pirate. Even so, the imaginary fight did illustrate a vital aspect of the fights between English men-of-war and pirates of Blackbeard's time: when the pirates "won," in reality they usually only broke even and escaped. And when they did claim a rare victory, whether the fight was a draw or the man-of-war was actually defeated, it was usually because the man-of-war was much smaller or grossly undermanned. Seldom did these pirates ever win against men-of-war. Blackbeard was one of the few who at least once truly intended to do so, or die trying.

By December 1718 Blackbeard was in the Caribbean, and there he may actually have first met Major Bonnet, with whom he was quickly unimpressed. He turned the unusual pirate captain out of his command, and put one of his own pirates in his place, leaving Major Bonnet to walk "about in his morning gown, and then to his books, of which he has a good library on board." Bonnet would eventually command a pirate vessel again, and would end his days as he and all cutthroat pirates deserved, with a rope around his neck.

In March and April of 1718, Blackbeard captured a few sloops in the Bay of Honduras, then sailed to the Bahamas and either lay in wait for ships "fishing" for sunken silver on lost Spanish galleons or passing through the nearby Strait of Florida, or fished the wrecks himself for a short time. From there, Blackbeard ordered a course to North America. His crew needed medicines—for syphilis, it has been suggested—and Charleston, South Carolina, was a likely prospect. Charleston was battered by an Indian war and lacked a man-of-war on station to protect it, so Blackbeard knew he could do as he pleased, at least for a short while.

The pirates arrived in late May, seized several vessels just off the town, and held them and their crews hostage, including Samuel Wragg, a member of the Charleston council. It was a shrewd move by Blackbeard. He dared not attack the town itself. Although beleaguered, it could certainly have raised a force of veterans sufficient to repel an attack by pirates, even if it dared not arm a sloop or two and attack the small but powerful pirate ship. This would have been a real concern to Blackbeard, for colonies often sent local sloops or small ships manned with volunteers against pirates, and with fair success. Hostages, however, prevented Charleston from taking such action. Now all Blackbeard had to do was keep an eye out for an errant man-of-war, or worse, one sent specifically to deal with him. But this threat he could easily deal with by keeping his visit short.

As soon as he had the medicine chest he needed and had plundered the vessels he had captured, Blackbeard released his hostages "almost naked" and sailed away, leaving the residents of Charleston both angry and chagrined at their impotence. Without doubt his fearsome reputation, built on little more than an image, had helped terrify Charleston merchants and their council.

By now, though, Blackbeard had a real problem on his hands. The fact was, pirates could not long survive without a base of some sort. If they were to be profitable, pirates needed a place where they could get rid of their goods, provision and refit their vessels, and spend some time in relaxation and recreation, which really meant a place with rum, women, and dice. New Providence was lost. There were areas in the Caribbean and on the African coast where a pirate could temporarily set up shop, but nothing permanent. Blackbeard had to either keep on the move or accept the amnesty the British government had recently offered.

For whatever reason, Blackbeard made a momentous decision. He chose the Outer Banks of North Carolina as his new home, a place where there were plenty of places to hide and good access to merchant shipping along the North American coast. However, his *Queen Anne's Revenge* was unsuitable to such shallow, often treacherous inner waters. He had to get rid of her. Off Topsail Inlet at North Carolina in June 1718, while pretending to beach his ship to careen her—to clean her bottom, in other words—he instead ran her aground. He took a handful of men with him and marooned another handful. The rest he treacherously abandoned. Immediately, he surrendered to the governor of North Carolina, who granted him the king's amnesty, although others would argue that this action was improper, for Blackbeard had committed piracies after September 5,

1718—and only those who had surrendered by this date could accept the amnesty. Any piracies committed afterward would void it. The "reformed" pirate set up headquarters in Bath-Town—and soon returned to piracy.

As soon as he had the medicine chest he needed and had plundered the vessels he had captured, Blackbeard released his hostages "almost naked" and sailed away, leaving the residents of Charleston both angry and chagrined at their impotence.

The primitive economy of the region provided Blackbeard with everything he needed: an outlet for goods and a governor willing to look the other way in return for such goods. As long as Blackbeard kept his depredations fairly small-scale, he would be safe enough, at least for a while. North Carolina governor Charles Eden even did him a favor and first "condemned" Blackbeard's sloop *Adventure* as a legitimate prize, although in fact it was not, and then similarly condemned a sugar-laden French merchantman that Blackbeard had captured. Eden went along with Blackbeard's obviously ludicrous claim that he had found the ship abandoned at sea. Blackbeard proceeded to sell the ship's cargo at Bath-Town, then burned the ship itself so that there would be no evidence. Of course, we should note that some historians have defended Eden as innocent of any piratical complicity. It seems far more likely, though, that he was entirely complicit, as many then believed, and did his best to hide any evidence against him, as corrupt political leaders have always done.

Unfortunately for Blackbeard, no such arrangement could last forever. In Virginia, the deputy governor, Alexander Spotswood, was well aware of the situation just to the south, and neither he nor Virginia's economy could permit it to go on. A nest of pirates next door was unacceptable. Fearing Eden would warn Blackbeard, Spotswood secretly decided to take action himself, although his authority to attack the pirate in North Carolina was debatable. He garnered the support of the guard-ships and pirate-hunters HMS *Pearl* and HMS *Lyme* to deal with the threat. The ships were too large to sail into Ocracoke where Blackbeard's sloop lay, so the governor hired two sloops to carry out the attack on the pirate ship. Virginia sloops of the time ranged from twenty to a hundred tons (18 to 91 metric tons), but most were between twenty-five and fifty tons (22.6 to 45 metric tons), small vessels indeed. Captain Ellis Brand of the HMS *Lyme* led a force over land to attack the pirates at Bath-Town, while Lieutenant Robert Maynard led the sloops, manned with Royal Navy fighting seamen, against the pirate himself in Okracoke Inlet.

Blackbeard would soon come face-to-face with men who were not afraid of his fearsome beard and manner.

"THAT COURAGEOUS BRUTE"

The accounts differ, as they always do in such cases, as to what happened after Blackbeard and Maynard made the terms of the engagement clear, so we must make the best of them. Maynard had fifty-four men under his command: twenty-one men and their commander, an officer named Hyde, in the "little sloop" *Ranger*, and thirty-two men, Maynard included, in the larger *Jane*. Blackbeard had somewhere between nineteen and twenty-five pirates aboard, himself included, as well as eight to ten great guns and probably some swivels. Until it came to boarding, Maynard's men had only muskets and probably a few swivels.

Maynard pressed forward toward the pirate, who by now knew he had no choice but to fight. Pirates knew well how to lie in wait, and Blackbeard was as ready as any to explode upon his approaching enemies. As soon as the two hired sloops came within point-blank range of Blackbeard's broadside, he gave the order to fire. The four guns spat smoke and flame, and their volley of hot metal killed Hyde and wounded five of his men. Immediately, the *Ranger* "fell a-stern," having lost her commander. Maynard shouted for his men to keep up their fire and try to suppress Blackbeard's guns. Largely by circumstance, the pirate hunters "shot away Teach's gib, and his fore-halliards," perhaps with a swivel. Losing control of his sloop, Blackbeard ran aground in the light airs and calm water. The pirate was in trouble.

Maynard, many of his men at the oars, the rest firing at the pirate, maneuvered to board Blackbeard. The pirate hunter's men were massed on deck, with no protection from gunwales or barricade—and the great pirate intended to take advantage of this. At an unknown range, but probably within 100 yards (91.4 m), Blackbeard fired another broadside with his three-pounders, and all were loaded with "swan shot, spick nails, and pieces of old iron." The effect was devastating. Swan shot were small shot, roughly buckshot size. Mixed with old iron scraps and nails, this shot and shrapnel swept Maynard's deck, killing or wounding as many as twenty men. In all probability, Blackbeard's men cheered and hurled foul curses across the water at the bleeding, dying naval seamen.

Maynard knew he could not afford another such broadside. He ordered everyone below. It was probably easy to hide that he was doing this, given the thick smoke drifting slowly in the light airs. He kept only three men on deck: himself, a seaman named Abraham Demelt, and a man at the helm whom he ordered to "lie down snug." Maynard had already lightened his sloop to ensure that he would not run aground on a sandbar as he approached the pirate sloop. On his orders his crew had heaved much of the ballast overboard, staved the water casks, and pumped the water out. Now, having no men at the oars, they approached more slowly, and feared another broadside at any moment.

But luck was on their side. Maynard's *Ranger* crashed alongside Blackbeard's *Adventure* before the pirate commander could fire another slaughtering broadside. Blackbeard ordered his men to hurl "several new-fashioned sort of grenades" made from case bottles (often used for gin) "filled with powder and small shot, slugs, and pieces of lead or iron, with a quick match at the end of it" onto Maynard's deck. He wanted to keep Maynard's men from boarding, or at least thin their ranks out before they did, or even make it so that he and his pirates could board the pirate hunter. But Maynard's men were hidden below, so whatever effect Blackbeard's grenades might have had, it was wasted on air.

In fact, there was nothing really new about these grenades, and it is surprising that they were not also fused with two or more slow matches wrapped around the outside and lit on each end, as such grenades usually were. Perhaps they were, and Johnson simply failed to mention this. This "double priming," as we would call it today, served a valuable purpose: if the grenade did not break, the quick match would soon ignite it, but if it broke, the slow match would light it immediately. Further, the burning powder was far more dangerous than the shrapnel, for these grenades were not very powerful, and especially not with their shrapnel mixed with the gunpowder.

Certain he had cleared Maynard's decks, the pirates boarded, Blackbeard leading the way, cutlass and pistol in hand. As he did, Maynard's remaining men surged from below. The naval officer had wisely had a second ladder built into the hold, so that his men raced topside in half the time. According to Johnson, Blackbeard boarded with fifteen men, including himself, against Maynard's thirteen. Maynard wrote that it was thirteen of him and his own against eleven pirates.

At such close quarters, the usual tactic was to close aggressively with cutlasses and pistols. The cutlass, its blade ranging from two to two and a half feet (61 to 76 cm), was the close-quarters weapon used to clear the decks and deliver the coup de grace after other weapons had been used. Firearms and grenades were the weapons of choice—grenades to help clear the decks, muskets to kill men at longer range, pistols to kill men within a few feet, and seldom beyond six or seven yards (5.5 or 6.4 m). But once grenades had been thrown and pirates had boarded and discharged their pistols, the cutlass by default was the primary weapon at hand. A well-balanced cutlass could be used effectively for short but powerful cutting and cleaving strokes, and, if its wielder knew what he was doing, delivered well. It was the perfect edged weapon in the close confines of the deck of a vessel and with one's comrades-in-arms close by.

Long blades and long strokes were not ideal here—they made it more likely that a blade would get caught on deck rigging or fittings, and were more likely to injure one's own people. Further, long blades were difficult to "free" at close distance: in grappling, for example, it was much easier to pull back a shorter blade and bring it to bear than it was a longer one. In this environment, the difference of a few inches (cenitmeters) could mean life or death. Even so, some men carried these longer blades, as we shall see.

On the deck of the *Jane*, men, fearfully enraged, fought one on one, two on one, and many on one. There was no duel or gentleman's fight: this was a fight to the death. There were no rules. Maynard and Blackbeard each fired a pistol at the other. Blackbeard was wounded. They closed, cutlasses in hand, until Maynard's broke at the hilt, where most blades are the weakest and have the most stress applied to them. Maynard leaped back and drew another pistol. As he brought it to full-cock, Blackbeard swung at him with his cutlass just as a Scottish Highlander, one of Maynard's men, "gave him a terrible wound in the neck and throat." Maynard was only scratched on the hand.

"Well done, lad," Blackbeard is reported to have said after the Highlander struck his probably lethal blow.

"If it be not well done, I'll do it better," the Highlander reportedly replied, and with his broadsword struck off the pirate's head. The battle was soon over. Only nine of Blackbeard's men survived, all "much wounded." None had surrendered while they could yet fight. Blackbeard himself had fallen, probably in age somewhere in his thirties, with "five shot in him, and twenty dismal cuts in several parts of his body."

BLACKBEARD'S GHOST

Today Blackbeard is considered to be the United States' arch-pirate, although there were many, many more who were far more successful, far more brutal, and survived far longer. It is his image that survives. He was larger than life, and he went out fighting, unlike most of his contemporaries, who often surrendered themselves and were hanged. We will never know for certain whether he was trying to escape from Maynard and was trapped into fighting or whether he intended all along to fight to the death, giving and taking no quarter.

Folklore and myth surround Blackbeard. In one tale, he swam around his sloop after being killed. In others, he appeared as a ghost in his old piratical haunts, and still does today. Johnson even wrote that while Blackbeard was alive, his crew found one man more among the crew one day at sea, and they believed him to be the devil himself. We'll never know whether this and similar tales were invented by a pirate crew having fun at the expense of credible listeners, or by others later. And it is always possible that some pirates came to believe in the myths they themselves created. We shouldn't forget that seamen, including pirates, were fond of "sea stories" told to the credulous.

Tales of Blackbeard's purported buried treasure have been around since soon after his demise. Only a few years after his severed head was hung from the bowsprit, a Portuguese seaman named Anthony de Silvestro, who had worked his way by sea to India, claimed that he had "belong'd to one of the sloops in Virginia, when Blackbeard was taken," and that on Mulberry Island the pirates "had buried considerable sums of money in great chests, well clamp'd with iron plates." Naturally, he did not explain why he or anyone else had not found the treasure for themselves, or why he was giving up such a valuable secret.

Charles Johnson gave the myth credence with some invented dialogue. Johnson was factually very accurate by the standard of the day, but much of his dialogue smacks of being invented to make his stories more interesting, and almost certainly was. According to the famous chronicler, in answer to a pirate who asked whether Blackbeard's wife knew where he had buried his money, the notorious rover replied, "Nobody but himself and the devil knew where it was, and the longest liver should take all."

CHAPTER 9

☠

BARTHOLOMEW ROBERTS

1682-1722

A GENIUS FOR FINDING THE GAME
AND AVOIDING THE WARDENS

For eight days in October 1719 they had fought contrary winds and currents, which in the end had left them ninety miles (145 km) to windward of their flagship anchored at Devil's Island in the Suriname River, which flowed from the Guiana Highlands in South America to the sea. The pirate captain—indeed, he was also the captain of their flagship, the *Rover*, in whose company was a recently captured rich Portuguese merchantman—had foolishly given chase in a captured sloop to a brigantine loaded with provisions without bothering to see how well the sloop itself was provisioned. As the pirates quickly discovered when they realized they might be at sea for days fighting wind and sea, the sloop was poorly stocked, by no means able to support forty men for any length of time. Nor would there be relief by capturing the brigantine, for they had lost sight of it soon after sailing in pursuit.

Worse, the captain did not even have a boat to send for water, having sent it back on the eighth day with a message for the flagship to rendezvous with them. But this might take several days. Thirst began to rage among the pirates, and the knowledge that streams and lakes of freshwater were readily available within the visible, verdant shore almost drove them insane. The pirate captain ordered a small vessel built so that a few pirates might get to shore for water. His crew tore up the cabin floor, fashioned a "tub" from its planks by tying them together with rope yarns, and managed to make it safely to shore and back with enough water to keep the cutthroats from perishing.

After several days, the pirates sighted a sail, but it was only the small short sail of a boat, not the large sails of their *Rover* or their great, tall Portuguese prize. It turned out to be the boat the captain had sent for help, and he was soon to learn that both the *Rover* and the prize were gone, taken in a mutiny by an Irish pirate named Kennedy, whom the captain had left in command.

The captain and his forty men were enraged, for they had lost not only their ship but also their great prize—and what a prize it had been! Its capture had been a brilliant showcase for this new pirate captain's courage and intelligence: after nine weeks of sailing without "purchase," as pirates called their captured prey and its plunder, they discovered a merchant fleet of forty-two Portuguese ships waiting for the two seventy-gun men-of-war designated as their convoy. Quickly the pirate captain ordered most of his men below decks and slipped among the fleet as if his *Rover* of thirty-two guns and twenty-seven swivels were just another merchantman. Some captains might wonder whom the *Rover* belonged to, but among so many ships, separated from each other by up to half a mile, it was hard both to know everyone and to tell what might be going on. This tactic of sneaking in was common among pirates and privateers, but it required nerves of steel and a willingness to fight against the odds if discovered.

Espying a deeply laden ship, the pirates came close aboard and ordered the ship's captain to send a boat or they would attack and give no quarter. A stampede of men on deck and a flourish of cutlasses were sufficient to show the merchant captain that the men on the nearby ship were pirates and meant business. Immediately, the Portuguese captain came over. The pirate captain demanded to know which was the richest ship of the fleet, and told the Portuguese captain that if he refused to say which it was, or if he lied about it, he would kill him immediately.

The Portuguese captain quite naturally complied, pointing out a ship of forty guns and 150 men. It was a ship of much greater force than the pirate vessel, for it was not only the number of guns that determined a ship's force, but also the size of the guns. The Portuguese ship was stoutly built and heavily armed, a ship intended to carry and defend rich cargoes.

But the pirate captain was not dismayed, as chronicler Charles Johnson noted. He ordered the *Rover* to steer toward the rich ship, and soon came within hailing distance. He forced a Portuguese prisoner to invite the captain aboard to discuss a matter of consequence with him. The pirate captain soon received his reply across the short distance of water between the two ships: the merchant captain would "wait upon him immediately."

It was just as immediately apparent, however, that there was more activity aboard the rich merchantman than was necessary to launch a boat. Indeed there was too much activity—the ship was being made ready for action, its crew was rushing about, casting off cannon lashings, bringing charges, arms, and grenades up from below deck, and preparing to fight from "closed quarters"—from behind barricaded bulkheads, that is. The pirate captain immediately ordered his gunports opened and guns run out, and soon the ragged thunder of a sixteen-gun broadside shattered both air and merchantman.

A thick, slowly dissipating cloud of smoke hung between the two ships, and under its cover the pirate ship quickly closed the short distance and came alongside to board. The pirates flung grappling hooks onto the rails and into the shrouds, and probably dropped one each from the main and foreyards as well. They massed on their forecastle, then behind a hail of exploding grenades and firepots they boarded, leaping from the pirate vessel into the waist—the deck amidships—of their prey.

Boarding was dangerous. Pirates not only had to contend with enemy muskets, swivel cannon, half-pikes, cutlasses, and exploding mines called powder chests, but also with the dangers of jumping from one ship to another. If a pirate fell, he might drown or be smashed between the two ships. The pirates boarded so quickly that the Portuguese had no time to retreat to closed quarters. The "dispute was short and warm," according to Charles Johnson, "wherein many of the Portuguese fell and only two of the pirates." The ship quickly belonged to the pirates.

The rest of the fleet panicked and scattered, sending signals to the anchored men-of-war, which, although they took their time about it, eventually came up. The foremost, which outsailed the captured merchantman, declined battle when the pirate captain offered it, perhaps fearing that the odds of two against one were too great. The pirate prize, sailing too slowly, had no choice but to fight, and doubtless duty should have provided the same answer to the man-of-war. Instead, the Portuguese warship preferred to wait for its consort to arrive, and by the time it did, the pirates were away with their prize.

Aboard the rich ship were sugar, hides, and tobacco, plus 40,000 gold Portuguese moidores, and gold chains and other gold jewelry, including "a cross set with diamonds, designed for the king of Portugal." Its cargo was a pirate's dream come true, and a fair portion was spent in "all the pleasures that luxury and wantonness could allow," which is a poetic way of saying that the pirates spent their moidores on local rum and women.

159

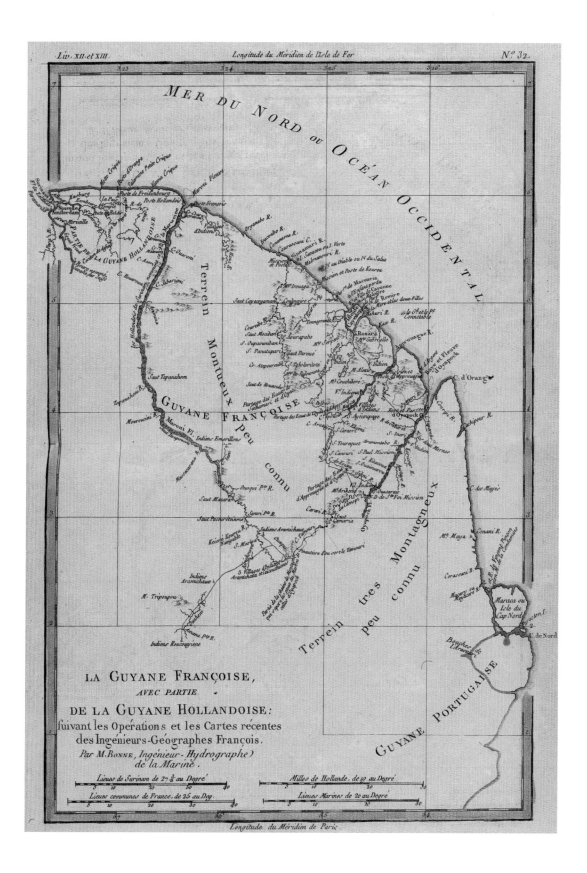

LA GUYANE FRANÇOISE,

AVEC PARTIE

DE LA GUYANE HOLLANDOISE:

suivant les Opérations et les Cartes récentes

des Ingénieurs-Géographes François.

Par M. Bonne, Ingénieur-Hydrographe)

de la Marine.

And now this rich prize was lost, largely though the rashness of the pirate captain, who, rather than send another man in his place, had sailed in pursuit of provisions without provisioning his own vessel, and in doing so had left his ship and crew vulnerable to the opportunistic Irish pirate he had left in charge. The chagrined, enraged, and now far less richer captain was Bartholomew Roberts, and he could never again abide an Irishman. Roberts was a man to nurse a grudge, and if revenge could not be had on those who deserved it, he would have revenge on all who resembled those who deserved it—and this soon became a hallmark of his pirate tactics.

THE CRIMSON TEETOTALER?

Bartholomew Roberts had not been a pirate captain for more than three or four months when he lost his great prize, and had probably not been a pirate for more than four or five months. Formerly the second mate of the merchant ship *Princess* out of London, the tall, black-haired Welshman was captured by the pirate Howell Davis in the spring of 1719. However, we should point out that an inconsistent and quite probably exaggerated 1737 account of the pirate John Plantain claims that Roberts had turned pirate in Rhode Island as early as 1718 and later consorted with pirate Edward England along the coast of Africa and in the Indian Ocean.

Averse at first to joining the pirates, Roberts eventually relented and signed their articles, lured by the freedom and obvious lucre of piracy. Advancement to rank might have been just as difficult among pirates as among merchant seamen, but among the pirates it came by vote of the company, and even the common pirate had a full share of the plunder, and his captain and quartermaster only two. It was a far more equitable arrangement than aboard a merchantman.

Nonetheless, Roberts did not become a pirate out of need, revenge, or a strong sense of injustice, but out of boredom, "novelty," and "to get rid of disagreeable superiority of some [ship] masters he was acquainted with." Of course, Charles Johnson, in his usual romantic and quite probably invented or highly edited language, quotes Roberts as saying that "since he had dipped his hands in muddy water and must be a pirate, it was better being a commander than a common man." Reportedly, he took as his motto, "A merry life and a short one"—and would spend the rest of his life proving it.

Roughly a month after Roberts first turned pirate in the spring of 1719, Howell Davis and several others were killed in an ambush at Prince's Island in the Gulf of Guinea, leaving Davis, with several musket balls in his body, to be tossed

The death of Bartholomew Roberts, as depicted in a nineteenth/twentieth century illustration. The pirates' defense against the attack of the pirate hunting HMS *Swallow* was desultory at best, and when Roberts was killed, his crew lost its spirit and soon after surrendered. The pirate style of leadership was both a strength and weakness. In the latter case, unlike men-of-war crews, who had a regimented chain of command with subordinate officers immediately stepping in to take over when a superior was killed or wounded, pirates often relied heavily on their captain and quartermaster, and often had no other officers designated for command should they die in action.

about in the surf lapping on the shore, and leaving the pirates without a captain and several other officers. Roberts was proposed as captain by the veterans among the crew—the lords, as they called themselves—in spite of his limited piratical experience, for he was said to be a man of "courage, and skilled in navigation; one who by his counsel and bravery seems best able to defend this commonwealth, and ward us from the dangers and tempests of an instable element." Or so Charles Johnson has it. Almost certainly Roberts had exhibited either wise or loud counsel during the aftermath of the ambush, but there had been little other opportunity since his capture to demonstrate his potential as a pirate captain.

It's possible that Davis, a "most generous humane person," had taken Roberts under his wing, but there is no record of this, only speculation based on the fact that both were Welsh. But many seamen and pirates were Welsh. At the very least, Roberts doubtless learned tactics from Davis, if only via stories of the pirate's adventures. Davis was a master of tactical deception and knew how to take a prize with the least fight, and often without a fight at all, and thus capture it with the least damage done to both the prize and the pirates. Add to this that Roberts was a skilled navigator, a specialty often in short supply among pirates of this day, and it is somewhat reasonable to see how he came to be made captain. Most likely, Roberts was elected via a combination of apparent ability and pirate politics.

As soon as the pirates had voted Roberts captain, they resolved by vote to attack the Portuguese at Prince's Island, having vowed a "severe revenge" for Davis's death. They destroyed the small fort, then rigged a small ship, brought it close to shore, and bombarded the town.

However, an account written by Captain William Snelgrave, a former prisoner of Davis's, which he in turn heard from two Capuchin monks who were witnesses, does not mention an attack on the fort, but only a small one on the town, in which Roberts's men built a raft, mounted it with several guns, and bombarded small homes but did very little damage, as one would expect. The pirates next contemplated landing a party of men to burn the town, but, realizing there was a large force of armed Portuguese in the dense wood adjacent to it, abandoned the idea, probably at Roberts's counsel. These pirates had little experience as soldiers, and did not sack towns and cities as their forebears had done.

Indeed, no more was the musket the primary weapon of pirates. These early-eighteenth-century pirates bore the cutlass and pistol with pride instead, although in fact they used them far more often for show than for fighting. The mere sight of 100 pirates, each with one hand waving a cutlass and the other on a pistol hanging from a silk sling, was enough to make most any merchant seaman surrender. But if pirates did have to fight with them, they used them to clear the decks and spaces of men, usually after stunning them with grenades and other "fireworks." Even the pistol was used almost as close as the cutlass was, and sometimes just as close, for it was also an excellent club.

Boarding their own great captured ship, the pirates set fire to two others and "sailed out of the harbor by the light of two Portuguese ships which they were pleased to set on fire there." It would have been an impressive sight, the flames bending in the wind, their light on the water, accompanied by the crack of burning timbers and the smell of burning wood, pitch, and tar.

Three or four months later, in October 1719, Roberts was anchored in the Suriname River in his small sloop. He had neither his *Rover*, which had originally been commanded by Davis and now belonged to the Irishman Kennedy, nor his great prize. Many of his crew were gone with the ships. Roberts was a curious figure among the pirates, a group that invariably had a variety of notable personalities and noticeable peculiarities among its members. He enjoyed drinking tea daily, but probably was not a teetotaler as he is often depicted. Even so, he was abstemious by pirate standards, and he despised the conflicts and lack of discipline common among his often drunken crew. In the ship's articles, he specified that there would be no drinking below after 8 p.m., although it may have been written in nautical language: after eight bells of the first watch. Given that the crew approved the articles says much about Roberts's influence over them. On the other hand, according to Charles Johnson, the pirates largely ignored the article and got drunk as they pleased, Roberts's attempt to promote brief bouts of sobriety notwithstanding.

Bartholomew Roberts was also known as well for his ostentatious dress, although many pirates dressed in such a fashion, in imitation of the gentlemen and princes of the world, for were not pirates princes of the sea? At times he wore a "rich crimson damask waistcoat and breeches, a red feather in his hat, a gold chain around his neck, with a diamond cross hanging to it," proclaiming his status as captain as brightly and loudly as any merchant captain ever did, no matter that he despised many of his superiors in the merchant service.

Soon these merchant captains would learn what a former second mate aboard a merchantman could do when made a pirate captain. From the Suriname River Roberts set forth to prove his worth.

OF FIRE AND FEAR

With what was left of his pirate crew, perhaps only a few dozen, Roberts drafted new articles, hopefully to enforce more discipline and prevent mutiny or the separation of the company. All voted on them and swore an oath on a Bible to uphold them. The sloop then set sail for the Windward Islands, where the pirates quickly took several small prizes, satisfying their need for provisions. Roberts's tactics would remain unchanged throughout his career: go where the merchantmen were, chase everything, fire a gun and hoist the black flag when close aboard, and wait for the prey to surrender. And nearly every time they worked.

While near Barbados in late February 1720, Roberts sighted a merchant galley, which in this case was simply a ship that could also row slowly and maneuver with oars, and also a sloop. He gave chase in his sloop to the galley and soon came up with her and fired a gun. But instead of surrender, he was greeted with three loud "Huzzahs!" and a broadside. Roberts turned and ran from the onslaught. Forced to lighten his sloop by throwing his guns and heavy stores overboard, he just barely escaped. The hue and cry was raised throughout the Windward Islands, and the galley's captain, a stout merchant commander

named Rogers, along with two sloops outfitted at Martinique, pursued him independently through the islands and for all practical purposes chased him away. Never again could Roberts abide a Barbados vessel, and he even fashioned a flag with his figure planting one foot on the skull of a Barbadian, and the other on the skull of a Martinican, out of spite for those who dared stand up to him.

Knowing well where the prey was and the predators were not, Roberts set sail for the North American coast and arrived off Newfoundland in May. In June he swept down upon the fishing fleets like a wolf among sheep. Fishing boats, fishing sloops, and merchant ships, he captured them all, burning many simply out of spite or delight. In Trepassey harbor alone he captured twenty-two sloops and a Bristol galley. In all, he took between thirty and forty vessels in the area, not including the many small open-decked fishing boats called shallops. He mounted the Bristol galley with sixteen guns, and with it captured nearly a dozen French merchantmen, one of which he mounted with twenty-six guns, named it the *Fortune*, and made it his flagship. With this ship Roberts captured even more prizes. Woe be it to any Bristol captain he captured, for he would abuse him mercilessly. After all, it was a Bristol captain who had given him a drubbing off Barbados.

With a ship under his feet again, Roberts sailed south to the Caribbean, arriving in September 1720 at Deseada in the Windward Islands, where many ships entered the Caribbean from Europe. But here he met with little luck and soon ran low on provisions. He tried to buy some at St. Christopher Island, but the governor would not treat with pirates, so Roberts fired on the town, captured one ship, and burned two in the harbor. Such retaliation sent a message that only at one's peril did anyone stand up to Bartholomew Roberts. But at St. Bartholomew he and his crew were treated better. Doubtless the governor and merchants were in need of goods. Or perhaps they were simply intimidated.

From there Roberts set a course for the Guinea coast of Africa, intending first to stop at the Cape Verde islands to refresh and careen the ship's hull. The pirates captured a French merchantman en route, which they exchanged for their *Fortune* and named her the *Royal Fortune*. In this vessel, according to a secondhand English account, was the governor of Martinique, whom the pirate summarily hanged from the yardarm in revenge for the sloops outfitted against him. But once again, Roberts ineptly found himself to windward, and, caught by the trade winds, had to head west for weeks. Once more, he and his crew were soon in danger of dying of thirst. So desperate was their situation that each man was allotted but one mouthful of water a day. Only landfall at Suriname in December 1720 or January 1721 saved them.

Roberts ordered a course north, once more to the Windward Islands, capturing more prizes en route. For revenge he sailed to Martinique, came safely into the harbor by pretending to be a Dutch smuggler, and burned twenty vessels. He continued raiding through the Windward Islands, then sailed to Hispaniola, settled into one of its many isolated coves, and careened.

At one point, Roberts's West Indian rampage was marred by an incident that provides some insight into his captaincy. Furious with the insult given him by one of his drunken crew, Roberts ran the man through with a sword, killing him, which so incensed one of the dead pirate's mess-mates, named Jones, that he cursed Roberts and said he "should be so served himself." Hearing of this, Roberts ran him through too, but surely did not predict the man's reaction. His wound notwithstanding, the angry pirate threw Roberts over a gun—a cannon, that is—and beat the hell out of him. The crew took council among themselves, and decided the assault on their captain deserved punishment, and so the offender was lashed twice, probably with a rope's end, by each man in the crew.

Bartholomew Roberts, as depicted in Charles Johnson's *The General History of the Robberies and Murders of the Most Notorious Pirates*. As in the case of Blackbeard, the illustration is based on Johnson's written description. Whether Roberts actually looked like this is unknown, although his resplendent clothing is accurate. Unfortunately, perhaps no illustrations of pirates of the late seventeenth and early eighteenth century are accurate. All are likely conjectural. At best, a few may have been based on descriptions of pirates by men who knew them or had seen them.

Soon enough, Roberts set sail for the Guinea coast again, this time successfully. He knew that sooner or later he would be treated in the Caribbean as he had been previously, and it was only because there were so few men-of-war on station that he had been so successful. Further, he had no base, and pirates must have one to survive. He had to go elsewhere, and the slave coast of Africa was the likeliest place. There he could find rich slave ships to plunder, and many safe coves where he could refit as necessary.

En route, though, the voyage was marred as a result of his recent violent altercation with one of his crew. Resenting his whipping, Jones and several of his mates joined Captain Thomas Anstis, who commanded an accompanying brigantine they had captured at Dominica in the West Indies. Due to the anger that had built up around Roberts's domineering attitude, a large number of others joined as well, and one night, roughly 400 miles (644 km) from Africa, the brigantine deserted and went on its own way.

On the African coast, Roberts and his men captured dozens more ships, most of them slavers, nearly all without anything resembling a fight. Only once was he threatened by two lightly armed French coast guards, but each quickly surrendered when they realized whom they faced. Roberts's flag, the Jolly Roger, a name known for certain to have been used by only two pirates, inspired the fear it was intended to.

At the end of June 1721, Roberts learned of the pirate-hunting *Swallow* and *Weymouth*, and also that they would be away until December. The coast was clear, Roberts might do as he pleased, and indeed he did. Here along the Guinea coast of Africa he also captured a fine French ship named the *Onslow*, which he took for his new ship, altered as necessary, mounted with forty guns, then made her his new *Royal Fortune*. Roberts and his pirates had reached the pinnacle of piracy, but in their arrogance they had forgotten to keep an eye on the horizon.

SWALLOW VERSUS ROYAL FORTUNE

In February 1721, two English men-of-war had sailed from Spithead in England. Stopping at the Madera and Cape Verde islands, they sailed to the West African coast. By October they had reached as far as Whydah, Prince's Island, and St. Thomas. Their mission? To capture or kill Bartholomew Roberts and his crews, and any other pirates they might encounter as well.

The last ship of Bartholomew Roberts to bear the name *Royal Fortune*. To its left is the *Ranger*, and in the background are prizes captured in Whydah road (anchorage). The flag on the left is based on a written description, and the one on the right is known only from this illustration. Whether they reflect the images on the actual flags is unknown, as no pirate flags of the period have survived. Similarly, no illustrations of actual pirate ships of the era have survived, making even contemporary depictions conjectural. Pirates used the "black flag" to sow terror among their potential victims, making it likely that would surrender without a fight. While pirates were willing to fight, most preferred to plunder without one.
Pirates of the New England Coast, 1923

Not yet having discovered any pirates, they "stretched our starboard tacks to the westward, designing to reach as far to windward as possible, that if any pirates should be on the coast, we might have them under our lee." In other words, the pirate hunters wanted to be able to run down upon them with the wind at their backs, so to speak, and not "beat to windward"—sail a zigzag course in the direction of the wind, in other words—toward them, and thus possibly lose them. Plus, being to windward of an adversary in an engagement had certain tactical advantages. From windward it was easier to aim broadsides at the hull, to board, and in general to control the engagement.

The HMS *Swallow* was a fifty-gun fourth-rate English man-of-war commanded by Chaloner Ogle, a capable seaman and naval tactician who would later, by refusing to pay his men their proper shares, prove himself almost as much of a pirate as the men he pursued. The *Swallow* was mounted with a full deck each of eighteen-pounders and nine-pounders, and carried six-pounders on her forecastle and quarterdeck. A heavily armed ship with clean, swift lines, she outmatched any pirate on the seas, and for this reason had she and her consort been dispatched to seek out and destroy the notorious saltwater thieves.

But by November, many among the crews of both pirate hunters had fallen ill, as crews often did in the tropics. The *Swallow* left the *Weymouth*, which did not have sufficient men well enough to even raise her anchor, behind at Cape Corso on the Guinea coast of Africa to impress merchant seamen and heal her own sick crew. At about the same time, Captain Ogle began to get word of the pirates, and also learned that some merchant seamen had deserted to them, claiming bad treatment aboard merchantmen. Curiously, the pirate hunters also received volunteer seamen who, also citing ill treatment, had deserted from merchant ships and chose instead to serve under the strict discipline of a man-of-war. Harsh treatment notwithstanding, most men in these conditions did not choose to become pirates.

By January 1722, the *Swallow* was in close pursuit of Roberts and his gang, and for them the game of cat and mouse would soon be over. Having relied on largely unprotected coasts and shipping routes, not to mention a dearth of pirate-hunting men-of-war tasked to find and destroy pirates, these rovers of the black flag, who had wrought terror and confusion among the merchantmen and slavers of the Atlantic, were about to be put to the test by officers and men who regarded pirates not as something to fear, but as vermin to be eradicated.

Learning that the Royal Navy was in the area, Roberts quickly quit Whydah on the Guinea coast after ransoming the ships he had captured. Only by twenty-six hours did he miss meeting the *Swallow*. Little did Roberts know that the *Swallow* had learned that the pirates had kept a French ship, a former privateer, as a prize, and that Ogle rightly assumed that they would refit the ship as a pirate ship, and would need a nearby place to do so. Roberts believed he had safely escaped yet again. Ogle, though, was busy searching for areas that "had depth of water sufficient" for a pirate to careen and refit.

At dawn on February 5, 1722, Roberts and his men sighted a single ship well below the horizon. Sails can be seen above the horizon long before the hull of a ship is, and at any other time of the day the pirates on the shore would have spotted the *Swallow*'s topsails when the ship was nine or more nautical miles away. And if any pirates had been keeping lookout in the maintops, they might have spotted the *Swallow* as far away as twenty-one nautical miles, if the weather was clear. But the *Swallow* arrived at dawn, and close enough to recognize three ships at anchor. Two were Roberts's main ships, the *Royal Fortune* and the new *Ranger*, and the third was the old *Ranger*. The pirates had very little warning.

Changing course to avoid a sandbank called Frenchman's Bank, roughly four and a half nautical miles north-northeast of Cape Lopez, the approaching ship suddenly appeared to the pirates as if she were running away, as would a merchantman who recognized pirate ships at anchor. Roberts ordered the *Ranger* to be "righted," for the ship was "on the heel" or "on the careen," which meant that she was being leaned slightly to one side to be cleaned for several feet (60 or so centimeters) below the waterline. Within an hour, with some volunteers from the *Royal Fortune* aboard as well, the *Ranger* and her crew slipped her cable, bent sails to the yards, and set off in pursuit, certain they were chasing a merchantman. It must have been quite an accomplishment, getting sleepy-eyed and quite possibly hungover pirates into action that early in the morning, but the lure of plunder was doubtless sufficient.

But this was no merchantman, and her captain did nothing to dissuade the pirates of their mistake. He ordered his helmsman to steer badly, and set a course before the wind, surely the image of a frightened merchantman. By late morning, three to four hours later, the *Ranger*, sailing a knot or two faster, had drawn within gunshot range, or 300 yards (274 m). How far out to sea the ships were depended on how fast they were sailing, but they were probably between sixteen and twenty-

four nautical miles from Cape Lopez. The latter is more likely, for it would have put them completely out of sight of the pirate ships at anchor, and more importantly to Ogle, hopefully beyond the distance at which gunfire would be heard. It is a tricky thing, the sound of gunfire, and how far it can be heard depends on the size of the guns and their charge, as well as a variety of atmospheric factors.

The *Ranger* was commanded by Welshman James Skyrme, formerly a mate aboard the *Greyhound* sloop. He had been forced into piracy, and even claimed that a pirate had "drubbed him and broke his head" in the process. Time, however, had turned him into a real pirate and he now paced the deck of the *Ranger*, sword in hand, ordering men to their duty and beating any who were "negligent or backward" in it. The *Ranger* hoisted her colors—an English red ensign at the stern; a black flag with

a skeleton "with an hour-glass in one hand and cross-bones in the other, a dart by it, and underneath a heart dropping three drops of blood" at the mizzen; a Dutch pendant at the main masthead; and an English Union Jack at the bow—brought her sprit yard in line with her bowsprit so that it would not tangle when they boarded, and fired several chase guns. Normally, this was enough to force a merchantman to surrender. And this ship, the pirates believed, was filled with Brazilian sugar, a "sweet" prize indeed.

When the *Ranger* came within "musket shot," or roughly fifty yards (45.7 m) closer, the *Swallow* "starboarded" her helm and turned suddenly, while simultaneously opening her gunports and hoisting her English colors. Before the *Ranger* could react, she had sailed within "pistol shot" range of the man-of-war—between 120 and 150 yards (109.7 and 137 m)—and was hit with nearly 350 pounds (159 kg) of iron, or even twice that if the guns were double-shotted or loaded with grapeshot on top of round. The rude assault came in the form a broadside of eleven each of eighteen-pounders and nine-pounders, and a handful of six-pounders as well. It was an old trick, one worthy even of Captain Davis, yet the pirates had not recognized it, so sure were they that the ship was a Portuguese merchantman.

The *Swallow*'s broadside probably raked the *Ranger* from bow to stern. Down went the black pirate flag—perhaps it was shot down, perhaps a pirate lowered it as a sign of surrender, then was overruled—yet even as it did Captain Skyrme turned his ship to starboard and gave a broadside in return, but one much less deadly, for the *Ranger*'s guns were much smaller. Up went the black flag again as the pirates turned and wisely tried to escape, likely to windward, given the *Swallow*'s position to leeward. This was unfortunate, for the *Swallow* sailed best "upon a wind."

The pirates had little choice but to run: the *Swallow* was powerful, and there would be no profit in this fight, except for the victorious naval seamen—and the hangman. The *Ranger* slipped ahead at first, and the *Swallow* could not bring most of her guns to bear. For an hour and a half the ships fought, in large part

"The Careening of the Corvettes in the Canal Mauvais, Torres Strait" by Louis le Breton and Auguste Mayer, 1846, very accurately illustrates two ships "haled over" for careening. This consisted of burning and chiseling marine growth from the hulls, caulking loose seams, making other repairs, and coating the hull with sticky preservative mixture, typically a various concoction of tallow, tar, pitch, and lime. Careening was critical to both pirates and pirate hunters. A clean hull was a fast hull, while a dirty hull was not only a slow one, but could lead to the loss of the ship if teredo worms, common in tropical waters, bored through the hull.

probably a running fight at close range, the *Swallow*'s bow chase guns versus the *Ranger*'s stern chase guns, until the *Swallow* came broadside to broadside with the *Ranger* again. The pirates considered boarding, but against the large trained crew of a man-of-war this might have been suicide, and so was voted down. Even so, many pirates "vapoured" with their cutlasses from the poop, waving them at the naval seamen as if to show they were not afraid.

But when the *Swallow* shot the *Ranger*'s main topmast down, or "by the board" as seamen called it, the pirates struck their colors and threw them into the sea. Ten of their number were dead and twenty wounded, out of a crew of sixteen Frenchmen, seventy-seven "English," and twenty Africans. Captain Skyrme had a leg shot off, yet remained truculent to the end. The English man-of-war had not lost a single man. Unbeknownst to him, Bartholomew Roberts had just lost half of his force without weakening his enemy in the least. Worse, he did not even know he had an enemy only a few miles away. It was not unusual for a consort pirate ship to be gone for days before she returned with a prize, and it might be two or more weeks before she was missed.

Five days later, the *Royal Fortune* and the old *Ranger* still at anchor at Cape Lopez, the pirates sighted the masts of another ship in the offing across the cape, this one under French colors. She appeared at first to be lying by—waiting, that is—at the distance of "random shot," or roughly two nautical miles, until the wind took her ahead. She tacked twice to reach the bay. When informed of the approaching ship, Captain Roberts was at his breakfast, eating a bowl of "Solomon Grundy," as salmagundi was popularly known, of which there were a variety of recipes. Most often it was a salad more or less of pickled herring, hard-boiled eggs, chopped meats such as chicken and bacon or other pork, plus onions, olives, pepper, vinegar, oil, and often other condiments such as parsley and capers. Roberts was unconcerned by the announcement.

The pirates lightly debated whether the ship might be a Portuguese merchantman filled with sugar, a French slaver, or even the *Ranger* herself. But one man recognized her. A deserter from the *Swallow*, he knew his former ship well, and his pronouncement threw the pirates into consternation. Roberts cursed as cowards those who knew her for what she was, and feared her appearance. But it was one thing to offer battle to a tentative Portuguese man-of-war, however large, but quite another to engage an English pirate-hunting fourth-rate man-of-war whose skilled crew had one purpose: find and destroy Bartholomew Roberts and his men.

Roberts swore a "first-rate oath," vowing they would "get clear or die," and ordered the anchor cables slipped and the sails set. He planned to set all sail and run alongside of the *Swallow*, then receive her broadside before firing a shot. If the *Royal Fortune* were too shattered by the broadside to fight or run, Roberts planned to run his ship aground or try to board the *Swallow* and blow up both ships. Pirates often swore they would blow themselves up before letting themselves be captured, but they never did. Talk is cheap, and greedy, plundering men are rarely the sort to commit suicide.

The crimson-clad pirate captain was as good as his word, and ran up under most of his sail within "pistol shot" of the *Swallow*, an English ensign at the stern, an English jack at his bowsprit, and a black pennant at his main masthead. Then down came the French colors flying at the stern of the *Swallow* and up went the English naval ensign, and with it a shattering broadside, probably of round shot with grapeshot on top. The timber-shivering round shot would have crushed men and sent large jagged splinters, a source of many wounds, among them, while the grapeshot, which at the time consisted of a heavy canvas bag filled with small iron shot and wrapped with cord, would have cut rigging and killed men. Why Roberts chose to receive the first broadside is unknown, for it was a foolish gesture. Charles Johnson wrote that most of Roberts's men were "drunk, passively courageous, unfit for service." But the sound of great guns and the smell of burned powder had a way of waking men up. It is likely that the trained and, especially, sober English gun crews simply got off the first broadside.

The *Royal Fortune* immediately hoisted her black flag—it had figures of a skeleton and of "a man portrayed with a flaming sword in his hand"—and unleashed her own broadside. Immediately, she set every sail she could and tried to run, but the *Swallow* hung on to her tenaciously. Engagements were usually waged under "fighting sail," which consisted of fore and main topsails, sometimes the foresail as well. This fight, however, was a running fight made under full sail and broadside to broadside, a classic and usually incorrect Hollywood image. But not this time.

For whatever reason, Roberts is reported to have sailed close-hauled, rather than before the wind, which might have given him an advantage in speed over the *Swallow*. The *Royal Fortune* briefly slipped ahead roughly half gunshot, or 150 yards (137 m), but was soon caught once more broadside to broadside with the man-of-war. Roberts by all accounts did his best to keep his men effectively at their guns, but even sober they were no match for the professional gun crews they faced and the professional officers who commanded them. Early on, the *Royal Fortune*'s mizzen topmast was shot by the board, and after an hour and a half, the mainmast was as well.

Roberts, dressed in his finest crimson, with "a sword in his hand and two pair of pistols, hanging at the end of a silk sling, flung over his shoulders," looking every inch the pirate commander on his quarterdeck during a fight to the death with the Royal Navy, had fallen to the deck early in the engagement. One of the pirate helmsmen found him near a great gun and cursed him violently as a coward hiding from the enemy, telling him to "get up and fight like a man." Only when the pirate noticed that his captain was bleeding to death from a grapeshot wound in the throat did he break into tears. In moments, Roberts was dead. Per his wish the pirates immediately heaved his body overboard. With his spirit went what little that remained in his crew. The pirates, who had lost only three out of a crew of 152 (fifty-two of whom were Africans), soon called for quarter and surrendered. This time, their black flag was trapped by the fallen mainmast, and they could not toss it into the sea. The *Swallow* had not lost a man. Most of the white pirates were soon tried and hanged at Cape Corso. The Africans were largely sold into slavery.

THE GREATEST PIRATE EVER?

Like Blackbeard's before him, Roberts's death turned him over time into a folk hero, coloring the views of some historians to the point that they have fashioned Roberts as the greatest pirate ever. This is quite a compliment, but it is a bit of a stretch as well. Although Roberts reportedly captured between 400 and 500 vessels, more than half were fishing boats, and many others were small sloops of little value. In fact, we should cut the number in half, given that it has been padded based on a newspaper report recounting how in Trepassey harbor Roberts "made himself master of said harbour and of all the ships there, being 22 sails of and 250 shallops." Roberts probably ignored these small fishing shallops as being of little value, and it is unlikely that he boarded or inspected them all in a single day. But even the revised number of two hundred is still extraordinary.

Further, Roberts lost perhaps the richest prize of all, his first. He had but few battles as a pirate, and, as in the case of his richest prize, he lost the most important one of all. In judging Roberts, it's all a matter of the standard used. Is the pirate who sacked Portobello, Maracaibo, Panama, and other towns and cities a lesser pirate than Roberts? That Roberts was the greatest pirate, during the short period from 1715 to 1725, at least in terms of the number of vessels captured, is undoubted. But the greatest pirate ever? It is a judgment likely to start arguments forever.

Some historians have also tried to fashion Roberts as something of an antislavery hero, as a man who despised slave ship captains, who brought former slaves into his crews, who captured and destroyed slave ships and so brought down the Royal Navy upon his back in defense of the slave trade, without which England's colonies could not profit. One has even stated that the demise of Roberts was a victory for slavery and capitalism, in spite of the reality that Roberts, like all pirates, was a businessman of the most extreme form. In fact, the only distinction Roberts made among captured captains was of their origin, reserving his ire for those of Barbados, Martinique, and Bristol. And although he took Africans into his crew, some of them probably as slaves while others possibly as freemen who volunteered to serve, he also traded in slaves and even deliberately burned a cargo of slaves to death because it was inconvenient to take the time to release them from their shackles.

In the end, Roberts was successful in spite of himself, and in particular in spite of his often drunk, often "unfit for service" crew. He was inexperienced as a pirate when he took office, was at times rash to the point of incompetence, twice made fundamental and nearly fatal errors in navigation, and could reasonably be characterized as moody and domineering, yet he led the most successful pirate cruise of the early eighteenth century. He knew where the game was, as Charles Johnson might have put it, and knew where the game wardens were, and he was adept at finding the former while avoiding the latter, until the end.

Perhaps his greatest attribute, though, was that once he became a pirate, he made piracy his life's purpose. One success led to another; there was no going back. "Damnation to him who ever lived to wear a halter," he reportedly said. As with his motto of a merry life and a short one, he was true to his word.

☠

CHAPTER 10

EDWARD "NED" LOW

1692/96?-1724

BY FAR THE MOST BLOODTHIRSTY OF ALL

Just before he was hanged for piracy on March 20, 1724, Nicholas Lewis—formerly quartermaster to Edward Low the pirate and when captured a member of the pirate George Lowther's crew—"gave a most terrible relation" of the capture of a Spanish prize. Perhaps he was repentant, or at least felt the need to clear his conscience. His last-minute testimony even prevented the hanging of two innocent men, by giving evidence that they were "forced" men. One he had even "whip't ... twenty-six time[s], but could not prevail with him to sign their articles," and so he testified. But eleven other men were hanged with him at St. Christopher Island (now St. Kitts) in the Leeward Islands of the Caribbean. According to John Hart, governor of the Leeward Islands, all of the pirates "behaved themselves with greater marks of sorrow and contrition than is usually found amongst those wretched sett of people."

The prize to which he referred, a sloop of six guns and sixty or seventy men, had sailed in mid-March 1723 from the Bay of Honduras with five captured English sloops and one English pink—a small ship with a "pinked" or narrow stern—following in her wake. She was a Spanish *guarda costa,* or pirate, depending on one's perspective, and had obviously been busy in the large bay where English pirates commonly plied their bloody trade, where English "traders by stealth," as smugglers were called, conducted their business in small coves near Spanish towns, and where logwood cutters called "Baymen" stole the Spanish dyewood on the shores of a place known today as Belize.

Espying the sloop, almost a year earlier to the day, the Spanish vessel, whose tragic fate Lewis would one day recount, was under sail in the Bay of Honduras. Captain Edward Low of the pirate schooner *Fancy* espied her and did what he always did in such cases: he "stood to cross her forefoot"—sailed a course to intercept her—hoisted false colors, in this case surely the Spanish Cross of Burgundy, and soon caught up with her. Perhaps that day the Spanish pirates were not wary, or perhaps they believed none would dare assault a Spanish pirate, and only a friend would approach under Spanish colors.

But when Low and his pirate schooner drew near, they struck their false colors, hoisted their black pirate flag, and fired a broadside into the Spanish sloop. It was an effective tactic, and one often used: approach as close as possible under the guise of being a friend, or even of being a weak vessel, then fire a broadside into the unsuspecting prey. At close range even a handful of guns loaded with scraps of metal, canister (cans filled with musket balls), or grapeshot was devastating, especially to unsuspecting men massed on deck. If loaded on top of round shot, such a broadside would shatter timbers and slaughter men indiscriminately.

But whether the broadside killed many or wounded only a few, by all accounts the tactic worked, for the pirates took the sloop without a fight. This was a curiosity, considering who the prey were. Spanish *guardas costas* and pirates were known for their ferocity in battle and for their cruelty in the aftermath. They were not known for asking quarter unless there was no other choice. Surely this time there was none. It may well be that of the sixty or seventy Spaniards, several manned each of the five prizes as prize crews, reducing the *guardas costas'* crew by twenty or thirty. Caught off-guard, they had no choice but to signal their surrender by striking their colors, lowering their sails, or waving a white rag. Without doubt they also shouted, "Good quarter!" This meant that in return for surrendering they would not be harmed or killed. Why none of the Spaniards' captured vessels escaped with their Spanish prize crews was never explained.

As the pirates began to plunder the Spanish sloop, they quickly discovered the captains of the captured vessels, and all were English. The pirate crew did not hold a consultation as it often did before engaging in acts of great moment. Instead, the crew members simply asked their captain what they should do with the Spanish prisoners. He gave them a simple order: kill them all.

Immediately, according to Charles Johnson, the pirates "without any ceremony, fell pell-mell to execution with their swords, cutlasses, pole-axes, and pistols, cutting, slashing, and shooting the poor Spaniards at a sad rate." Those

who tried to hide in the hold were butchered as they huddled in terror—much like the terror they themselves may have inflicted at times. It is impossible that the deck was not covered in blood, that scuppers did not bleed into the sea, that pirates and victims alike were not covered in wet, glistening crimson. Pirate swords cut throats, sheared flesh from faces, and opened great gaping wounds in chests and bellies, while their axes split skulls and their pistols did their simple ugly duty of filling torsos and brains with lead.

More than a dozen men leaped into the sea to escape, but the pirates followed in a canoe and "knocked [several] in the head," cracking their skulls with cutlasses, boarding axes, or pistol butts, and leaving the helpless men to drown, if the blows had not already killed them. Roughly a dozen reached the nearby shore safely and hid themselves, but whether any survived long enough to be rescued later is unknown. The pirates in the canoe landed and came ashore. One of the Spanish survivors, severely wounded, came to them and begged for quarter. It had not worked the first time, but in the face of death men will hope beyond reason. "God damn him," a pirate reportedly shouted as he grabbed the fugitive, he would "give him good quarter instantly." The bloodthirsty rover then shoved the barrel of his musket into the man's mouth and throat, and fired. It was a brutal, merciless, bloody massacre—there is no other sort—of men who had been granted quarter.

For Edward Low, this slaughter was neither an act of pretended patriotism nor of purported pride in national origin. Nor was it an enormity intended to send a message, for if he had had his way none would have survived to tell the story. Perhaps he merely wanted no Spanish witnesses, but Low usually let most of his prisoners live. Rather, this was merely an excuse to butcher men on a large scale. Low did it because he enjoyed it. Perhaps he believed he could more easily get away with killing Spanish and Portuguese, but this did not stop him from coloring his hands scarlet with the blood of Englishmen, too.

BORN TO BE HANGED

Edward Low was born in Westminster, a suburb of London, probably in the last decade of the seventeenth century. Small for his age, he quickly compensated with an unbounded aggressiveness and willingness to fight any boy who was foolish enough to refuse to give up his money or goods. Even as an adult he was described as a "little man," as opposed to a "lusty" one.

Edward Low, as illustrated in Charles Johnson's *The General History of the Robberies and Murders of the Most Notorious Pirates*. As in all such portraits, Low's features are conjectural. He is shown here with the great 1722 hurricane in the background, although his vessel was not struck by the hurricane, but by a different storm. Low's armament—a brace of pistols and a cutlass—was the common armament of early-eighteenth-century pirates, although many affected a silk sling from which to carry their pistols. *Pirates of the New England Coast*, 1923

His upbringing probably left much to be desired. His brother Dick had been a thief since childhood, and later became an especially accomplished pickpocket and housebreaker as well, although not good enough in the long run, for he was eventually hanged at Tyburn in 1707 along with his associates Stephen Bunce and the famous Jack Hall, the chimney sweep, after they broke into a bakery, assaulted and robbed its elderly owners, and threatened to cut their servants' heads off and kill and eat their six-year-old granddaughter.

His eldest brother was apparently a more honest sort. When Low "came to a man's estate" at the age of twenty-one, he relented and went to sea with his brother, and there he spent the next three or four years. In Boston he took his leave of seafaring and worked in a rigging house for one or two years, and returned once, probably as a seaman aboard a New England merchant vessel, to visit his mother in England. After returning to Boston he worked another year or two in the rigging trade, but being "too apt to disagree" with his employers, he shipped aboard a logwood sloop destined for the Bay of Honduras in 1721. Based on what we know about his life to this point, he was between twenty-six and thirty years old.

Men have become pirates for a variety of reasons, need and greed foremost among them, occasionally with elements of revenge and rebellion thrown in for good measure. Often, there was a specific incident involved, a trigger of sorts that did not excuse a man of piracy, but provided the opportunity or helped push him into choosing the sea thief's trade. For Ned Low, it may have been the loss of his wife Eliza, whom he had married in Boston in 1714. She first gave birth to a son, and in the winter of 1719 gave birth to a daughter, Elizabeth. Eliza died soon after their daughter was born, and, as some men have done throughout history, Low abandoned his children after their mother's death, only to regret it later. An eyewitness would later describe how Edward Low, the pirate, when drunk would "weep plentifully upon the mentioning" of his daughter, and how he refused to permit married men to become pirates, for they would be "under the influence of such powerful attractive, as a wife and children" and desert him.

It is difficult to resist the temptation to play amateur psychologist in Low's case. Brought up among criminals and quite possibly abused as a child, he quickly turned to petty crime accompanied by violence that made up for his small stature. The loss of his wife, and more painfully, his abandonment of his children, surely added to his mental trauma and the violence that ensued from it. Even so, few persons brought up in such circumstances go on to attack the world in bloodthirsty criminal violence. Low was to become a notorious exception.

A wounded Spaniard murdered by one of Low's men, from an illustration in the 1725 Dutch edition of Charles Johnson's *The General History of the Robberies and Murders of the Most Notorious Pirates*. Low's crew might have argued that they were meting out murderous justice upon the crew of a Spanish *guarda costa*, which had probably practiced similar cruelties on English seamen. Even so, it is hard, knowing Low, to believe that this cruelty was practiced for anything other than its own sake.
Pirates of the New England Coast, 1923

It was in the Bay of Honduras—the old Caribbean pirate haunt in a western corner of the Spanish Main—that Low took his first steps as a pirate. Arriving as a member of the crew of a small logwood sloop, Low was given the job of coxswain of the boat that ferried the logwood cutters ashore and the cut logwood back to the sloop. A dozen men were with him, tasked to cut and load the dyewood logs. All were armed with muskets as usual, out of concern for Spanish attacks. After all, the Spanish Main still belonged to Spain, as did the logwood Low and his crew were cutting.

One late afternoon in the fall of 1721, as the boat came alongside with the dozen logwood men and a load of logwood, Low asked the sloop captain whether they could remain aboard and eat, then return to shore. The captain, however, wanted his sloop loaded, or "laded" as he would have actually said, as soon as possible, and imperiously ordered them back to shore.

This did not sit well with the men in the boat; Low was incensed. Grabbing a musket in what might reasonably be described as a psychotic rage, he fired at the ship's captain—an act not only of attempted murder, but also of mutiny—but missed him, killing the man next to him, which was indeed an act of murder. Immediately Low fled, probably first to shore with his companions to provision their small craft for a sea voyage. The next day Low led them to sea. That same day they captured a small, unidentified vessel, probably a sloop or ketch sent to fetch logwood, and then, according to chronicler Charles Johnson, "made a black flag and declared war against the world."

CRUELTY WITHOUT A PURPOSE

From the Bay of Honduras Edward Low ordered a course for the Caymans, small islands south of Cuba and northeast of Jamaica, where English sloops went to catch sea turtles for profit. "Turning turtle" the process was called, for the "turtlers" turned the hapless animals on their backs so they could not get away, and returned for them later. There Low doubtless intended to provision for a longer voyage—turtle was often salted in barrels for use at sea—and grab any small vessels that happened to be there. With only a dozen men under his command, his prey for now had to be the small and the weak, for even the average merchant sloop could stand against them if its crew was willing to put up a fight.

But instead of prey, Low ran into pirates—George Lowther and his crew, to be exact—not long after Christmas in 1721. The two pirate captains, one

A Newfoundland fishing port, with a ship taking on a cargo of cod in the background, from Herman Moll's *Map of North America*, circa 1717. Typically unprotected, such fishing ports were easy, if not necessarily lucrative, pickings for pirates such as Edward Low and Bartholomew Roberts. Unprotected and abounding in small fishing vessels called shallops, these ports served primarily as sources of provisions and vessels for pirates. Roberts once trapped 250 fishing shallops in harbor, the basis for the claim of his capturing more than 400 vessels, in turn making him in the opinion of some "the greatest pirate ever."

Pirates of the New England Coast, 1923

A View of a Stage & also of ÿ manner of Fishing for, Curing & Drying Cod at NEW FOUND LAND.
A. The Habit of ÿ Fishermen. B. The Line. C. The manner of Fishing. D. The Dressers of ÿ Fish. E. The Trough into which they throw ÿ Cod when Dressed. F. Salt Boxes. G. The manner of Carrying ÿ Cod. H. The Cleansing ÿ Cod. I. A Press to extract ÿ Oyl from ÿ Cods Livers. R. Casks to receive ÿ Water & Blood that comes from ÿ Livers. L. Another Cask to receive the Oyl. M. The manner of Drying ÿ Cod.

a veteran, one a complete novice, saluted each other, made the appropriate compliments, which consisted largely of firing pistols in the air and drinking lots of rum, and agreed to sail together with Lowther in command and Low as his lieutenant.

Very quickly Captain Lowther set the example of cruelty, for which Low was admirably suited. On January 10, 1722, in the Bay of Honduras, Lowther's sloop chased the *Greyhound*, a merchant ship of 200 tons (181.4 metric tons) commanded by a stout and resolute captain, Benjamin Edwards. Lowther hoisted his colors, expecting the ship to lower its colors and topsails, but instead received a refusal. The pirates gave the *Greyhound* a broadside, and she one in return. For two hours the vessels fought until the outmanned *Greyhound* was forced to strike, or lower, its sails and colors. The pirates cruelly abused her captain and crew, whipping, beating, and cutting them. Low was right at home.

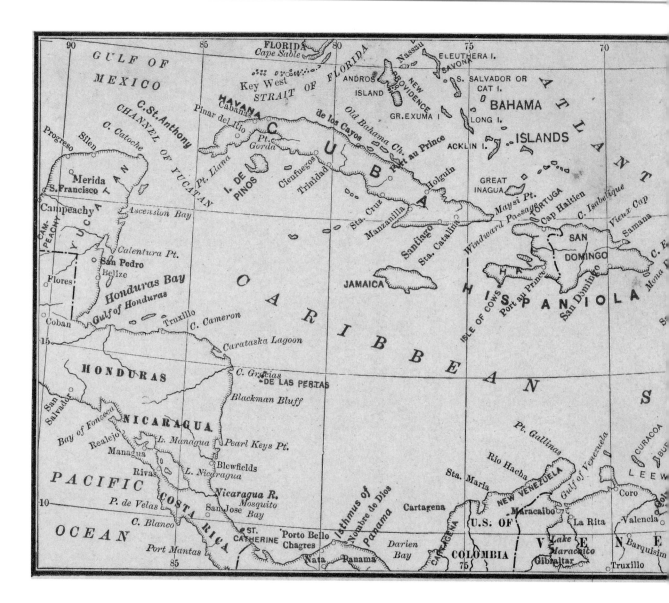

Soon after in the same area, the pirates captured a Rhode Island sloop, and gave Low her command. The second mate of the captured *Greyhound*, Charles Harris, had turned pirate, and was given command of another captured sloop. This unholy trinity sailed to the Bay of Amatique in the southwest corner of the Bay of Honduras to careen their vessels (i.e., clean their hulls by beaching their vessels on one side, then the other) and prepare for a great plundering cruise from North America to the farthest reaches of the Caribbean. Hardly had they begun when a force of Native Americans, allied with the Spanish, swept down upon them, forced them back to sea, and in the process burned Lowther's sloop, the *Happy Delivery*. Lowther, as pirate-in-chief, took command of Low's sloop,

Haunts of
Brethren of the Coast"

SCALE OF MILES
150   250   350

and the pirates abandoned the rest of their small vessels and headed north.

At the end of May 1722, they captured a small brigantine off the coast of Virginia or Maryland. Forty-four men volunteered to go with Low in the prize, and at the same time voted him as captain. The brigantine was small and unarmed, so from Lowther's sloop to the brigantine Low and his men brought two great guns, as carriage-mounted cannon were called, four swivel guns to mount on the rails, six quarter-casks of gunpowder, and some provisions. Low doubtless wanted to get away from Lowther and not lose his command again, and Lowther was glad to be rid of an unruly lieutenant who was "always aspiring and never satisfied with the proceedings of the commander," according to Charles Johnson. With this puny vessel and armament, Low and his men sailed away on their own, intending to make themselves rich, infamous, and feared throughout the Caribbean.

Low ordered a course north and began a rampage not unlike that of Bartholomew Roberts. Even his tactics were similar: chase everything in sight, hoist the black flag, and fire a broadside if necessary. It worked almost every time. Sometimes, however, more subtlety was required. Sailing to Nova Scotia, Low directed his brigantine into Port Roseway on June 15, 1722, and "came to an anchor" as sailors would have said. He ordered some of his men into the brigantine's boat, and they rowed from fishing vessel to fishing vessel, each time pretending to be friends.

Philip Ashton, a twenty-year-old fisherman from Marblehead, Massachusetts, described how it was done. The pirates "came alongside of us, and the men jumpt in upon our deck, without our suspecting anything but that they were friends, come on board to visit, or inquire what news; till they drew their cutlashes and pistols from under their clothes, and cock'd the one and brandish'd the other, and began to curse & swear at us, and demanded a surrender of our selves and vessel to them." Ashton would endure repeated threats against his life, not to mention physical abuse, as the pirates tried to force him to become one of them. "You dog you! If you will not sign

The map in "Haunts of 'The Brethren of the Coast,'" from Frank Stockton's *Buccaneers and Pirates of Our Coast*, clearly illustrates why mariners referred to any intricate passage as the "Caribbees," and why pirates such as Ned Low were able to prey on vulnerable merchantmen so easily, and escape just as easily. Islands and cays are numerous, the coastlines often tortuous, political territories are mixed together almost randomly, and choke points are numerous. It is easy to see how Low or any pirate could cruise the south Cuban cays then slip south to the Bay of Darien, then work north along the Mosquito Coast of Nicaragua and from there into the Bay of Honduras, plundering all the way.

our articles, and go along with me, I'll shoot you thro' the head!" was the mildest of the abuse he received. He always refused, and eventually ran away in the Bay of Honduras and marooned himself. In 1725 he was rescued and returned to Marblehead, where Puritan minister John Barnard helped him write a famous account of his adventures.

Low and his pirates ranged along the far northern coast, capturing fishing boats and sloops, and often torturing their crews. He was fond of cutting and slicing his prisoners up, especially the captains if they had resisted at all. But Low was cruel not only to captains. He also abused crewmen, especially unmarried men who would not join him. Often, though, there seemed to be no reason at all to his savagery. For example, he viciously beat two "Nantucket Indians," part of the crew of a fishing vessel, and then hanged them.

One of the prizes Low captured at Port Roseway was a swift schooner, a fairly new form of two-masted vessel gaining in popularity. Each mast carried a large gaff sail, making the schooner both easy to handle and very easy to sail to windward. Low knew that it would be the ideal vessel for him. He put ten great guns in it, named it the *Fancy*, and made it his flagship. He gave command of the brigantine to Charles Harris.

Low and Harris knew that soon someone, probably the merchants of Boston, would send armed vessels in pursuit. It didn't pay to tarry too long in any well-traveled place. Figuring they would try to seize a few more vessels before they departed the area, they sailed north to St. John's, Newfoundland, and discovered a large ship at anchor. Low planned well. He put most of his men below deck to pretend that his schooner was a fishing vessel. When they came alongside of the fat merchantman, his men would surge on deck and board the hapless prey. But by chance, as the pirates were entering the harbor to capture the ship, they hailed a small fishing boat and asked what the ship was.

"A large man-of-war," came the reply.

According to Ashton, the "very name of man-of-war struck them all up in a heap, spoil'd their mirth, their fair hopes, and promising design of having a good ship at command." The pirates fled north, sacked a small, undefended village called Carbonear, then, fearing pursuit, set sail east for the Azores. Charles Johnson, however, wrote that they went to the West Indies and barely survived the famous hurricane of 1722, which tore a swath through the Caribbean and the Gulf of Mexico, from the Windward Islands to Jamaica to New Orleans, where it destroyed more than thirty-five buildings and sank all the vessels anchored there. But Johnson was wrong, and probably wanted to liven up his narrative of Low's adventures. Ashton was still a prisoner of Low, and he did not write that they sailed to the West Indies at the time, or that they suffered through the hurricane.

Near the Azores, Low and Harris easily captured seven vessels by their usual tactic of running up the black flag and waiting for their prey to surrender. If any hesitated, Low threatened to kill them all. One was a thirty-four gun French ship, and another was a Portuguese ship known as the *Rose Pink* or *Rose Frigate*, which had once been a small English man-of-war. In typical pirate fashion, Low traded up again, swapping his schooner for the pink, and appointing one of his quartermasters,

Nineteenth-century woodcut of "turtlers"—turtle fishermen—loading green and loggerhead turtles on an island off the south Cuban coast. The process was no different from two centuries earlier. Turtlers used handspikes to turn turtles on their backs, then dragged them to a staging area where they were loaded in boats and ferried to waiting sloops. Turtlers and turtle sloops were common pirate prey. The south Cuba islands were ideal for pirates to hide, sloops could be captured and turned into pirate vessels, and turtlers could be forced to provide provisions in the form of turtle meat.

© The Print Collector/ Alamy

Farrington Spriggs, also called both Francis and Frank, to command the schooner. He took several cannon from the French ship and mounted them in the pink. Having no more use for the French ship, the pirates took her crew out, except for the cook. Him they tied to the ship's mainmast, and then set fire to the ship. According to Charles Johnson, they said that the cook, "being a greasy fellow would fry well in the fire." Ashton, however, mentioned neither the French ship nor her cooked cook.

> *Having no more use for the French ship, the pirates took her crew out, except for the cook. Him they tied to the ship's mainmast, and then set fire to the ship.*

The pirates committed other enormities as well. They "cut and mangled" the captain and crew of the *Wright Galley* after the merchant seamen seemed inclined to defend themselves; they repeatedly hanged two Portuguese friars by the neck from the yardarm, hoisting them up and then letting them down just before they were dead, over and over, until finally they were dead; and one pirate split open the belly of a Portuguese passenger, literally spilling his guts because he "did not like his looks."

SIMPLE TACTICS

It was easy for Low and his pirates to get away with their captures and cruelties. There were seldom any men-of-war around, and merchant vessels were usually poorly armed, and even when they had good armament, they seldom had a crew large enough to man it. It was all about economics. Merchant owners considered large crews too expensive. What this amounted to was that pirates seldom had to do more than get within range of their prey and hoist the black flag.

At some point, probably early in his independent career, Low and his men created their own pirate flag. Few pirate flags were alike, and many did not use the now famous skull and crossed bones, but used full skeletons instead. In Low's case, he and his consort captains, Harris and Spriggs, and probably a pirate quartermaster named John Russel as well, used the same symbol on their pirate flags. Although Low sometimes used a "black flag with the figure of death in red at the main-top masthead," he and the others used a black flag as an ensign (a vessel's main flag) "in the middle of which [was] a large white skeleton with a dart in one hand striking a bleeding heart [with three drops of blood], and in the other an hour-glass," a flag very similar to that of Bartholomew Roberts. The only difference, noted in a newspaper account and in a trial deposition, is that Harris's black flag was actually a "deep blew flagg." Perhaps it had faded from black to blue, or perhaps the color was by choice to make it distinguishable from Low's black flag. Spriggs and his crew referred to their flag as the Jolly Roger, and Harris and his crew to theirs as Old Roger—probably the rest did similarly.

Now that Low had a new pirate ship of fourteen guns, he had to make it ready to serve its purpose. This was an important part of being a successful pirate. Again, this meant careening, and possibly cutting more gunports in her so that she could mount more cannon. From the Azores, Low ordered a course to the Canary Islands, where they easily took more prizes, and from there he commanded his little fleet to the Cape Verde islands. At Boa Vista Island the pirates made the *Rose* into a true pirate ship, and at nearby São Nicolau Island the pirates filled their water casks.

But before we follow Low any farther, we need to note the existence of a journal written by Captain George Roberts, who was both captured by pirates and later set free by them at sea, where he soon found himself marooned ashore. His book was obviously written by a mariner, but of particular interest are the two chapters in which he details the ten days he spent in October 1722 as a prisoner of the pirate Spriggs. Low was there also, commanding the *Rose Pink* as the pirate admiral, and also John Russel, a Portuguese it was said, commanding the schooner *Fancy*. In perhaps too much detail to believe it was all written by Roberts himself, or at least without the hand of an active editor, he describes the numerous conversations he had with Low, who in many ways came across as the most decent of the three pirate captains. According to Roberts, who was often threatened but never otherwise abused, Low was both a heavy drinker and a good conversationalist, one perhaps leading to the other.

Soon after, probably by the end of October, Low ordered a course for Brazil—and here came the real storm that almost destroyed them. For "five days and nights together" the pirates hourly feared for their lives, knowing they might well be "swallowed up by the violence of the wind and sea." Ashton said the pirates began to fear the Almighty, an odd thing for men who, according to Roberts, "had no god but their money, nor savior but their arms." Of course, Ashton's coauthor was a Puritan minister who doubtless had his own agenda.

The storm cast Low and his *Rose Pink* near three small islands called the Triangles off the coast of Suriname. The pirates had repair work to do, and got right to it—and in a foolish accident, heeled (leaned) the *Rose* so far over that water sped in through her open gunports and sank her in six fathoms. Two of the pirates drowned. Once again they clambered aboard the schooner *Fancy* and set sail, this time north to the Caribbean.

Low ordered one of his men to cut the Portuguese captain's lips off, and Low himself "broiled" the lips in front of the captain's face.

There Low plied his usual tactics and captured a dozen or more vessels, mostly small. One of them, a Rhode Island sloop, Low took for his flagship, leaving the schooner *Fancy* to Spriggs. However, according to both Johnson and pirate quartermaster Nicholas Lewis, the pirates espied a rich Portuguese ship while en route to the Caribbean. They gave chase in the schooner, then attacked and captured her. Low's pirates searched the ship high and low, but discovered no money, which they were sure the ship carried. Low ordered several prisoners to be tortured, and soon enough one of them blurted out in pain the truth: the captain had hung 11,000 gold moidores from a rope outside the great cabin, and when he realized his ship would be captured, he cut the rope and let the gold fall into the sea.

Low was enraged. He ordered one of his men to cut the Portuguese captain's lips off, and Low himself "broiled" the lips in front of the captain's face. His point made, Low then ordered the murder of the entire crew. Ashton, however, makes no mention at all of the capture of the ship, or of Low's crazed, murderous rampage. But this is of little consequence, for many of Low's cruelties are well documented.

CLOSE CALLS

No one's luck holds out forever. The pirates ranged through the Caribbean, from the Windward Islands to Curaçao along the coast of Venezuela, then south toward Cartagena in modern-day Colombia, then southeast toward

Portobello. They encountered two "tall ships," as large, three-masted ships were then called—great prey indeed, for doubtless they would be filled with slaves and merchandise, given their location on the Spanish Main. But Low should have learned to be wary of large ships by now. Indeed, one of the ships was a Guinea-man, as slave ships were often called, but the pirates quickly discovered that the other was the HMS *Mermaid*, an English man-of-war of fifty-four guns. To engage even a small frigate would have been suicide, but this was a large ship—a single broadside from the HMS *Mermaid*'s "large range of teeth," as Ashton called the warship's armament, would have shattered the pirate sloop and schooner from bow to stern.

Naturally, Low and Spriggs ran for it. In their flight the pirates wisely separated, Low ordering a course to sea and Spriggs one toward shore. Although a large ship, the HMS *Mermaid* was swift and chased the pirates before the wind (sloops and schooners were faster sailing "on" a wind—toward the wind, in other words). Wanting to capture the larger of the pirate vessels, the man-of-war pursued Low and soon gained on him. But Low had a scrap of fortune on his side—one of his men knew of a shoal over which the sloop could pass but the HMS *Mermaid* could not. Over it they sailed freely, but not the man-of-war, which ran aground and could not get off in time to catch Low.

Spriggs, however, still feared that the man-of-war might catch them now instead. He and one of his "chief companions, took their pistols, and laid them down by them, and solemnly swore to each other, and ledg'd the oath in a bumper of liquor" that if they could not escape, they would each shoot the other in the head. Fortunately for both, the man-of-war could not catch them.

For five weeks the pirate vessels were separated. Low and Spriggs continued toward the Bay of Honduras separately. Here the two were reunited and celebrated in drunken revelry after Low fired a shot at Spriggs's schooner, thinking it had been captured; here Ashton ran away and marooned himself on Port Royal Key near Roatán Island; and here the pirates murdered the crew of the Spanish *guarda costa*. It was now April 1723, and time to cruise again along the coast of North America.

Low had now two sloops in his "pirate fleet," his *Fancy* and Harris's *Ranger*. Spriggs and his crew were off on their own somewhere. Perhaps Spriggs had had a falling out with Low—he had been angry with Low for abandoning him near Portobello. Off Cape San Antonio, Low captured the sloop *William*. He and his men tortured the prisoners to reveal their money: they cut them, beat them, and put slow matches between their fingers until they were burned to the bone. Low similarly abused other crews.

But if one waits long enough, often there is justice, even if it is only by accident—and in such cases, none ever call such judgment accidental. News of Low's rampage along the North American coast had spread far and wide, even to the HMS *Greyhound*, which protected New York. Learning of the pirates' location from some of Low's victims, her captain, Peter Solgard, set sail. Surely Low knew that by now word of his brutal plundering would bring a response. Perhaps he still trusted in his good fortune, although if he had examined it closely, he might have noticed that much of it consisted of close calls.

On June 10, 1723, the HMS *Greyhound* came in sight of the Low and Harris sloops. Immediately the pirates assumed the ship was a prize in the offing and gave chase. Solgard let them, knowing well it would give him time to make his ship ready to fight, and would make the pirates believe he was but a merchantman. After all, a man-of-war would turn and fight.

And as soon as the sloops "came up" with her, the HMS *Greyhound* did. The pirates fired first, then, realizing their prey was a man-of-war, they hoisted their red flags of no quarter, indicating that they intended to fight to the death. The HMS *Greyhound* sailed close to the sloops and opened fire with a combination of round shot and grapeshot, shattering the pirates so much that they immediately bore away to escape. For two hours it was a running fight. The pirates got out their oars and tried to row away from the man-of-war. In desperation they threw their backs into it, trying to save themselves from the noose.

But the man-of-war, of twenty guns and 120 men, had oars, too. Eventually, the HMS *Greyhound* rowed between the sloops and released her furious broadsides on both, shooting down the schooner *Fancy*'s mainyard. Now Low knew exactly what to do: he ran, leaving Harris and his survivors to be captured and, most of them at least, were hanged.

After the capture of Harris's sloop, Low went into an active rage. He abused all those he captured. He cut, whipped, and murdered. He had the heart cut out of one man, roasted it, and forced the man's mate to eat it. He cut one man's ears off, salted and peppered them, and forced other prisoners to eat them. He cut off another man's head and committed other outrages. But perhaps it was not revenge that motivated Low's rage. Perhaps instead it was the shame of his cowardice, and every cut, every blow, every murder he inflicted was one he knew should have been reserved for him.

NOT HANGED TOO SOON...

Some historians have referred to Edward Low as a minor pirate, hardly worthy of note. And perhaps by some standards he was just another cruel pirate who briefly terrorized the Caribbean Sea and shore. And yet, he lasted at least as long as pirates of greater fame, such as Blackbeard and Bartholomew Roberts. He captured more than 100 vessels, a notorious number and far more than Blackbeard's total, although but a quarter or half of Roberts's, depending on who does the counting. So infamous was he that English governors considered him in the same light as Roberts, and noted that with the demise of Roberts, only Low and Spriggs remained significant pirate threats.

How did Low, a man obviously insane, do so well as a pirate? Easy—he kept his tactics simple.

But just how did Low, a man obviously insane, do so well as a pirate? Easy—he kept his tactics simple. He never stayed too long in one place. He knew when to run. He was a pirate at a time when merchantmen were everywhere and pirate hunters were not. He was also lucky. Above all, though, he was a charismatic leader. If the journal of George Roberts can be believed, Low was one of the best, his mood swings and violent outbursts notwithstanding. His leadership may have ultimately been his best tactic.

Edward Low left an indirect legacy as well, beyond his captures and cruelties. We have already noted that the pirates he variously sailed with were responsible, along with Bartholomew Roberts, for the "Jolly Roger" becoming our common name for the black flag of the pirate. In an even darker part of this legacy, we have also pointed out elsewhere that although pirates of Low's time often boasted that they would kill themselves rather than be taken, they nearly always surrendered instead. Of course, a few did fight to the death, but at least two even kept their word and killed themselves rather than be taken alive, and both were members of pirate crews with whom Low had been associated.

According to the *Boston Gazette*, one "desperado," a member of Charles Harris's pirate crew captured by the HMS *Greyhound* in June 1723, "as soon as the others had surrender'd ... took his pistol and shot himself through the head." The other who killed himself was Captain George Lowther, with whom Low and some of his men had cruised for a few months in 1722, and perhaps also in 1723. While he and his crew were careening their ship at Blanquilla Island, off the coast of modern-day Venezuela, they were attacked by the *Eagle* sloop out of Barbados. Lowther quickly led a dozen of his men through the stern windows and escaped ashore, only to find themselves marooned. Not long after, in May 1724, he shot himself after the crew of a Spanish *guarda costa* captured most of his companions. Perhaps all of these captains—Low, Spriggs, Harris, Russel, and Lowther—made vows to kill themselves if capture were imminent. We know Spriggs did. But even if all did, not all carried them through.

Low, his men, and the other pirates he sailed with were the hardest of hardcore pirates, and the last of the short-lived decade of early-eighteenth-century pirates who robbed and murdered from 1715 to 1725. They were a terrible lot, and no punishment could have been too severe. And this was something Edward Low would soon discover.

After the capture of Harris, Low and his men headed north to their old "fishing" grounds off Nova Scotia and Newfoundland. Again, using his old tactics he captured roughly forty vessels, including a twenty-two-gun ship he turned into his flagship. In July 1723, the pirates captured the *Merry Christmas*, mounted her with thirty-four guns, and set sail across the Atlantic for more piratical rampage and cruelty among the Canary and Cape Verde islands. There they murdered Portuguese passengers and cut a ship captain's ears off because he had the temerity to at first resist capture. There also Low appears in some accounts to have briefly joined with Lowther again. From the islands Low set a course to Africa, where on the Guinea coast he and his pirates captured a small ship and put Spriggs with whom he had reunited, in command of it. Spriggs soon parted company with Low and sailed on his own account.

By January 1724, Edward Low's new crew had apparently had nearly enough of his combination of moodiness and violent outbursts, which had probably grown worse over the past two years. According to some newspaper reports, Low and Spriggs had returned to the Bay of Honduras, where they were marooned by their crews. True or not, in May of 1724, Low was with only thirty men in the Windward Islands, where he captured an English sloop. Soon, a French man-of-war from Martinique was in swift pursuit.

The final straw came when Low grew angry at his quartermaster, who among pirates was second-in-command, for opposing him over the course of their pirate cruise. That night, while his quartermaster slept, Low put a pistol to the man's head and pulled the trigger, blowing out his brains. That Low was the captain was irrelevant—even a pirate captain was not permitted to murder his own men. Low's crew put him adrift, along with two or three of his cronies, in a small boat or sloop without provisions, leaving him to the mercy of the sea. Soon after he was taken up by a French vessel, probably the pursuing man-of-war. Dying of thirst, Low and his foul compatriots doubtless signaled to it, hoping to be rescued from a long, painful death. Recognizing Low for who he was, the French crew put him in irons and carried him to Martinique, where he was summarily tried and hanged, as almost assuredly were his two or three cronies as well.

Or so it was reported, first in the 1725 French edition of Charles Johnson's great work on pirates, and a year later in his second English edition. Even so, there is a report published in 1726 of Low with eight men and Spriggs with three marooned on Roatán Island in the Bay of Honduras, but we have no further details. More curiously, there is a report of Low and Spriggs off the coast of New England in 1726, at the same time that William Fly, a short-lived but brutal pirate in the mold of Low, was attacking vessels in the area.

How did anyone know it was Low and Spriggs off the coast of New England? Simple. The idea was put into the heads of captured seamen by William Fly and his pirate crew, most likely as a joke intended to frighten mariner and lubber alike, and proves just how famous these two pirates were. The report of Low and Spriggs at Roatán seems more difficult to put to rest, but it apparently refers to a period in early 1724 when Low may have been marooned in the Bay of Honduras. Further, the two men were not noted as alive in 1725, the year in which large-scale piracy in the Caribbean came to an end, and are never again reported as alive after 1726. Nor did captains or crews ever come forward after 1724 to claim they were attacked by these butchers.

It is safe to assume that Low was indeed captured and killed in 1724, as he long deserved, a mercilessly cruel man who, in the opinion of many and especially of those who suffered at his hands, could never have been hanged too soon.

CHAPTER 11

☠

KANHOJI ANGRIA

unknown-1729

THE INVINCIBLE ADMIRAL OF THE PIRATE COAST OF INDIA

For half a decade the pirate chief avoided preying on the vessels flying the red-and-white-striped ensign with the Cross of St. George in its canton. It was not that he was afraid, for a veteran sea rover whose sword had many times been bloodied and who commanded a fleet of swift sea vessels carrying hundreds of warriors and an army as many as 20,000-strong ashore was not likely to fear merchant ships sailing from a nation half a world away. Rather, his interest at first was to rob the ships of the Portuguese, Mughals, and Siddi. But this had changed a decade past, in 1702. Since then the Honourable East India Company, as it was formally known, had refused to pay tribute—and thus the pirate chief sent his swift, rakish vessels against its ships.

In sight, just north of Karwar, India, were three vessels flying the foreign merchant ensign, although now it bore the Union flag in its canton. They were a small frigate named the *Defiance* (a redoubtable name indeed), an armed company yacht, and the *Anne*, an armed ketch. Aboard the *Anne* were Thomas Chown, the company agent at the English trading post at Karwar, and his pregnant wife, Catherine. From Karwar north to Bombay they were sailing, there to lay claim to the estate of Catherine's deceased first husband. Her life so far had been one of sorrow mixed with understandable relief. Only four years before, when she was thirteen or fourteen, her parents had given her in marriage to John Harvey, a "deformed," much older man. Mr. Harvey soon had the perhaps fortunate grace to die of age or disease, and his widow married Thomas Chown not long after.

The commander of the pirate flotilla in the offing had no interest in the joys and tragedies of the passengers aboard the merchant prey. His concern was tactics. He gave an order, and a *gallivat* surged swiftly forth to inspect the vessels

BOMBAY on the Malabar Coast, belonging to the East India Company of ENGLAND.

from a distance. Only if the wind were calm would this oared vessel come close. It was too lightly built to defend against a broadside of great guns, but in calm airs it could maneuver to avoid the large guns of its prey. The *gallivat* kept its distance as its captain counted the gunports cut into the side of each vessel and the swivel cannon mounted on their rails, and confirmed the ensigns the vessels flew. Often it was difficult to tell one flag from another, except at close range, and especially if the wind was light.

A *gallivat* was an oared Indian vessel much like a Mediterranean fighting galley. It rowed with thirty or forty oars, but never fewer than twenty, and had two masts with triangular sails called lateens, although the mizzen, or aft, mast and sail were very small. Although of only forty to seventy tons (36.2 to 63.5 metric tons) burden and of shallow draft, a *gallivat* could still carry as many as 100 fighting men. In most cases, though, it carried only twenty, plus as many oarsmen as needed. Mounted on its rails were five or six swivel guns, fired from a light deck made of split bamboo fitted above the oarsmen. Occasionally, larger *gallivats* of up to 120 tons (108.8 metric tons) had a deck that could support great guns, and these mounted six to eight guns of two- or four-pound shot.

Bombay in the eighteenth century, from a copperplate engraving, 1755. The port was the Indian home of the British East India Company, also known as the Honourable East India Company. One of Kanhoji's principle bases, Khanderi Island, was located only nine miles south of the entrance to Bombay harbor, making Bombay vessels, including ships of the Honourable East India Company, prime targets for attacks by Kanhoji's grabs and gallivats.
© World History Archive/ Alamy

The *gallivat*, its flag flying from a staff mounted on its prow, soon returned to the pirate flotilla. Immediately the entire pack of sleek vessels set forth in pursuit of the small convoy, four *grabs* leading the way. Always these pirates preferred a wind and sea in which they could maneuver swiftly under oar or oar and sail, and in which their prey could not. Today was such a day.

The *grabs*, each of which always had at least one *gallivat* attending it, slowly moved forward, both under their own eight oars in the prow, and of the many belonging to the *gallivat* towing them. A *grab*, or *ghurāb*, was a swift, shallow-drafted Indian sailing vessel that somewhat resembled a *gallivat*, although it was much larger. One might even describe it as a ship, albeit an exotic one by Western standards. It carried two, and sometimes three, masts, was of 150 to 300 tons (45.3 to 272 metric tons) burden, and mounted sixteen great guns. Fourteen of these guns, probably three- or four-pounders, made up the port and starboard broadsides, and a pair of six-pounders were mounted under the small forecastle in the bow for firing in the chase. The *grab* had a long, low prow, resembling a sword or lance, just a few feet (about 1 m) above the surface of the sea, yet it also had a very high stern, giving it a unique appearance.

The crew usually averaged 150 men, but could be as few as 50 or as many as 250. Most of its fighters were armed with curved swords called *talwars*, small shields, and long lances with bamboo shafts, but roughly ten aboard each *grab* were armed with matchlock muskets. Unlike many of the European pirates, for whom the musket was often the most important weapon, these Angrian sea rovers relied foremost on their great guns until it came time to board.

The crews aboard the merchant vessels knew they were in danger. Quickly they broke loose their great guns from their lashings and prepared them for action. They knew how these Angrias fought, and so they made certain they had a pair of guns ready to fire aft. If necessary, they chopped ports in the transom, the curved portion of the stern at the base of the great cabin, so they could better "traverse," or aim, the guns. They poured water onto the decks and filled buckets, tubs, and even half-casks with seawater, not only to fight fires but also to keep the decks wet, vital for the fight that was surely to come. If the *Defiance* were doing its duty, its captain placed it between the other merchant vessels and the pirates closing in—assuming the wind let him. Most important, all three vessels were wisely trying to run away.

What the crew and passengers aboard the merchant vessels saw were four *grabs* and at least as many *gallivats* slowly approaching. The chase seemed inexorable yet its conclusion inevitable. The crews of the merchant vessels could now only wait until the fighting began. It is easy to imagine the fear and adrenaline among the crew and passengers, but for Thomas Chown, his pregnant, eighteen-year-old wife ensconced in the safest place aboard the ketch—the dark hold below—it must have been quietly terrifying.

The *grabs* and *gallivats* headed straight for the sterns of the three vessels flying the red and white ensigns. If the *Defiance* had taken its place behind the yacht and ketch, the leading pirates gave it a wide birth to avoid the point-blank range of its guns. Probably one each of *grab* and *gallivat* were headed toward the yacht and ketch, while the remaining pirate vessels, at the end of the pack, rowed toward the more powerful frigate. But this would be no battle of broadside to broadside.

Illustration of a typical great gun, or a cannon, with a bed carriage, used throughout the seventeenth century and well into the eighteenth century. The ships of the Honourable East India Company and the *grabs* of Kanhoji Angria would have been armed with similar guns. At the top of the illustration are loading implements, although pirates, privateers, men-of-war, and other well-armed ships usually loaded with a rope rammer and sponge, depicted at bottom right. The rope rammer, made from old rigging, was typically wrapped or "fortified" with marline (sea twine) to make it stiffer. From John Sellers's *The Sea Gunner*, 1691.

© Lordprice Collection/ Alamy

As the pirate vessels came within range—fewer than three hundred yards for six-pounders—the *gallivats* released their towlines, leaving the *grabs* free to engage. Carefully the gunners in the bow of each *grab* waited until all the masts of the prey were in line, then, as the sea lifted the *grab*'s bow and elevated its bow guns, they fired. Over and over they touched their slow match to the vents of the guns, firing the charges inside and sending hot iron shot at the masts while warriors shouted, waved their *talwars*, and waited to board and plunder. Although most shots missed the masts, by their repeated number they eventually shattered rigging and sails, leaving them in shreds. Soon the yacht and ketch could not escape even if the wind did rise. At the stern of the *Defiance*, two *grabs* fired on the frigate, first one, and then the other, towed in and out of line by the *gallivats* as necessary. Occasionally, a *gallivat* slipped in and quickly fired its own guns.

This was the ideal tactic for these pirates, for it permitted them to use their weaker, but far more numerous, vessels to best advantage, giving them the best chance of success while minimizing their losses. The smoke from the guns soon lay thick between the vessels, obscuring them and making aiming and firing a slow process, as crews waited for it to clear. But for the fact that men were wounded and killed by the exchange of fire, one might even call the battle tedious. Gun crews were soaked in sweat as they worked the hot guns on the sweltering day. Even those who had nothing to do but wait until the time came to repel boarders were drenched in sweat from the still, twice-heated air.

But the captains of the *grabs* and *gallivats* had no intention of speeding things up by making a hazardous run alongside the vessels to board. They waited until the time was right to board, and after several hours it was. One of the yacht's masts came down, then the other, leaving it unable to defend itself against the *gallivats* swarming around it. By now the *Anne* was no better off. She had fired all of her powder, and now tried to run. Swiftly two *grabs* came alongside and hurled firepots onto her decks. But the wet decks did little to defend against the bombs, and the *talwar*-wielding warriors quickly surged aboard, screaming and cutting. In moments they captured the small vessel, along with Mrs. Chown and a cargo of pepper and wax. Only the *Defiance*, a well-armed ship, escaped, as the *grabs* and *gallivats* probably abandoned their attacks and went after the wounded yacht and ketch instead.

For Catherine Chown, her situation could not get much worse, for her husband's right arm had been carried away by a round shot, as cannonballs were called. Taken below, he bled to death in his wife's arms. Once more a widow, she was also the prisoner of a great pirate, who, according to East India Company officer Clement Downing, had "stately houses built with stone, fine strong fortified castles, and fine horses, pleasant gardens to recreate themselves, pleasant fruits, good Persia wine, and plenty of Arrack [a strong liquor made from the coconut palm]."

But Mrs. Chown probably never saw these grand estates. Instead, she was carried to Khanderi, a tiny, heavily fortified island nine miles (14.5 km) south of Bombay (modern-day Mumbai). A pirate fortress such as only Hollywood might imagine, Khanderi was but a quarter of a mile (402 m) long and not even 300 yards (274 m) wide. It rested in shallow water, and on its eastern side was the only landing place, a tiny harbor fifty yards (wide, guarded by a dozen cannon that could rain slaughter on any vessel trying to land there. Virtually inassailable, even in the face of the English presence at Bombay, the island held Mrs. Chown firmly in its grasp.

The pirate chief demanded 30,000 rupees for her ransom, an extraordinary sum. And the Company paid it. The Englishmen who went to pay the ransom had to "wrap their clothes about her, to cover her nakedness," according to Downing. Whether she was handed over entirely naked, or her light Indian dress was considered naked by the standards of an English woman of the period, was not noted. The East India Company paid the ransom for more than just the release of Mrs. Chown and other English prisoners. It was tribute, but the peace that followed would last only two years. Mrs. Chown soon remarried, only to lose her third husband a few years later, again to a violent death in India.

The pirate chief who captured her was Kanhoji Angria (pronounced "Connagee Angry"), the *sarkhel* or *darya sarang*, the fleet admiral of the Maratha in whose service were Indian Hindus, Indian and Arab Muslims, and even Christians, including Dutch captains, Portuguese gunners, and English pirates. But in the eyes of the East India Company, two of whose vessels he had just captured, he was for all practical purposes a very dangerous prince of pirates by sea and land.

THE MAKING OF A PIRATE PRINCE

Little is known of Kanhoji's ancestry and youth, and many of the historical accounts are confusing and unreliable. As such, we should treat all of his history prior to 1698 as tentative. To set the scene, India in the late seventeenth century was an enormous hodgepodge of competing peoples, faiths, kingdoms, and fiefdoms often at war with each other. Those that concern us most are the Maratha, a confederacy of Hindu peoples that claimed much of the west coast of

India, and the Mughal Empire, an enormous and powerful Muslim state whose emperor Aurangzeb was trying to conquer all of India. On all sides, princes competed against each other for power, even within a kingdom or empire, and at times even fought against their own rulers. Complicating the situation further were the powerful Western trading companies from Portugal, the Netherlands, and England, which often fought with each other and the various Indian states.

At sea, the situation was no less complicated. For millennia, pirates and other sea rovers had ranged along the Indian coasts, and some had sailed beyond the Horn of Africa. The Indian states plundered the vessels of their enemies, and often everyone else's. Sometimes they plundered solely for profit, and sometimes as a form of profitable warfare.

On the west coast of India, the various Malabar pirates, including the Maratha, took their *grabs* and *gallivats* to sea for plunder and tribute. Records as far back as 2,000 years tell of these Malabar pirates, and Marco Polo even wrote about them. There were also Arab pirates who entered Indian waters for plunder, and Western pirates, such as William Kidd, Henry Every, and Edward England, who did the same. India, like the Caribbean and Mediterranean of this age, was a maritime crossroads, the perfect place for piracy and privateering to flourish.

In any place of ships and riches, some men are bound to make a name for themselves, and Kanhoji Angria was one. Almost certainly he came from a seafaring background. His father, Tukoji Sankhpal, sometimes given as Tukoji Angria, may have been born in the tiny village of Angarwadi, near Poona, India, roughly sixty miles (96.5 km) from the west coast, and from which the name Angria was derived. However, some old English histories claim that Tukoji was Kanhoji's grandfather, and was an African born on an island in the Strait of Hormuz and raised as a Muslim. In this version, Tukoji later became a seaman or pirate, served under Shivaji, the *chattrapati* (king) of the Maratha, became a devout Hindu, and married either Shivaji's sister or the sister of his *peshwa* (a combination office of prime minister and military leader). His son Purab would have been Kanhoji's father.

Assuming, however, that Tukoji was Kanhoji's father, around 1658 he volunteered as a soldier in the Maratha army, which was fighting against the powerful Mughal Empire, although some English histories say he served the "Grand Sedey" against the Mughal emperor. (The "Grand Sedey" was one of the two Syed brothers, powerful Mughal rajas, or kings, who competed for control of the Mughal Empire.) Tukoji quickly distinguished himself in battle by taking charge when his commanding officer fled at the sight of 500 Mughal troops. He rallied the remaining Maratha, and in the night led them through a ravine to attack the Mughals by surprise, routing them. For this valiant service he was rewarded with the command of 200 soldiers at Suvarnadurg, a great island fort from which Maratha naval forces—English and Portuguese merchants called them pirates—plundered the Indian shores and coastal waters.

Kanhoji may have been born at Suvarnadurg, possibly around 1669, and here he may have spent many of his early years, although one story claims his father was killed in battle when he was very young and he was raised by an uncle. An almost certainly frivolous account claims that Kanhoji was not the real son of Tukoji, or Purab as they name him, but a teenage imposter who drowned the real son and his brother at sea, and returned years later to claim that he was Kanhoji. Yet another account claims that Kanhoji was born in Bombay, and when he reached adulthood he set forth with several companions, took over the unoccupied fortress on tiny Khanderi Island, called "Kenerey" by the English, nine miles (14.5 km) from the mouth of Bombay harbor, and turned pirate.

More likely, Kanhoji worked his way up from common seaman to captain, although he may have begun as an officer of sorts, given his possible family history. In his early years he fought for the "Grand Sedey" against the Mughal fleet. In

Grabs and *gallivats* attacking a **British** ship (center right, flying the striped company ensign) belonging to the **"Honourable Company,"** from a probably mid-eighteenth-century painting. The large vessel on the left is a grab. Note especially its long jutting prow, unlike the bow of European ships. Otherwise, the grab's masting and rigging is similar to that of European ships. In the foreground are *gallivats*. Note the large mast and sail, with a much smaller mast and sail aft, and the sharp prow with a small flagstaff flying Maratha colors (usually orange).

return for his valor, around 1689, Kanhoji, perhaps only twenty years old, was given Khanderi Island to command. But it was not command of the fortress that mattered, for the walls and cannon were merely a means of protecting the several piratical *gallivats* based there. With these swift vessels Kanhoji was in the perfect position to plunder as he pleased. Before long, he extended his reach far beyond Bombay and the waters of the Maratha. He preyed upon the vessels of his neighbors, and those of the Portuguese as well. Kanhoji was the first of the Angrias, who, for the next sixty-seven years, would threaten trade on the west coast of India.

But Kanhoji's first prizes were not princely ships filled with rupees and silks. Instead, perhaps around 1689 or 1690, he led his five *gallivats* to the fishing grounds off Bombay, plundered the fishing fleets, and probably demanded tribute from them as well, in return for which he would leave them unmolested. At first, the East India Company tolerated these petty pirate attacks on Indian fishing boats. Rather than take military action against a small but almost impregnable fortress, the Company built a small twelve-gun vessel to protect the fishermen, and also an armed yacht to protect the English governors of the Company's factories, as their trading posts were called.

Kanhoji next attacked and captured a Portuguese *grab*, giving him the combination of *grab* and *gallivats* he needed to make even greater conquests at sea. In Downing's words, "After Angria had taken this grab, he mounted several guns on her, and declared open war with all nations." Soon after, he attacked another Portuguese *grab*, this one much more powerful, and, after a stout battle, captured it. At this time the Maratha were waging a war against the Mughal Empire and its allies, the Portuguese and the Siddi, a piratical people on the west coast of India, of Muslim faith, African origin, and guerilla warfare expertise. Kanhoji made the best of this, and began carving out a seagoing empire of his own by attacking his enemies as they grew weak from war and unrest.

So successful was he that in 1698 he was named admiral of the Maratha, whose lands were but a sliver on the west coast of India, and whose population was 13 million. With this appointment came control of the Indian coast from Bombay to Vengurla, 225 miles (362 km) to the south. Kanhoji had a fleet of both *grabs* and *gallivats*, as well as control of numerous forts along the coast, including the great fort at Vijaydurg, where he made his first headquarters, and the island fort Suvarnadurg. Any ships that passed his part of the coast were in danger of attack or extortion—and ships from the Middle East to the Far East and vice versa all traveled along the Indian coast. But Kanhoji Angria did not limit his sea roving to his own waters, or to those of his enemies, the Mughals, Siddi, and Portuguese. He attacked vessels and villages as far south as the kingdom of Travancore, which reached the southern tip of India. By 1700 the East India Company considered him a notorious, daring pirate. In 1702, probably feeling strong enough to take on even the most powerful of the foreign traders, he for the first time attacked one of the East India Company's vessels.

A KINGDOM OF SEA ROVERS

It was only a small vessel, though, and doubtless he was trying to test the waters. But when the English agents from Bombay petitioned for the release of the six men captured at Cochin (modern-day Kochi), he refused and advised them that they would soon come to fear him. Two years later, after a dispute with the Maratha *peshwa*, he claimed independence and was in turn proclaimed a rebel by the Maratha king and *peshwa*. This mattered little to him, for he was powerful enough that soon even the king himself would have to come to terms with him.

At first the Maratha tried to fight him with its navy, but he recruited as much of the Maratha fleet as he could to his command, via his charisma and successful record—then attacked and destroyed the rest. Still unwilling to accept the independence of the renegade Kanhoji, the Maratha built three forts across from Suvarnadurg, but the pirate admiral soon captured them all. During this time, the death in 1707 of the Mughal emperor Aurangzeb caused disruption in the empire and greater civil war among the Maratha. Kanhoji seized the opportunity and claimed even more power, going to war both by sea and by land against anyone who stood in his way.

The East India Company immediately realized what this meant—that Kanhoji, now no longer under the control of the Maratha king, might do as he pleased. They advised him that Bombay belonged to them, and that he must leave its vessels alone. Had Kanhoji been English, he might have said, "Go to hell," for that was exactly the substance of his reply: he would attack whom he pleased. The Company was now at war with the pirate king.

At first, it did not seem much of a war, for Kanhoji was busy fighting the Maratha, Portuguese, and Siddi, but in 1707 his *grabs* and *gallivats* attacked the *Bombay*, a well-armed, well-manned Company frigate. The fight was long, as *grabs* and *gallivats* swept under the ship's stern repeatedly, violently unloading their guns into masts, rigging, and hull. The crew of the *Bombay* fought back hard for hours, trying to sweep the decks and shatter the masts of the *grabs* with their stern guns, and trying to sink any *gallivat* foolish enough to come within range.

Fights at sea in this age were dangerous for many reasons. There was the obvious danger from the round shot of the great guns, which could mash a man into jelly, take off a limb, or severely lacerate him with the splinters they caused. There was the danger from other shot as well: chain shot designed to cut rigging and sails, but which could sever a man in half; bar shot, which could do likewise; and grapeshot, canister shot, and "langrage," whose small projectiles of iron and lead balls and scrap metal shredded sails and rigging, not to mention the flesh of men. There were the dangers of small arms and cold steel: of musket and pistol shot, of thrust and cut, from musket and pistol butts, and even from the handspikes used to aim great guns.

But there were also the many dangers of fire and flame. Grenades and firepots were more dangerous for the fire of their explosions than they were for the fragments they flung among men. Wads rammed down upon cartridge and round shot in the barrels of great guns burned when the guns were fired. At close range they could set fire to sails and other combustibles, as could firepots. Often they ignited powder cartridges on the enemy's decks, burning nearby men to the bone. In the worst cases, a trail of powder might have been left from the gun decks to the powder room, or there were too many cartridges on deck, and when one caught fire from a firepot or burning wad and exploded, it might set fire to another, and then another.

Some version of this probably happened during the fight with the *Bombay*, for she suddenly exploded and burned. Writers who witnessed such terrible events invariably described their horror at seeing men blown into the air and into the sea, first shattered and burned, and then, if not yet dead, drowned. Survivors were often burned in places to the bone. The *Bombay* was lost to Kanhoji, but he had made his point. He was not afraid to attack even a ship as well armed as any man-of-war.

In 1710, Kanhoji decided to base *grabs* and *gallivats* at his former headquarters on Khanderi Island. He had long since left it behind, perhaps when he was made admiral of the Maratha. The problem was, it was now occupied by forces of the Grand Sedey with whom, among others, he was at war—not to mention that the Company might have something to say about the pirate Angria setting up shop again only nine miles (14.5 km) south of Bombay. Kanhoji had a powerful fleet of ten *grabs* of sixteen to thirty guns each, some as great as 400 tons (362.9 metric tons), and fifty *gallivats* of various sizes. He could carry a landing party thousands of men strong in his *gallivats* if necessary. With his forces he assaulted the island, and at the same time the Company ship *Godolphin* engaged his *grabs* and *gallivats* nearby, or vice versa. The fight lasted for two days. In the end, the *Godolphin* escaped much battered to Bombay, and many of the *grabs* and *gallivats* to Khanderi, which was now in Kanhoji's possession. No one would ever take the island back from him, although they would try.

The pirate admiral now made every effort to strike even more fear and awe into his enemies. To those at Bombay, according to John Burnell, a Company army officer, Kanhoji sent several captured Indian residents "whom he caused to be burnt with hot irons in the forehead to the bone, and then ordered them to go tell the general that that was his chop [mark] which he designed to fix upon all the English in Bombay." Immediately the alarm was sounded and the Company's army "marched and quartered" every night in the garden near the bay where they expected him to land. But Kanhoji did not come. The fear alone served its purpose. From Surat on the northwest coast of India to Dabhol 250 miles (402 km) south he took every merchant vessel that came his way. His swift *grabs* and *gallivats* often ventured more than 700 miles (1,126 km) farther south than Dabhol, raiding and pillaging as they went. Pirates dreamed of being princes upon the sea, of being able to do as they pleased. Kanhoji actually did.

By 1712, Kanhoji held the power of a sovereign prince and was treated as such, his piracies notwithstanding. Indeed, there was no other choice, so powerful was he. No longer did he take to sea to raid and plunder, but sent his commodores and captains in his place. Some were foreign: one was Dutch, another Portuguese. It was rumored that if his commanders were successful, he rewarded them well— but if they failed, he had their heads cut off. Finally, in 1713, after his successes on sea and land against the Maratha king, including the defeat of the *peshwa*'s general, the king and *peshwa* made peace with their admiral, confirming him in command of the Maratha fleet and granting him the right to ten great forts and sixteen small ones, along with all associated lands and villages.

At roughly the same time Kanhoji had made peace with the English at Bombay, namely in the form of the tribute paid to him in early 1713 after the capture of the *Anne* and the Company yacht. Kanhoji was at the peak of his power, and the English had only once handed him a setback, and it was but a small one. This did not, however, mean that the East India Company would not retaliate if the great admiral attacked them again. They considered his mere existence a

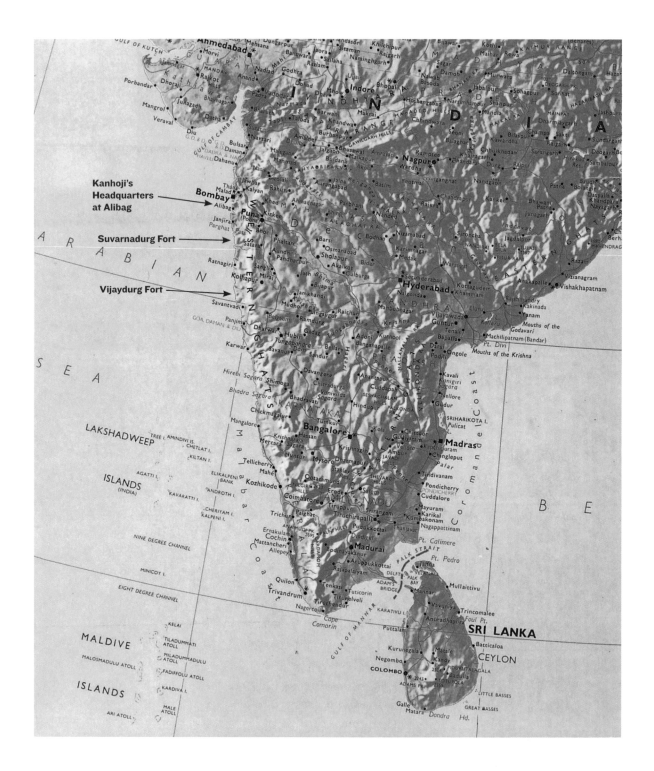

Kanhoji's
Headquarters
at Alibag

Suvarnadurg Fort

Vijaydurg Fort

threat, especially with his fort at Khanderi and his headquarters at Alibag, only a few miles (kilometers) farther south. Kanhoji's power at sea had made him an enemy of what soon would be one of the greatest colonial empires in history.

DETERMINED TO BRING HIM DOWN

Indeed, for all practical purposes, Kanhoji was so far undefeated. Only once could the East India Company arguably claim to have defeated him, and only in the sense that the *Godolphin* had escaped capture, which in many ways was a victory. By 1715, either Kanhoji had grown weary of peace with the English traders or they had done something to offend his sea-roving sensibilities, for he released his *grabs* and *gallivats* to attack the Company again. This time they went after the East Indiamen *Sommers* and *Grantham*. But the ships fought back vigorously—by now, Company ships were well armed and manned against the Indian pirates.

The East Indiamen were unable to maneuver due to the calm air, but their guns managed to keep the warriors aboard the *grabs* and *gallivats* from boarding. Knowing that they could not bring their full broadsides to bear, the ships manned their boats and sent them against one of the pirate *grabs*, whose crews now found the tables turned on them. One boat managed to board the *grab* at its low prow, but the Indian pirate warriors fought back fiercely with spears and *talwars*. The pirates repelled the boarding party. For more than four hours pirate *grab* and *gallivat* fought back against the merchantmen's armed boats until the *gallivats* finally towed the battered *grabs* away. With no wind, the Company ships could not follow, and their boats were too battered to pursue; furthermore, if the wind rose, Kanhoji's men would head to windward if they feared capture, where it would be impossible for the ships to catch up with them. One English officer, Midshipman Henry Cave, was speared in the chest while trying to board the *grab*. He survived, and kept the lance as a souvenir for the rest of his life.

But even this setback, and others like it to follow, proved how difficult it really would be to truly defeat Kanhoji. It was easy for him to make profitable war on his enemies, and indeed on anyone he pleased, as long as they came to the west coast of India. He owned more than 200 miles (322 km) of heavily fortified coastline along which merchant vessels had to travel in order to take advantage of the land breezes, for they extended only forty miles (64.3 km) out to sea. His *grabs* and *gallivats* kept close to shore and often hid until they sighted their prey. If the wind was in their favor, they rowed swiftly to the attack, and if the attack turned against

Map of India, from Bombay (modern Mumbai) to Ceylon (Sri Lanka). Kanhoji Angria's attacks ranged as far south as Trivandrum, and probably even beyond Cape Comorin. At the height of his sea-roving reign, Kanhoji controlled the coast of India from Bombay to Vengurla (a coastal town near Savantvadi). The entire coast of India was a major trade route for merchant traders from both Europe and Asia, and Kanhoji's piratical kingdom lay at its center.

them, they had only to retreat under their oars to one of the many forts along the coast, or even into a small cove or river. They did not keep far to sea, so they could never be trapped there. To destroy them, their enemies had to come ashore where they had an army of 20,000 or more, and forts so strong that it would take a great army and much artillery to bring them down. It was pirate heaven.

The pirate admiral kept up his plundering reign at sea and often at shore, enriching himself and the Maratha, and growing ever more powerful. Although the Portuguese often took arms against him, they were also accused of providing him with gunpowder, gunners, and even Dutch deserters. He continued to recruit foreigners into his navy, and after 1715 recruited some of the English pirates who took to sea at the end of Queen Anne's War. One of them, John Plantain, would even build his own small pirate empire at Ranter Bay on the island of Madagascar.

Tired of his "insolences," as doubtless the Company called them, the English at Bombay under Governor Charles Boone dispatched forces against Kanhoji. Boone was tireless in his efforts to build ships and develop forces to protect Bombay. In 1719 an alliance of the East India Company and Portuguese forces attacked Khanderi Island, but were badly beaten back. Even the presence of one of Kanhoji's former commodores, a Portuguese named Manuel de Castro, who had once commanded his *gallivats* and who knew the ways and tactics of the pirate admiral, failed to grant them victory. Three times the Company's forces attacked Vijaydurg, and three times they were sent away well bloodied and empty-handed. In 1721, in company with Portuguese forces, they attacked Kolaba, the fortress that defended Alibag, but were beaten and battered back in this case as well. Kanhoji knew that if he was strong enough by land, he could never be defeated at sea. And he never was.

PIRATE OR PATRIOT?

Until recently, Kanhoji's sea-roving and naval actions had received little attention, even in his own country, but this has finally begun to change. Today he is a source of national and naval pride, and is recognized in India as one of the fathers of the Indian navy for two reasons. Not only was he an early Indian admiral, but also his attacks led the British government to establish a force that would one day become the Indian navy. Today, Indian Naval Station Angre, home of India's western naval command, is named after him.

But was Kanhoji really a pirate? More often than not, no. For certain he was a sea rover, but most often as a privateer or commander of a plundering navy. To the English and other Westerners, however, only a *civilized* state could authorize privateers or navies to plunder, and they did not consider the various small Indian rulers civilized. Thus they were pirates. At least part of the time Kanhoji did engage in what many nations would define as piracy, and for the merchantmen of the Honourable East India Company he was never anything but a pirate, albeit a noteworthy and redoubtable one. Even Kanhoji's *real* piracies were in the same vein as those of Sir Francis Drake and Sir Henry Morgan, men who were sent to sea to steal and who afterward were knighted and regarded as heroes.

Kanhoji Angria died in 1729, not only unconquered but also undefeated. The forces of the Mughal emperor, as well as of the Siddi, Maratha, Portuguese, and English, were never able to stop his rise to power on land and sea. His descendents would rule after him, but never as successfully, and much of the Angrias' power was broken in 1756 with the capture of the fortress at Vijaydurg by a combined English and Maratha force of soldiers and sailors. Great Britain intended to rule India, and soon would, the Angrias and their sea warriors notwithstanding.

But through whatever lens he is viewed, whether as a ruthless pirate, marauding privateer, plundering opportunist, or patriotic naval hero—and indeed, he may have been all—Kanhoji Angria belongs on the list of the greatest sea rovers in history, alongside Kheir-ed-Din Barbarossa, Sir Francis Drake, and Cheng I Sao. Perhaps an English factor in Bombay said it best: "Thus fortunate and invincible was Connagee Angria, who ravaged and plundered the English, and other nations for a long time with impunity, and died full of glory ... and still fuller of riches."

CHAPTER 12

☠

CHENG I SAO

1775?-1844

LEADING A THOUSAND DEADLY "WASPS OF THE OCEAN"

The Chinese pirates lying at anchor nearby rarely attacked European vessels, which were mostly well armed. Some indeed were powerfully so, with experienced crews, and might wreak havoc among the fleet of pirate junks. Worse, attacks on European vessels, especially on those of the English, might invite retaliation. In general, it was wise to leave them alone, but for the smaller sort, and even then the boats of the English men-of-war were to be avoided. Local fishermen and coastal traders knew that the pirates would rather not tangle with these men-of-war and their offspring, and if one of these armed boats happened to be making its way along the coast or up the Pearl River, often an entire fleet of local vessels, hundreds even, would follow along, their protection assured.

The captain of the pirate junk had no way of knowing who was in the cutter—a type of ship's boat—that had foolishly come near to ask for directions to Macao on this day in September 1809, or that it belonged to the East India Company ship, the *Marquis of Ely*. Nor had he any way of knowing that weather had forced the boat away from the ship it belonged to, or that its crew was poorly armed and their powder wet, or that only a day before the crew had rowed hard for six hours into the wind, trying to run from three pirate boats, after having eaten little except green oranges for three days. Overnight the cutter and crew had lain anchored near the shore, where the background hid them from lookouts at sea. The next morning, its coxswain hoping soon to be in Macao, the cutter headed to a nearby shore, then fled from the threatening appearance of the men there, all of whom were armed with pikes and lances. And now, as they rowed toward a fleet of junks anchored across the way—which the Chinese pilots in his boat told him were "Mandarin" (Chinese) junks and salt boats, not pirates—both coxswain and crew were in for a surprise.

The captain sent a boat to intercept it, and as it came alongside of the cutter, twenty of his men leaped up from where they had hidden themselves in the bottom of the boat. With a sword in each hand they jumped aboard the cutter, putting one to the throat and the other to the breast of each man, "keeping their eyes on their officer, waiting his signal to cut or desist," as English mariner Richard Glasspoole, who commanded the boat, would later write.

The pirate officer sheathed his sword, followed by his men, who did the same. Screaming and shouting for joy, the pirates, whom Europeans usually called Ladrones, from the Portuguese word for "thieves," hauled their prisoners into their boat. This handful of captured men were lucky. Often these pirates killed their captives immediately, depending on who they were. Those who resisted or insulted their captors were routinely killed. Those who were told to join the pirates, usually for skill in handling a ship's great guns (cannons) or muskets—as Glasspoole would soon be—but refused, were likewise put to death. In 1805, every member of the crews of two Portuguese vessels, one captured among the Lema Islands (fifteen miles (24 km) south of modern-day Hong Kong) and the other just off the coast soon after departing Cochin, were cut literally to pieces after refusing such service.

The English prisoner was brought before the captain of the junk, "a stout commanding-looking man" dressed in purple silk pajamas and a black turban. He asked the Englishman who he and the others were, threatened them with death, and ordered the interpreter tortured to make sure he was telling the truth. This was but a minor, incidental capture, but it would be reported up the chain of command nonetheless.

The captain was but one of a thousand pirate captains commanding 40,000 to 60,000 pirates divided among six great pirate squadrons that were identified by their flags—red, yellow, green, blue, black, and white. He reported to a squadron leader, who reported to the admiral of his fleet, and he to the admiral of the great Red Flag fleet who commanded all and whose more than 500 junks outnumbered all the five other fleets together. Such strict military order was unusual among both pirates and privateers, but most unusual of all was that the admiral of the Red Flag fleet—and thus of the 1,000 pirate junks and as many as 60,000 pirates—was a woman. As for Richard Glasspoole, whose English nationality and association with the Honorable East India Company concerned his captors, he would soon witness her greatest acts of piracy.

FROM PROSTITUTE TO PIRATE

In the early nineteenth century, the coastal waters and villages of China catered to an enormous population of seagoing traders and fishermen who plied their cargoes and took their catch along one of the world's great sea lanes. In addition to fish markets, merchant trading shops, and ship chandlers, some of which operated from boats and junks, there were other businesses that appealed directly to the sailor's social needs and addictions—specifically, gambling halls, tea, tobacco, and opium houses, and brothels. Seamen of all sorts visited these houses of recreation, and in 1801, probably as a result of such visits, a pirate leader named Cheng I married a Cantonese prostitute named Shih Yang. How well he knew her before he married her is unknown. Although some fictional accounts romantically describe the bride as having been taken as a prisoner during a pirate raid, there is no evidence for this, although it is certainly not impossible.

Cheng I was a powerful man, the leader of a pirate fleet, although by no means was he the most powerful of pirates. He could have taken wives from among his many female prisoners, and perhaps he did. But he must have seen something more than mere beauty in this woman whose body was sold for sex, if indeed she was beautiful, for we have no description of her. She was not a teenage prostitute, although she probably began as one. Rather, she was in her mid-twenties, and by now was probably both experienced in the world and business savvy, for prostitution, like piracy, is an ancient trade practiced out of need or greed, or both, and is most successful when practiced according to the principles of good business.

Very likely, Cheng I saw wit or intelligence in her, and fighting spirit, all characteristics not necessarily in accord with Confucian values that demanded submissiveness in a woman. But they were definitely in accord with what a great pirate leader needed in a wife who might in many ways be his co-commander. On the other hand, the woman may have seduced Cheng I, subtly or overtly, realizing how much further he might elevate himself—and her as well—if he had a partner of great intelligence and ambition at his side.

At the time of their marriage, Cheng I still often sailed as a legitimate privateer in the service of the Tay-son dynasty in Vietnam, which had been fighting a decade-long rebellion led by Nguyen Anh and assisted by a small number of French mercenaries. This is not to suggest that his fleet did not engage in outright piracy, for certainly it did, and its origins were in piracy, albeit petty. The Ladrones had begun small, as most pirates everywhere did. Their first pirate vessels were small boats propelled by oars, and their first crews numbered only thirty to forty. Working together, a few of these boats captured a few junks, and with these junks they captured others, including some of the Mandarin war junks, as the ships of the Chinese navy were called.

Now, in the service of the Tay-son, the pirates had grown much stronger. They were protected in Vietnamese waters, and even better, the Tay-son provided them with good, strong junks and better "great guns," or cannon, than they typically had. They could strike out northwest from the Gulf of Tonkin,

War junks as used by Chinese pirates, or Ladrones, from Charles Elms's *Pirates Own Book*. The junk was highly suited to Chinese waters, both coastal and river. Difficult to distinguish from merchant or fishing junks unless very close, they were ideal pirate vessels. Their sails were fitted with battens that enabled them to be easily raised, lowered, and reefed. Junks were lightly armed with great guns, at least by European standards, and boarding was therefore a common tactic of Chinese pirates. Cheng I Sao commanded 1,000 such vessels.

REPUBLIC OF CH

SIN-KIANG

Su-chau

East Turkestan

INNER
Si-ning
Lan-ch

Yarkand

Khotan

HINDUKUSH

Kabul

Mt. Godwin Austen
28,280 ft.

KWEN-LUN MTS.

CHINESE EMPIRE

Cheng-tu

Sze-chw

Chaval
1895

KARA KORUM MTS.

Gilgit

Chung-k
1891

AN Peshawar

Khaibar
Pass

Kashmir

Srinagar
1846

CHINESE TIBET

OUTER

Chillianwala

Gujrat

HIMALAYA

1904-1914

Autonomous 1914

Lhasa

Punjab

Lahore

Amritsar

Sobraon
1849

Mulwa

Simla

Kurnaon

Tsanpu R.

Chang-ts

Kathmandu

NEPAL

Multan

Patiala

Meerut

Bareilly

Mt. Everest
29,002 ft.

Chumbi

Punakha

BHOTAN

Bikaner

Delhi

Jaipur

Mutra

Agra

Oudh

Nigam

Khatmandu

Brahmaputra R.

Hadbu

Yun-na

Rajputana

Jodhpur

Ajmer

Etawah

Lucknow

Cawnpur

Ganges

TEESTAN

Assam

Manipur

Bhamo

Yun-nan

Mong

Gwalior

Jhansi

Allahabad

Rewa

Benares

Patna

Berhampur

Dacca

Bham

Kotah

Udaipur

1818

INDIA

Ahmadabad

Narbada

Indore

Rewa

1812

Bengal

Chandarnagar

Calcutta

Chittagong

BRITISH

Mandalay
1886

Tong

Cambay

Baroda

Surat

Damán

Assaye

Narbada

Nagpur
1853

Nagpur

Orissa

Cuttack
1803

Upper

Burma
1886

1893

Bassein

Bombay

Berar

Aurangabad

Godavari R.

Jaipur

Circars

Puri

BAY

Minbu

Poona

Satara

Dom. of the

Haidarabad

Bijapur

Nizam

Krishna R.

Yanaon

OF

BENGAL

Pegu
1852

Lower

Burma

Kolhapur

Dharwar

Masulipatam

Rangoon

Moulmein

SIA

Goa

Bellary

Nellore

Irawadi R.

Tenasserim

Bangkok

Seringapatam

Mangalore

Mysore

Bangalore

Madras

Andaman

Islands
1858

Tenasserim

Pnom

Gulf of

Cannanore

Tellicherri

Mysore

Pondicherry

Ca

Mahé

Calicut

Karikal

Siam

Cochin

Trichinopoly

Tanjore

Negapatam

Quilon

Tuticorin

Trincomali

Nicobar

Islands
1869

Georgetown

Penang
1786

Tantala

C. Comorin

1796

Ceylon

Kandy

G. of Manar

Colombo

Kota Rajah
(Achin)

Sumat

F.M.S.
1874

Maldive

Is.

1802

INDIAN OCEAN

Malay Peninsula

Straits

10

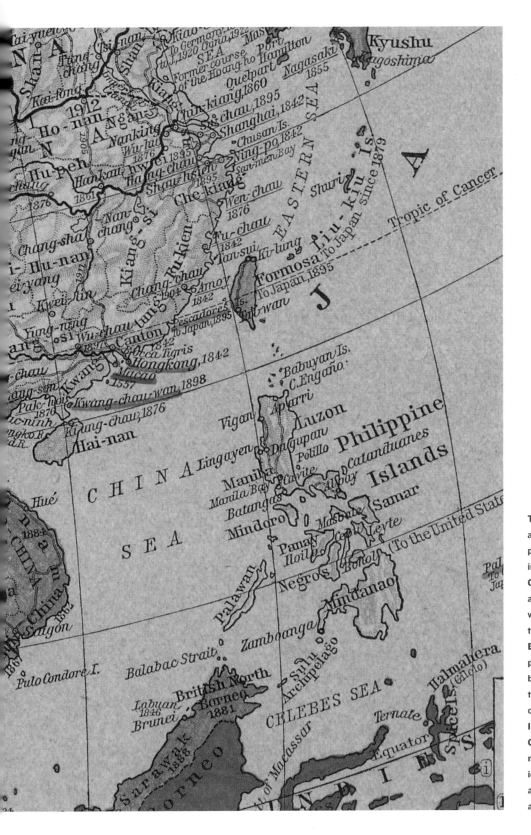

The South China Sea and environs. Chinese pirates operated primarily in Vietnamese and Chinese waters. The area around Hainan Island was a critical chokepoint through which much European and Asian trade passed, and pirates often based themselves here to take advantage of its central position. Cheng I Sao's great attack on Cochin began at the mouth of the Pearl River, identified here as the area between Hong Kong and Macao.

pass between the mainland and Hainan Island, plunder the Chinese coast and coastal waters, then retreat back to Vietnam, where other profitable fighting and plundering was to be had. Under the Tay-son, the Chinese pirates grew from perhaps a few hundred pirates and a few dozen pirate junks to tens of thousands of pirates and hundreds of junks.

Throughout history many upsurges in piracy have followed immediately upon the heels of war's end when privateers find themselves suddenly out of work. And so it was that in 1802, a year after the marriage of Cheng I to Shih Yang, who afterward was known as Cheng I Sao ("wife of Cheng I"), the Tay-son dynasty fell. At roughly the same time, Cheng Ch'I, a great leader of Chinese privateers and pirates in Tay-son service, was killed in action near Hanoi, leaving a power vacuum among the pirates. Cheng I, perhaps led or encouraged by his wife, quickly stepped in to fill it.

The pirates, whose number had grown manyfold during the Tay-son rebellion from 1792 to 1802, were now in disarray. Not only had they lost their leader, but also shortly after his death they were defeated by the Nguyen fleet at Son Nam, Vietnam, and forced back permanently into Chinese waters. They needed leadership and a new structure, now that their old way of Tay-son privateering was gone. Cheng I provided it. He established pirate bases, first at the Luichow Peninsula across from Hainan Island, then at Lantau, a long, narrow island just south of what today is known as Hong Kong. He ordered his pirates to treat the nearby villagers well, so that they would always be well supplied. At these places entire pirate fleets would lie at anchor in plain sight, their crews and families living aboard, seldom venturing ashore except to plunder. Yet in many ways, Cheng I Sao appears to have emerged as a power behind the throne. Without doubt, she was learning firsthand how to manage a pirate empire.

For the next five years, Cheng I's pirates ranged from Vietnam to the north China coast in fleets of as many as 300 junks, each of which carried a large number of women who were there not only as wives and mothers, but often simultaneously as sailors and sometimes even as captains. These junks were pirate ships as well as the floating homes of the many seagoing pirate families crammed between their decks, each—husband, wife, and children—living in a space as small as four feet by four feet (1.2 m by 1.2 m).

But in November 1807 Cheng I was killed off the coast of Vietnam. Accounts of his death vary. In one, he died in a gale at sea, and in another, from a round shot (cannonball) while in action as a mercenary pirate or privateer against the Nguyen usurper. In either case, the result was the same. The pirate fleets were without a leader, and someone had to claim the right of succession. Enter Cheng I Sao, the mother of two of Cheng I's sons. She knew that her own sons, only two and four years old, could not be promoted to command of the great pirate fleets for many years. But another of Cheng I's sons could. The fifteen-year-old, Cheng Pao, had been taken prisoner by the pirates in 1801, the same year Cheng I married Cheng I Sao, and was now on his way to becoming a talented pirate. Cheng I had immediately taken an interest in the boy, reportedly developed a homosexual relationship with him, and over the next few years groomed him for command. At some point, Cheng I and Lady Cheng adopted the young man and made him captain of a pirate junk.

After her husband died, Cheng I Sao went immediately to work getting Cheng I's kinsmen on her side and backing Cheng Pao for command of the fleets. Historian Dian Murray has suggested that at times she may have been able to use "male fear of her 'mysterious potency'" to gain an advantage in negotiations, and perhaps this was the case here. Further, it was not unusual in China for a woman to succeed her husband upon his death. But often those who help a leader succeed are abandoned in the end, and Lady Cheng, as she would become known by the English, had to ensure that this would not happen in her case. She therefore seduced adopted son Cheng Pao, violating the incest taboo even while consolidating her power over him, thus over the succession, and thus over the pirate fleets. A few years later she married him.

This done, she set about with an almost bureaucratic mania for rules, regulations, and records. She codified Cheng Pao's pirate articles (she may have even written them), and applied them to all six pirate fleets. It was agreed that 80 percent of plunder went into a general fund from which junks were provisioned and repaired and other expenses paid. All plunder was "registered"—recorded in plunder books, that is—and no division was made until all plunder was noted and its value ascertained. Pirate junks were registered as well; each had a registration number and flew the flag of its fleet. She established a system of "Ladrone-passes," as Europeans called them: a system of safe passage in return for tribute, and also for those negotiating tribute or ransom. In other words, it was "black rent" or a "protection racket," which pirates have often engaged in everywhere. She had a system of financial agents and negotiators, much as the Somali pirates do today. Far more important, Lady Cheng mapped out a pirate strategy that would take them farther than her husband or any other pirate leader in memory ever had.

SCOURGING THE CANTONESE COAST

Broadly speaking, the waters from Hainan Island to the Bocca Tigris (Tiger's Mouth), a strait on the Pearl River roughly fifty miles (80.5 km) above Macao, was the most dangerous stretch of Chinese coast, at least in regard to pirate attacks. In particular, the passage between Hainan Island and the Luichow Peninsula, where the pirates made one of their bases, and the waters from Macao to the Bocca Tigris, just shy of Cochin (modern-day Guangzhou), were feared by both Chinese fishing and trading junks, and smaller European merchant vessels. Even well-armed merchant ships and men-of-war were on their guards here. The islands at the wide entrance to the open sea were aptly named the Ladrones, for here Chinese pirates had for many centuries lain in wait in their junks for passing merchant vessels.

The pirates operated in great fleets of junks of many sorts. Chinese junks were constructed according to purpose and varied by region, but most had three masts, each with a single lug sail, which was a mostly square sail of which roughly one-third projected beyond the mast. It could be easily shifted from one side of the mast to the other when tacking (sailing against the wind), and it could be easily shortened as well. Rather than being "reefed" like European sails, which were shortened by tying them to the yard via "reef points," the junk's sail was stiffened every foot or two (30.5 cm or so) by stout bamboo "battans," which made shortening sail much easier. It was like drawing up a Venetian blind.

Most junks carried only eight to twelve guns, and even though this was only a small armament, many of the guns were of large caliber, including nine- and twelve-pounders, and occasionally eighteen-pounders. Unfortunately, the pirates had few firearms to augment their great guns, which would have gone far to make up the deficiency. And those they did have were matchlock muskets that they used inexpertly, or captured modern flintlock muskets with which they were even less adept. Chinese pirates often forced European prisoners to use captured flintlock muskets in battle. Prisoners had little choice: it was fight or die. Far more common were the bow and arrow used in place of muskets, plus various spears, and invariably each pirate carried a pair of "long knives" or "cutlasses," as Europeans typically referred to the different Chinese swords.

The crews of Lady Cheng's junks were a variety of veteran Chinese and Mongol pirates who had served during the Tay-son rebellion. Many, although not the majority, were married and had their wives and children with them. There

"Madame Cheng" in action, from an eighteenth-century engraving. No descriptions or illustrations of Cheng I Sao's actual appearance exist. Further, it is unknown whether Cheng I Sao actually engaged in close combat, or limited herself to directing it. There is at least one account of a female Chinese pirate engaging in close combat, and there are numerous accounts of female victims fighting fiercely against Chinese pirates. Leadership by example was but one of several sources of power available to pirate captains.

Private Collection/ Peter Newark Historical Pictures / The Bridgeman Art Library International

were fishermen and other mariners who joined the pirates later, and criminal gangs from the mainland, of which there were many in China. Some Europeans were among her crews as well, most of them not of their own choosing.

With these vessels, men, and women, Lady Cheng scourged the Chinese coast. Most of their prey, far outnumbered by the attacking junks, their large crews, and the number of guns they carried, surrendered without a fight. Anything other than running was suicide. But other attacks were not as easy or as successful. In August 1809, one of her flotillas of eighteen or twenty large "Ladrone" junks espied the *Atahulpa* of Boston, an American merchantman, at anchor at Macao. It looked to be an easy conquest, for the *Atahulpa* carried only six guns, and these were only six-pounders. Further, part of her crew was ashore.

The junks swept forth and attacked, some of them remaining in reserve while others fired their great guns. For hours the junks attacked, cutting the *Atahulpa*'s rigging to pieces and striking her hull many times. Even so, the merchantman's deadly gunnery forced the junks to keep their distance, preventing them from slipping alongside to board in violent frenzy. Now it became a waiting game. The *Atahulpa* could go nowhere in the stale, smoke-darkened air—the pirates need only batter away at her until she submitted. There was no way she could escape from so many pirate junks. Suddenly, the breeze freshened and the *Atahulpa* cut her cables. The Ladrones, caught by surprise, chased her, fighting a running battle, but too soon the merchantman had taken shelter under the guns of the Macao fort. The large artillery of the fort could turn junks into splinters. They had no choice but to withdraw. There would soon be other merchantmen to assault and plunder.

The attack illustrated the tactical problem of Lady Cheng's great fleet. The dozens and even hundreds of junks sailing together were perfectly suited for attacking fleets of merchant trading junks and for raiding villages. But attacking a large, well-armed merchantman was another thing entirely, for it was impossible to put an entire fleet to work attacking a single vessel. Only a handful could get near without great confusion, and even then the junks might accidentally fire into each other. No single junk was a match for these large armed merchantmen, and if the fight lasted long, help in the form of a man-of-war might be on the way. Many attacks took place near Macao and Canton, areas heavy with European presence and armed force.

The Ladrones were fierce in battle, but one has to wonder whether having their families aboard the pirate junks caused them to take fewer risks than they otherwise might have. On the other hand, when cornered, the pirates fought desperately, perhaps in part because they knew they must defend not only their lives but those of their families as well. In "their defense [they are] most desperate," wrote Glasspoole, "yielding in the latter instance to no superiority in numbers."

The failure of the Ladrones to capture the *Atahulpa* should not suggest that they had little in the way of tactics, and that their success was due largely to their large numbers, their organization, and, as will be seen, the fear they induced through their cruelty. Indeed, although these factors certainly made Lady Cheng's pirates an effective force, their tactics easily matched them. In 1807, J. Turner, a British mariner captured by the Ladrones the year before, was aboard a pirate squadron leader's junk when it went in pursuit of two "Chin Chew" junks—beautiful seagoing junks, with fine, swift lines, from Ch'uan-chou.

The Ladrones would even dive into the water to attack vessels, first tying a "short sword...close under each arm," then swim in large numbers out to anchored junks or brigs and board them quickly before defenses could be organized.

The pirate squadron, of four large junks and three small, soon came up with one of the large merchant junks. The prey refused to surrender. Immediately, the Ladrones attacked, battering the junk with their great guns. The pirates intended to beat them until they surrendered. If the merchant junks still refused, they would slip alongside, hurl firepots onto the decks and stones at the crew, then board, each man armed with two short swords and hewing his way through any of the enemy still standing. But the Ch'uan-chou junks were strong, with sturdy timbers, and they were well armed and manned. They fiercely resisted all pirate efforts.

Now the pirates were desperate. If they could not have both junks, they would be satisfied with one, and pay the other for its stubborn resistance. The Ladrones removed the guns from one of their small junks, filled it with combustibles, and sent it to crash alongside the "Chin Chew" junk. The merchant vessel would catch fire and burn. The fools who had resisted would be punished, and the crew aboard the remaining junk would know that the same fate awaited them if they did not surrender.

But the Ladrones were disappointed again, for the merchant junk's sails were on the opposite side of the fireship, and only the hull would burn, and where it did the fire was quickly put out. Soon enough, the merchant junk's crew shoved the fireship away, probably with spare yards or other booms, and the pirates once more had to wait another day for victory. But again, there were many potential prizes on the sea. Soon there would be others. They had but to wait and keep their eyes open.

The Ladrones had other tactics as well. Sometimes, they would even dive into the water to attack vessels, first tying a "short sword ... close under each arm," then swim in large numbers out to anchored junks or brigs and board them quickly before defenses could be organized. Tactics like these were a great source of Lady Cheng's profitable piracies. But in spite of the many successful forays of her crews along the Chinese coast and into Vietnamese waters, never had the Ladrones ventured beyond the Bocca Tigris, where many rich, fertile towns and villages lay on the banks of the Pearl River. Lady Cheng was determined to change this.

BEYOND THE TIGER'S MOUTH

On September 25, 1809, the fleets of the Red Flag and Black Flag, 500 junks strong, prayed to their gods—Cheng Pao even had a small temple aboard his junk—then weighed anchor and ascended the Pearl River delta via several paths. It was to be an audacious invasion, but perhaps only in the sense that no one had yet been daring enough to lead it. If the Mandarin war junks feared to attack Lady Cheng's fleets, what was to stop them from ascending the great Pearl River delta and stealing as they pleased? The fertile region was wealthy, and one grand successful raid might make the pirates wealthy, too. Her fleets were now well organized, with an effective chain of command. As long as they operated together, there would be no stopping them.

The plan was a simple one, and they put it into action at every village they came to. First, the pirates demanded tribute. Naturally, the residents of small villages that could not defend themselves against pirates either fled to the hills or paid tribute. But when a town or village failed to pay the tribute, the pirates attacked, looted, and burned it—and murdered its residents, sparing only those who might be well ransomed.

Glasspoole described the usual scene well: "Early in the morning the Ladrones assembled in rowboats, and landed; then gave a shout, and rushed into the town, sword in hand. The inhabitants fled to the adjacent hills, in numbers apparently superior to the Ladrones. We may easily imagine to ourselves the horror with which these miserable people must be seized, on being obliged to leave their homes, and everything dear to them. It was a most melancholy sight to see women in tears, clasping their infants in their arms, and imploring mercy for them from those brutal robbers! The old and the sick, who were unable to fly, or to make resistance, were either made prisoners or most inhumanly butchered!"

But some did fight back. When the pirates reached Kan-shih, roughly a dozen miles (19.3 km) south of Canton, they found that the town had prepared its defenses and was waiting for the attack. The Ladrones demanded tribute, but the residents killed two of them. The pirates waited for their entire fleet to come up, then, furious because the townspeople had killed two of them, attacked the small town's main entrance. Quickly they surged over the outer fence, planted their flag, and, swords and spears swinging and thrusting, charged the defenders in the streets. But the defenders were ready for them, and killed many as they tried to force their way into the town. The number of the Ladrones was large, however, and soon the battle was fought in the streets.

The pirates quickly came face to face with Chow Wei-teng, the local "boxing master"—a martial arts master—who led the resistance. The attackers tried to force their way in at the entrance to neighboring Lantou, but Chow Wei-teng alone killed ten pirates there. This resistance broke the will of the other attackers and they began retreating to their ships. Seeing this, Cheng Pao himself took command of the battle ashore, and the pirates again gained momentum. For perhaps hours the residents of Kan-shih resisted the fierce onslaught, but eventually the overwhelming number of pirates began to turn the tide. Chow Wei-teng fought desperately to the end, doubtless wielding sword or spear, his wife fighting at his side.

The pirates closely surrounded the redoubtable martial artists, pressing them hard. Seeing the peril they were in, one of their fathers—probably Chow Wei-teng's father-in-law—rushed to their aid and killed several pirates, forcing the rest to retreat from the close fight. By now the pirates, wary of engaging the fighting master and his wife on their terms, had to come up with another tactic. Keeping out of range of the deadly weapons of the warrior husband and wife, they killed the valiant pair from a distance, probably with bow and arrow. With their death, the town's defenses collapsed and the survivors retreated across a bridge that led to the hills beyond, cutting it behind them so the pirates could not follow.

But this did not hinder the sea thieves at all, for they simply swam across the waterway and chased the fleeing residents, capturing many. The pirates had killed 100 or more residents. But probably just as many pirates had been killed as well. By now most of the pirates were ashore. Dividing into four companies, they searched high and low, looting, pillaging, and murdering. They found women hiding in rice paddies and took them captive. Many women tried to run, but the practice of footbinding—of wrapping women's feet tightly from childhood to keep them small—left them unable to flee. The pirates burned homes and killed anyone left who resisted. Soon, the Ladrones loaded boat after boat with prisoners, clothing, pigs, food, and other goods, and rowed them to the waiting junks. According to one account, the pirates took 1,140 prisoners, male and female. Afterward, according to Yuan Yun-lun, who interviewed many witnesses and victims of the great pirate raid up the Pearl River, "in the whole village you could not hear the cry of a dog or a hen."

But the Ladrones were not finished. They continued to sack the region, stealing, torturing, murdering, and raping. They forced Glasspoole and other Westerners like him to bear arms against the innocent victims, or be killed. As the pirates descended the river on their return, some villagers fired on them from a hill. In response, the Ladrones surged ashore and for several miles (kilometers) destroyed rice paddies and orange groves. According to Glasspoole, male prisoners who refused to join the pirates had their hands "tied behind their back, a rope from the masthead rover through their arms, and [were] hoisted three or four feet from the deck, and five or six men flogged them with three rattans twisted together 'till they were apparently dead." The victims were tortured until they joined or died.

On October 20, Mandarin war junks attacked, but the pirates defeated them, killing many. Ten days later, the pirates prepared to attack a town named "Little Whampoa," but found its harbor blockaded by war junks and the town's inhabitants ready for a fight. Cheng I Sao sent her vessels to attack both the waiting junks and the town's fort. Three hundred of her men swam to shore, ran across a spit of land, then swam to the war junks and boarded them. At roughly the same time the pirates breached the fort, the defenders fled, leaving the Ladrones to do as they pleased.

And so they did, sacking the town. The pirate admiral—Cheng Pao, or perhaps even Lady Cheng herself—offered a bounty of twenty dollars per Chinese head. The Ladrones slaughtered all those they could find, decapitating them. They tied heads

together by their queues (ponytails) and slung them over their shoulders. Some pirates came away with five or six heads. The pirates plundered for nearly a month more, and on November 20 escaped from a combined force of Portuguese and Mandarins.

In all, the great raid lasted almost two months. Lady Cheng had devastated the Pearl River delta, exacting oppressive tribute from towns and villages willing to pay, and raping and pillaging those who were unwilling. Not even the Chinese war junks, assisted by Western vessels, had been able to stop her, leaving the entire region feeling enraged yet helpless against her great fleets.

PLUNDER AND CRUELTY

In the end, plunder was what it was all about. Piracy may have served a useful social purpose, keeping Ladrone families together and building a community, but sustenance was key, and this was had by stealing from others and sharing the profits among all. Women, of course, were popular plunder, perhaps most of all. That the great pirate leader was a woman appears to have had no bearing on this—male pirates sought women aboard captured ships and villages. Throughout history, female prisoners have seldom fared well as pirate captives, and many were raped soon after they were captured. Historians have often stepped delicately around this issue in the case of both Western and Eastern pirates. Strictly speaking, Cheng Pao's articles, doubtless approved by Lady Cheng, forbade rape as well as consensual sex between prisoners and pirates, and included harsh punishments in both cases, as well as in cases of theft and cowardice. Death—by decapitation for men, by drowning for women—was the usual punishment.

To marry or have sex with a woman without permission was to steal plunder, and among all pirates of all ages the theft of plunder has been punished severely.

Yet the articles do not appear to have forbidden the rape of prisoners per se, but only required that, as with all of Lady Cheng's piratical business, appropriate permission first be granted. Specifically, articles issued by Cheng Pao under her aegis held that "No person shall debauch at his pleasure captive women taken in the villages and open places, and brought on board a ship; he must first request the ship's purser for permission, and then go aside in the ship's hold. To use violence against any woman, or to wed her without permission, shall be punished with death." In other words, get permission first. What we do not know is how often permission was granted. Perhaps the provision was put in place not only to establish order over pirate crews but also in some small way to protect women prisoners. However, in spite of the prohibition on "debauchery without permission," there appears to have been much officially unsanctioned rape and other debauchery during raids ashore. There, the situation was chaotic and pirate officers had less control. Not only "wives and daughters" appear to have been raped without the required consent, but men and boys as well. Dominance, after all, often takes a violent, sexual form.

Female prisoners who could not afford to be ransomed would spend at least the next few years as pirate wives or concubines, or, if they were considered homely, they might simply be put ashore. The provision against marrying or having sexual relations without permission was doubtless included as a means of governing plunder, ensuring equality when dividing the spoils, and preventing outbreaks of violence among pirates competing for a particular female prisoner. Prisoners were property, and, all else being equal, a beautiful woman was assuredly seen as more valuable than one of average appearance. To marry or have sex with a woman without permission was to steal plunder, and among all pirates of all ages the theft of plunder has been punished severely.

Aboard the Ladrones, female prisoners who were not ransomed—ransoms ranged from 600 to 6,000, or in the case of the prisoners from Kan-shih and Lantou, 15,000 *liang* of silver (a *liang* was roughly one and a third ounces [37.7 g])—were usually sold as wives to pirates for forty dollars apiece, probably in Spanish dollars or pieces of eight, which was common currency in China. These marriages helped ensure order: pirates, who seldom went ashore, now had little need to, and soon enough would have families as well to tie them to the floating pirate culture. Ladrones who married these women were not permitted to abandon them, or to abuse them, and eyewitness accounts confirm this. Nor were crewmen permitted to have unmarried women aboard except in the instance of prisoners, and even then sexual relations with prisoners, not to mention forcible "debauchery," were to be conducted out of sight in the hold. Chinese pirate junks were floating homes housing many families, and a certain level of stability was required, even among pirates.

Some Ladrones did use violence other than rape against captured women, in spite of the prohibition against it—and the articles do not appear to have equated rape with "violence against women." Many female prisoners were dragged by the hair, beaten if they resisted, and confined in small exposed areas on deck. In one of what were probably many such instances, Mei Ying, a beautiful married woman captured at Kan-shih or Lantou during the great 1809 raid, hurled repeated insults at her pirate captor. Furious, he hoisted her up and tied her to a yardarm, yet still she insulted him, so he hauled her down and hit her as hard as he could, knocking out two of her teeth. As he prepared to tie her up again, she bit tightly into his clothing with her bloody mouth and held firmly, simultaneously grasping him as tightly as she could with her arms and hurling both of them into the sea, where pirate and prisoner drowned.

Some prisoners were treated even more brutally. Occasionally, entire crews were put to death. Those of the Mandarin war junks were invariably the object of cruelty and murder, and many would leap into the sea to drown rather than submit to the pirates' cruelty. Turner described how one Chinese prisoner "was nailed to the deck through his feet, with large nails; then beat with four rattans twisted together, till he vomited blood; and after remaining some time in this state, he was taken on shore and cut to pieces." This was not an isolated instance. He described another in which a prisoner, after being "fixed upright, his belly was cut open, and his heart taken out, which they afterwards soaked in spirits and [ate]." He went on to say that this was a frequent practice, often used on those who had "annoyed the Ladrones in a vigorous manner."

In part because of their cruelty, and sometimes in spite of it, the pirates profited well. On the one hand, it induced fear so strong that many intended victims gave up without a fight. Others, however, fought back because they knew all too well the cruelty that might follow even if they surrendered. But the Ladrone depredations could not go on forever. The great raid beyond the Bocca Tigris left both the Chinese government and the British and Portuguese merchants and navies little choice but to act, sooner or later. Certainly, the Chinese war junks could not conquer the Ladrones alone. Although often the captains and crews of the war junks fought courageously, more often they avoided engaging the pirates, especially those of the Red Flag, Cheng I Sao's own.

In 1809 one commander, while escorting trading junks, told his anxious captains not to worry because the pirates "not being the red flag, we are a match for them, therefore we will attack and conquer them." Without doubt, had he seen the red banners flying, the commander would have hastened away as quickly as possible with the junks he was escorting. An 1815 guide to maritime geography noted that Chinese war junks generally took every precaution to avoid a fight, "and for this purpose their war junks beat their gongs night and day, as it would appear, to give the pirates notice to keep out of their way."

There had to be a better way to put the great pirate empress, the dragon of the sea, to rest. Lady Cheng may have felt she had nothing to atone for, but both the pirate and the businesswoman knew the wind was about to change, and she would have to be prepared for it.

WHEN THE PEN IS MIGHTIER THAN THE SWORD

Cheng I Sao differed in several ways from other great pirates. Not only was she a woman pirate, but she was also a female admiral of pirate admirals in a profession that was invariably dominated, even in the East, by men. She knew well how to manage a great industry, even if it was piracy. She was also a true pirate, of the purest form. Although she had probably briefly been a privateer after marrying her first husband, she did not, and indeed could not, pretend that her depredations were justified by any government except her own criminal enterprise. Her fleets engaged in exactly what pirates have long been hated for: pillaging, murder, rape, and destruction at sea and ashore. Further, she led one of the largest pirate fleets in history, perhaps even the largest, in the number of both vessels and pirates, although her depredations do not quite equal those of some of the other great pirates in history. Yet they were enough. Certainly, if she had had a fleet of heavily gunned ships with crews to match, there is no telling what havoc and destruction she might have wrought.

Perhaps the most significant difference, though, is that she knew when to quit. She understood as well as any pirate—and probably better than most—that piracy was a business. She understood the economics of piracy and could see that quitting while she was ahead—and still young—was a far better prospect than raiding sea and shore forever. There remained the possibility that the Chinese government would get English naval support, and with a combined force would seek out, engage, and destroy her fleets. She had to consider all angles. After all, what was piracy but a means of wealth, of profiting by plunder? So successful was she that the only reasonable tactic left to use against her was to offer amnesty and hope she took it.

Lady Cheng knew a good offer when she saw it. Sooner or later all of her achievements could turn to dust. She might be usurped by a rival, or captured, leaving her worse off than when she married. Worst of all, she might find her head struck from her shoulders by an executioner's sword. After several months of careful, astute negotiation, she accepted an offer of amnesty and surrendered on April 18, 1810, but on her terms. After all, she was in a powerful negotiating position. She was permitted to keep all of the proceeds of her piracies, and her husband Cheng Pao was made a lieutenant in the Chinese navy, where he commanded twenty or thirty junks manned by his own followers. Those pirates who foolishly refused the offer of amnesty were eventually hunted down; many were killed.

Lady Cheng, however, lived another thirty-three years. Just before her death in 1844 at the age of sixty-nine, she was the proprietor of a notorious gambling house in Canton. Without doubt she was a legendary figure, and surely still there were those alive who had faced her fleets in action. They would have known her as the greatest of Chinese pirates, but she was more than that: she was one of the greatest pirates in history.

CHAPTER 13

☠

JEAN LAFITTE

1782?-1823

THE LAST GREAT PIRATE OF THE AGE OF SAIL

It should have been an easy capture, like nearly all were. These pirates invariably preferred not to fight, for after all, they were seamen looking for an independent lifestyle fueled by easy pickings on the sea. These seagoing swashbucklers were not military men or former military men, at least not most of them, nor did they have the discipline and training of an American or European naval crew, whose skills had been raised almost to a form of high art in the early nineteenth century. Their target was just another merchant ship under sail in the Caribbean making a passage south of Cuba, near Jamaica and the Cayman Islands.

The small schooner—it was either the *Minerva* or the *Blanque*—quickly overtook the large merchant ship. This was easy to do: merchant ships were typically built to carry a lot of cargo, and thus were comparatively slow. But schooners were built for speed. They had first become popular in the early eighteenth century, because of their swift lines and versatility. Many had a rakish appearance: a long bowsprit projecting forward, and two or even three masts sharply raked—tilted, that is—aft, giving them a sharklike, predator aspect. They carried a large gaff sail on each mast, and could carry two or even three square sails on the mainmast, and two or three headsails between the mainmast and the bowsprit. Some had ports for as many as eighteen guns.

All the pirate schooner should have had to do after overtaking the merchant ship was come within 200 yards (182.8 m), keeping of course to windward (i.e., between the prey and the wind), then fire a gun and hail the prize-to-be. A simple demand to surrender or receive a broadside—or perhaps worse, be boarded by pirates now angry that they had to risk their lives, when they were accustomed to do so rarely, as in a storm, for example—should have been sufficient.

Today, though, this day in late October or early November 1822, the intended prey fought back, firing a broadside, probably striking the sloop and taking her captain and crew by surprise. This was one of the best ways for a merchantman to deal with a pirate or privateer: lure her in close, then open fire without warning. With luck, the brutal volley would damage the attacker enough that the intended victim could escape. A round shot, as cannonballs were correctly called, might shatter the rudder or the helm, or kill the captain. One might "hull" the attacker—put a hole below the waterline—and this would force the attacker to bear away to repair the leak. Sinking the attacker was always possible, but unlikely, for wooden vessels were actually hard to sink. Round shot made only small holes that could be quickly plugged. No captain wanted his ship to have a hole below the waterline, but being sunk was usually one of his least concerns, unless his pirate enemies had very large guns.

And some pirates now did, in the form of a new sort of naval artillery called a carronade, a short-barreled gun of large caliber. Due to this large caliber it was devastating up close, but its barrel was too short to give it much range. A recent practice was the use of "Long Tom," a long gun of various caliber that was often shifted from a gunport on one side to one on the other as necessary, although it was cumbersome and even dangerous to do so. Most effective were those mounted on deck swivels or "pivots," usually on the forecastle or quarterdeck, that let the gun crew simply turn it from port to starboard and vice versa. In this way, privateers could carry fewer guns.

But the merchantman's sudden broadside did little more than prove her captain and crew's willingness to fight, which in turn inspired the pirate captain and crew to prove theirs. The vessels engaged each other, the merchantman trying to kill pirates and shatter rigging so that she could escape, the pirate trying to kill or wound enough of the merchant crew so that they would give up. The pirate captain did not want to shoot the ship to pieces. He wanted her intact for several reasons. A badly damaged ship took time to repair, and was less valuable. If by accident his guns set her on fire, he might lose both ship and cargo. This would be not only a great loss to the pirates, but also in the end might inspire a search intended to destroy him, his crew, and his schooner. Worst of all, if the ship were badly damaged and help suddenly appeared on the horizon, he would have to abandon her.

Tactics at sea had changed little in two centuries. Ships and other vessels were typically larger and sleeker now, and their guns bigger. The rest, though, was for the most part unchanged. Ships and other vessels still manouvered around

each other and slugged it out, firing at each other with great guns (cannon) filled with round shot, canisters of lead or iron balls or scrap metal, or sometimes both. Sometimes ships simply stood off from each other at 100 or 200 yards (91.4 or 183 m), firing broadsides into each other's hulls, decks, or sails, and topping it all off with musketry intended to kill anyone who showed himself. Small pirate schooners still relied heavily on musketry, and all pirates used it.

The pirate captain wanted and needed to end today's fight quickly, for there was one more reason to avoid long battles at sea: if the pirate schooner were badly damaged, not only would his prey escape, but he would also be vulnerable to attack by any man-of-war or heavily armed merchant vessel that happened by. And the passage south of Cuba was a busy one.

But schooners were light and maneuverable, so assuredly the pirate did his best to cross the bow or stern of the merchantman and rake her fore and aft—that is, send a broadside through her stern (the weakest part of a ship) or bow, where the shot would pass the length of the ship, killing or wounding men at the guns. If it came to it, the pirate would board, pushing his schooner's bow amidships of the prey and grappling with sharp irons made for the purpose. His men would toss grenades and firepots onto deck, then board, cutlass and pistol in hand, attacking and killing in a fearful frenzy until the merchantman struck her colors.

But it probably never came to this. Eventually the merchantman surrendered, perhaps after losing some of her crew, or after her crew grew fearful and refused to fight, or after her rigging became so damaged that she could neither maneuver nor escape. The pirates sent a party of men aboard her, examined her documents so that they would know what cargo was aboard, and probably "pillaged" her as well—that is, stole personal items from passengers and crew. Several of the pirates had been killed in the action, and others wounded, perhaps even the captain himself. The sea thieves would not therefore have been in a merciful mood as they boarded their prize, but doubtless their captain held them in check. He was a businessman, albeit foremost a man of adventure, and knew that cruelty to the merchant crew would only make ransoming the ship more difficult and might even invite retaliation.

The pirate captain sent word to Cuba of the capture, and provided his terms for ransoming ship and crew. The owners agreed to them, and payment was scheduled to be made near Santa Cruz del Sur, a small town on the northeast corner of the Gulf of Guacanayabo on the south coast of Cuba. In the area were numerous small cays, or islands, as is typical of the south Cuban coast.

A schooner is under sail in this nineteenth-century image. The schooner began to appear as a popular vessel in the early eighteenth century (although its sail plan had been around much longer), both for merchants who required a swift trading vessel, and for pirates and privateers. By the early eighteenth century it had become the preeminent vessel among pirates, privateers, and slavers. Swift, easily managed by a small crew, and able to sail close to the wind, it was the last great development of piratical craft under sail.
Alamy

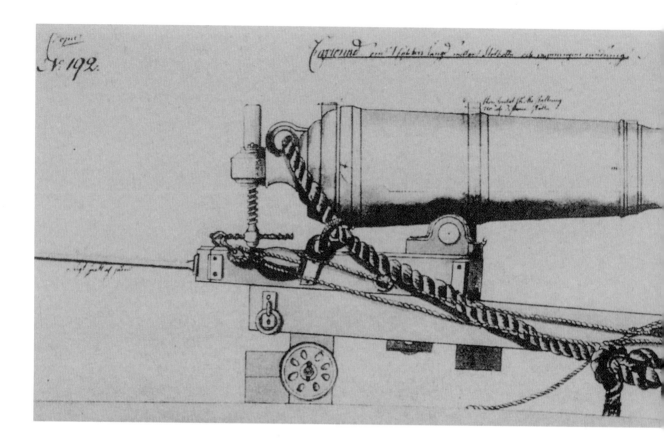

The pirate schooner escorted her prize to the rendezvous. A few pirates were aboard the merchantman as a prize crew, and they would return to the schooner as soon as the ransom was paid. As in the case of the capture of the merchantman, the exchange of ransom for ship should have been straightforward. And doubtless it would have been, but for the two armed Spanish vessels that suddenly appeared, probably from an anchorage near the shore where their masts would have been hidden by the background, or from among the many cays in the area.

The armed vessels meant business. Very quickly one recaptured the merchantman while the other attacked the pirate. Almost certainly the second armed vessel joined in the fray after recovering the prize, making it two on one. Furiously the pirates tried to beat off the attack, but to little avail. The Spaniards boarded the pirate schooner in overwhelming numbers. For the pirates it was fight and die, or surrender—or abandon ship. Several quickly did, including their captain, leaving their comrades behind to be captured and, sooner or later probably, killed.

We do not how the pirate captain and his few remaining crew made it to shore. They may have boarded a small boat they had in tow, for boats were often towed during a fight. Perhaps they lowered one from the stern davits, where often

a boat was stowed. Or perhaps they simply swam. In any event, they came ashore near Santa Cruz del Sur and tried to flee. But they had no weapons, other than knives perhaps, or a few small arms, and no food, probably no money with which to buy food or make bribes, and no friends nearby. Spanish authorities—Cuba had not yet thrown off Spain's yoke—quickly captured them and threw them in jail at Porto Principe, located about forty-five miles (72.4 km) north of Santa Cruz del Sur. Known in past centuries as Puerto del Principe and today as Camagüey, it was the provincial capital and the largest town in the area.

Here the pirate captain grew ill, although the actual ailment was not noted. His jail keepers moved him to the hospital of San Juan de Dios, where he was able to get word to friends who arranged his escape. How they did it is not recorded, but on February 13, 1822, Jean Lafitte escaped from Porto Principe and made his way to a small pirate settlement on Cayo Romano just off the north coast of Cuba. A month later he was in command of another pirate schooner cruising the Old Bahama Channel between the north coast of Cuba and the Bahamas—a principal route of slavers and traders.

But this free reign of the pirates would not last forever. Indeed, its end was in sight, and Cuba was its last refuge in the Americas. The world had turned modern, and with it its navies, and they were tracking down pirates left and right, leaving them little place to go. Even now the U.S. navy was searching for Cuban pirates, destroying all whom it found. Lafitte no longer had the Louisiana bayous to hide among, or the great fortress at Cartagena, Colombia, to protect him, or his base at Galveston, Texas, to shield his ships and men. He had only a small patch of sand, known as Rincón Grande, on the Cuban coast, and the U.S. navy was closing in. His days were numbered and he knew it. Even so, he could never give up the sea and its treasures waiting to be plundered. Hope was always on the horizon.

IN OLD NEW ORLEANS

Thirteen years earlier, in 1809, almost 10,000 French refugees arrived in New Orleans from Cuba. Roughly a third of them were white, a third free blacks, and

The gun, called a carronade, takes its name from the original manufacturer, the Carron Iron Company in Scotland. Although its short barrel significantly limited its effective range, its combination of light weight and very heavy caliber permitted small vessels to carry a heavy armament. Its carriage has two parts: the upper "bed" holds the gun in place, and the lower "bed," or slide, takes up the recoil and also permits the gun to be traversed. Beginning in the late eighteenth century, carronades were used to augment the main batteries of some men-of-war and privateers.

a third slaves. Originally from the French colony of Saint-Domingue, they fled during the slave uprising that turned Saint-Domingue into Haiti. New Orleans, located fewer than 700 miles (1,126.54 km) northwest of Havana, Cuba, and with a heavily French population, was the perfect place to emigrate.

Largely rebuilt after the great fire that destroyed almost half of it in 1788, the city sat on the edge of a crescent bend in the Mississippi River. Six blocks wide and fourteen blocks long, not counting the rapidly growing suburbs, with streets named after French royalty and other heritage—Rue Bourbon, Rue Dauphine, Rue Chartres, among many others—it controlled the waterway of the United States to be. It was an active yet sultry city at the time, of roughly 20,000 residents, including recent immigrants. Each afternoon in the summer the sky clouded over and delivered a torrential downpour for less than half an hour, turning the streets to mud and briefly making the air even more humid than before.

Among the refugees in this most cosmopolitan and youngest of U.S. cities—it had been acquired in 1803 with the Louisiana Purchase—was Jean Lafitte. His brother Pierre, a landlubbing businessman of often questionable money-making practices and for all intents and purposes the brains of the two, had preceded him there by six years, although the past three had been spent in nearby Pensacola, Florida. Jean was most likely born in the Bordeaux region of France, perhaps in the small village of Bages, probably around 1782. Doubtless he became a seaman at some point, perhaps locally at first, later on voyages abroad. Around 1800 he left France for the Americas. The nation was just getting over the throes of the French Revolution, and the Age of Napoleon had begun with Napoleon's coup the year before. For many of France's population, the Americas, which looked like lands of far more potential than economically depressed France, beckoned.

Many historians believe Lafitte emigrated to Saint-Domingue, where large numbers of French refugees sought a new life. But by 1804 most had fled the island in the aftermath of the slave uprising that gave rise to the Haitian nation. By 1806 Lafitte was in command of a French privateer. Britain and France were at war, and their privateers preyed not only on each other but also on each other's allies, and often enough on anyone, as privateers had done for centuries. Spanish colonies, inspired by the American and French revolutions, had also begun to overthrow their royal government—and privateers were a common means of sea power for a budding nation. For the French kicked out of Saint-Domingue,

Illustration of Lafitte accepting a chest of ransom, by noted illustrator Frank Schoonover, a student of Howard Pyle. Ransom was a common means of pirate plunder, both of towns and of vessels. In Lafitte's time, it was more difficult to dispose of captured vessels, owing to the lack of markets for them. Small vessels could be plundered and burned, but larger ships could be ransomed. Their cargos could also be ransomed, or sold elsewhere. In Lafitte's case, one attempt to ransom a prize almost got him hanged.

those of a plundering, seafaring bent went to Guadeloupe and Martinique in the Windward Islands of the Caribbean, where they were granted privateering commissions that amounted to little more than licenses to steal. The Americas, in other words, were in the midst of a small, brief golden age of piracy and privateering, not to mention of smuggling. Often the twain—sea roving and smuggling—went hand in hand.

Unfortunately, we know next to nothing about Lafitte's privateering at this time. Historian William C. Davis speculates that Lafitte could have been the "Captain La fette" who commanded the privateer *La Soeur Cherie* (the *Dear Sister*) and brought a captured British merchantman named the *Hector* to New Orleans in 1806. The ship's papers were false and intended as cover for a smuggling operation. Already the city was known as a great entry point to the United States and its territories. With the entire Gulf of Mexico to the south and the great highway of water known as the Mississippi River to the north, it was an ideal place for the privateer to trade both illegally and profitably.

We know almost as little about Lafitte's appearance and personality as we do about his privateering prior to 1809. He was said to be an inch or two over six feet tall (around 185 cm), with a pale complexion (odd for a seaman, but Lafitte was often ashore, and one description does note his dark complexion), dark hair, dark hazel eyes, and long sideburns. He was said to be handsome, too, although this is hard to judge from the only known illustration of Lafitte, a crude drawing made by a man who said he had once worked with him, and of which historian Davis has pointed out may not represent Lafitte at all. Unfortunately, much of what we think we know about Jean Lafitte is hearsay and invention passed down over the years, and most of it was probably fabricated as the pirate became a legend. Among other characteristics popularly attributed to him, many of which may be true, was a friendly, genial, helpful nature. This should come as no surprise. Contrary to the image of the pirate and privateer as a cruel, glowering sort, most were like other seamen—friendly and outgoing, with a cynical, occasionally dark sense of humor. Men who have to work and live together at sea learn both how to get along and how to lend a hand.

Lafitte was without doubt an excellent seaman, and may also have been a good swordsman, as he was said to have been by at least one contemporary. Swordplay was still in vogue at the time, both in France and in Louisiana. New Orleans, with its strong French and Spanish influence, was the center of fencing and swordplay in nineteenth-century North America, and was the only place

"Lafitte and his crew clearing the decks of the Indiaman," an illustration from *The Pirates Own Book* by Charles Elms. It was common for boarders to turn an attacked ship's own guns against it if the crew had not disabled them as they should have. Elms's book is one of several pirate books that have contributed significantly to the popular notion of pirates and piracy. Unfortunately, many of the books are combinations of both fact and fiction, and all too often more of the latter than the former. Note, for example, the skull and cross bones; Lafitte never flew this flag.

where the sword duel was at least as prominent as that of the pistol, and probably more so. Everywhere else, duelists used pistols, for they required far less skill to use. The city always had at least several fencing masters, and duels were common. Whether Lafitte ever actually engaged in any, however, is unknown, although local legends and popular histories usually claim he was a gentleman swordsman who fought many. Very likely he fought at least one, given his trade and the local proclivity for provoking armed encounters over one's honor.

Swordplay at sea, however, was limited largely to the cutlass, and most seamen, including pirates and privateers, could probably be considered as having limited skill. However, any man who professed any social standing in New Orleans had to be able to use a sword.

And in New Orleans, it paid to have social standing. The city and its surrounding area were infused with a multicultural, multiracial, multilingual population, a mixture of Old World traditions and hypocrisy, New World struggle and rebellion, and North American greed and industry. In its streets one heard a mixture of French, Spanish, English, and various slave patois. The population was equally diverse. Not only were there the descendants of the original French and Spanish populations, as well as those of the Acadians from Canada, but there were also recent French arrivals, many of them refugees from Revolutionary and Napoleonic France. White Anglo-Americans had recently arrived, and black slaves, too. Some of the slaves were descendants of Africans brought to America as slaves, but others had been brought directly from Africa. To this population were added the recent 10,000 French refugees from Cuba.

The slaves of these new immigrants, however, had been impounded aboard the ships they had traveled on to New Orleans. It was against U.S. law to import slaves, but the new immigrants relied on them to provide the labor for the lands they intended to buy and work, and other planters in the area demanded them as well. Privateers, always seeking profit over duty, not to mention over "hard knocks," aggressively sought slavers, given the value of their cargo and its high demand, and were always looking for a convenient port in which to sell it. The Lafitte brothers had a solution. Its name was Barataria.

BAYOUS AND BATTERIES

In the early nineteenth century, smuggling, primarily of slaves but of other goods as well, was done in a time-honored way. A ship would drop anchor in a harbor—in the Mississippi River at New Orleans, for example—and her captain would pretend that his ship had been damaged at sea or was in need of supplies. He then bribed officials as necessary, and at night his illicit cargo was offloaded. Such transactions had been taking place in the New World since at least the early seventeenth century. The United States banned the importation of slaves in 1803, followed by a ban on British imports three years later. After British ships began unlawfully boarding U.S. ones and seizing U.S. seamen, the United States retaliated by banning British goods, which prompted customs officials and naval vessels to search more aggressively for contraband. It was no longer as safe as it once was to sneak supplies into New Orleans across the city wharves.

Some thirty miles (48 km) south of New Orleans as the crow flies—but far longer via a tortuous route of lakes and bayous inhabited by alligators, snakes, crawfish, and mosquitoes—lay Barataria Bay. Inhabited by runaway slaves and other refugees from the law, difficult to infiltrate by sea or land, and with access via water routes into New Orleans, it was the perfect smuggler haven. New

Orleans needed slaves and goods, privateers and smugglers had them in stock, and Barataria lay in the middle.

The brothers Lafitte—Jean more often among the bayous, Pierre more often in New Orleans—quickly established themselves as purveyors of goods smuggled via Barataria. At Grand Isle, a barrier island at the entrance to Barataria, they unloaded slaves and goods from privateers and smugglers, loaded them in pirogues—flat-bottomed boats whose name descended from Spanish *piragua* and Carib *piraua*—and delivered them via several bayous into New Orleans. The city had a long history of smuggling and needed the slaves and goods; therefore, most residents saw nothing wrong with the trade. Everyone knew what was available and where it came from, and the two men who ran the trade freely walked the streets of New Orleans. Louisiana governor William C. C. Claiborne was not amused, but his naval and customs patrols failed to halt the influx, for they could seldom find any privateers, and they only rarely dared penetrate deep into the bayous.

Jean, however, was not satisfied with being a mere middleman between privateers and the purchasers of contraband. Far more a man of physical action than his brother, he surely longed to be at sea again, in command of an armed vessel, making a name for himself and a fortune for the Lafittes. Instead, he, and often his brother, too, were escorting Spanish cargoes through the bayous. In 1812 the smuggling brothers were ambushed by the U.S. army, and one of their number was killed. The brothers were taken to New Orleans and released, pending charges. Immediately they went back to work.

But the times had begun to change. In 1810 Cartagena rose up in rebellion against Spain, creating opportunities for privateers to attack Spanish ships, and in 1812 the United States went to war with Great Britain. The opportunity of plunder on the sea now seemed boundless. Rather than wait for privateers to carry their cargoes to Barataria, the Lafittes would command their own fleet. Their vessels could capture Spanish ships, steal their cargoes, then sell them in New Orleans as if they were legitimate trade goods—all it would take was a bit of ink and paper to create a new manifest—or put them ashore at Grand Isle.

In late 1812 they fitted out a small schooner and put Captain Jean Jannet in command. Soon Jannet returned with a prize, a hermaphrodite brig—a two-mast vessel, rigged with square sails on the foremast and a gaff sail on the mizzenmast—named *La Dorada* and filled with a cargo of seventy-seven

244

A plan of the entrance of Barataria, either by or supervised by Colonel G. T. Ross after the raid on Lafitte's base. Grand Isle (Grand Terre) is on the right. Sketched on the map on the right is the schooner Caroline, which could not cross the bar and enter the channel. The attacking force has been crudely sketched in just south of Grand Isle, and Lafitte's schooners are similarly depicted to the north of the island. One pirate schooner is noted as "aground and saved—Lt. Gordon," another as "on fire blew up," and a third as "on fire saved by Lt. Jones." Passages to New Orleans are noted on either side of Marsh Island.

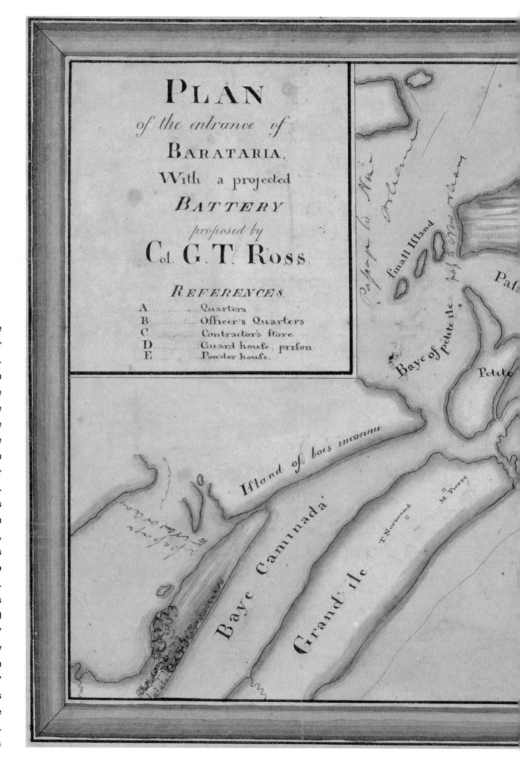

sh Island

course to new orleans

Grand' Terre

course to new orleans

main channel   15 16 20

place of the projected Battery

a well   encampement   a well

flood water

Schooner Caroline
could not approach
within two Miles

Parapet X feet high

Rampart

Place d'armes

Pit 3 feet
above water

A

B

C

D   E

gate

allude to Pirates
" " " to Gun boats
& Small boats of
the army & navy

slaves. The Lafitte brothers sold the slaves, and Captain Jannet transferred his command and crew to *La Dorada*, then put to sea for more prizes. Soon after, the brothers purchased a former French privateer schooner named *La Diligent* and outfitted her with twelve great guns, fourteen-pounders all—a very large armament for a Gulf or Caribbean privateer—along with eighty muskets, eighty cutlasses, and forty pistols. She was not only swift but also very well armed for a privateer. Many privateers were still armed as they had been a century past, with only muskets and perhaps a few swivels. It was expensive to outfit a privateer, and one armed with great guns was a threat indeed. But whether or not a privateer carried great guns, Lafitte knew how vital muskets were to all privateers, for the tactics and lessons learned in the days of the buccaneers and filibusters remained valid.

In May 1813, the *Dorada* captured a small schooner, the *Louisa Antonia*. The Lafittes renamed her the *Petit Milan*, and sent her to sea with the *Dorada*. The brothers now owned three swift privateers. Reports that they fortified Barataria with fourteen cannon were an exaggeration, but they did man the pirate haven with 200 to 300 privateers, pirates, and slaves.

One thing the brothers lacked, though, was a legitimate privateering commission. Without one, the Lafitte captains and crew were pirates, and thus subject to being hanged, as probably were the Lafitte brothers for fitting them out. Although Pierre would later claim they bought a commission in New Orleans, they probably never did, and if they did, it was of dubious legality at best and certainly would not have covered all three privateer vessels. Jean Lafitte might have considered himself at long last a privateer again, but he was in reality a pirate, even if he did soon claim that his schooners held commissions from Cartagena. Indeed, his schooners began to fly the flag of Cartagena, part of the new United Provinces of Grand Granada. Yet, even with a fleet of three privateer or pirate vessels, not to mention dozens of privateers routinely calling at Barataria, privateer or pirate Jean Lafitte had still not returned to sea. He remained a landlocked pirate lord.

THE BATTLE OF NEW ORLEANS

The brothers continued to build their bayou business. Governor Claiborne remained unamused by their activities, and believed the smuggling trade was a drain on the local economy. Certainly, it was a drain on customs duties, but, as Jean Lafitte himself argued, his trade was monopoly busting and brought money

The Battle of New Orleans as depicted in a circa 1890 lithograph by the Chicago art firm of Kurz and Allison. The battle is idealized. General Jackson rides a white horse while his artillery, regular infantry, and Tennessee and New Orleans volunteers fire upon the attacking British, with the British fleet depicted in the background. In fact, fog and gun smoke obscured much of the battlefield, and the battle began in the early morning. Many of Lafitte's men served in action during the battle, many of them as gunners serving cannon, and were pardoned afterward. However, like Lafitte, most probably returned sooner or later to piracy.

Library of Congress

into New Orleans. Privateers needed supplies to refit, and they could often pay in cold hard cash, which at the time was most commonly in the form of silver dollars.

These dollars were of all sorts, ranging from old irregular Spanish pieces of eight called cobs, to Spanish milled dollars stamped with the Pillars of Hercules and Spanish arms, to those stamped with the bust of the Spanish king. The Spanish piece of eight, or dollar, was the primary currency not only of the United States and the Americas in general, but also of much of the world. These dollars flowed through the hands of the Lafitte brothers.

But it was not just a matter of lost revenue that concerned Governor Claiborne. Call them privateers or pirates, the empire of sea rovers at Barataria—of armed schooners and men—could be a threat to the city itself. Already privateers using Barataria as a base had captured a New Orleans vessel and sold its cargo. The vessel had flown a Spanish flag to escape the British blockade, a very common practice, but the privateers used this as an excuse to seize it. This was an old pretense, and one of the reasons privateers often had a bad name. In fact, even if the privateer had a legitimate commission, knowingly plundering a friendly or neutral vessel was an act of piracy. Neither Claiborne nor New Orleans merchants could long tolerate a nest of pirates resting just below the most important city in the South. In November 1813, Claiborne offered a $500 reward for the capture of the pirate Jean Lafitte.

However, the Lafitte empire posed an even greater threat to New Orleans. British spies reported that the privateers and pirates of the fortified base at Barataria would be useful blockading New Orleans. They could be turned into British privateers. Such a force could devastate New Orleans shipping, and provide protection for a British thrust into the belly of the United States.

And there was a sure way to make certain this did not happen, notwithstanding that Lafitte had already turned down an offer to help the British and had sent a letter to Governor Claiborne offering his services and those of the Barataria smugglers, pirates, and privateers in defense of New Orleans. In September 1814, Commodore Daniel T. Patterson attacked Grande Isle. The Baratarians—800 to 1,000 "of all nations and colors" according to Patterson—saw before them a force of six "gun vessels," a small tender, and a schooner. Immediately the pirates put their schooners in line of battle and prepared for action. Yet they did not fight, and instead set fire to two of their schooners and abandoned many more. The pirates knew that although they had a large force of men, they lacked the guns to fight a professional force. Their schooners were armed in all with only twenty guns, a pittance against the naval vessels preparing to attack. Patterson captured eight schooners, one felucca, one brig, and eighty Baratarians, plundered Barataria of an estimated $200,000 worth of coin and goods, burned everything he could, and sailed in triumph to New Orleans.

Even so, Lafitte did not turn his anger on the Americans. With the threat of an imminent British invasion and the arrival in December 1814 of General Andrew Jackson and his army of regulars and Tennessee volunteers, Governor Claiborne offered the Lafittes and their Baratarians amnesty if they would join the fight. Lafitte never liked the British, nor did the many French who lived in New Orleans and the surrounding area. They were old enemies, and until only a few months ago had been at war. For whatever reason—profit, nationalism, or patriotism—Lafitte chose the side of the Americans. One observer wrote that "Mr. Lafitte solicited for himself and for all the Baratarians the honour of serving under our banners, that they might have an opportunity of proving that if they had infringed the revenue laws, yet none was more ready than they to defend the country and combat its enemies."

Quickly Lafitte and his men set forth in their pirogues and joined General Jackson's army. Some of the Baratarians formed themselves into companies of pirates to serve with Jackson's main force, while others joined existing companies at Fort St. Philip, which guarded the Mississippi River, Fort St. John, which protected the Lake Pontchartrain entrance to Bayou St. Jean, and Fort Petite Coquilles, which protected the entrance to Lake Pontchartrain. Lafitte told General Jackson that he had supplies enough to outfit an army of 30,000. This may have been hyperbole, but Lafitte was in many ways true to his word. He provided a large quantity of gunpowder, and Jackson himself wrote that "I procured from them 7,500 flints for pistols and boarding peaces [large, yoke-mounted muskets and blunderbusses] which was solely the supply of flints for all my militia and if it had not been for this providential aid the country must have fallen." And this is probably true, for until Jackson arrived, New Orleans was completely unprepared to defend itself against even a small British attack.

The main, famous battle itself is well known. In the darkness and fog of the morning of January 8, 1815, 8,000–9,000 British soldiers at Chalmette, Louisiana, marched toward Jackson's lines near New Orleans. Jackson's artillery, much of it manned with Baratarians, opened fire, punching holes in the advancing British regiments. The mixture of fog, gun smoke, and ankle-deep mud further hindered the attackers, and, with the loss of many British officers, confusion often reigned. Even worse, the British had forgotten the ladders and other tools they needed to assault the U.S. earthworks, even if they managed to advance that far.

But still the British advanced. At close range the mixed U.S. army of roughly 5,400 soldiers, militia, Tennessee volunteers, privateers, and pirates opened fire with muskets, slaughtering the British who had so far bravely survived the deadly march toward their enemy. The British managed to capture only a single U.S. redoubt, but quickly lost it to a counterattack. With many of their officers dead or wounded, the British regiments now held their ground in the open, not knowing whether to advance or retreat. The ragtag U.S. force slaughtered many more of them until a British officer finally took command and led the defeated force from the field.

In the end, the attackers had almost 300 killed (some accounts say far more), among whom was their commanding officer, Major-General Edward Pakenham, more than 1,000 wounded, and almost 500 captured or missing in action. The Baratarians had fought fiercely, and without doubt their presence helped turn the tide of battle. The problem was, the War of 1812 was already over, but no one knew it—the Treaty of Ghent had been signed the previous month, on December 24, 1814, but it would take weeks for the news to arrive.

The courage of Lafitte's privateer captains and crews was even noted in a military report by Adjutant General Robert Butler on January 15, 1815. He wrote that "Captains Dominique and Belluche, lately commanding privateers at Barataria, with part of their crew and many brave citizens of New Orleans, were stationed at [cannon] numbers 3 and 4. The general cannot avoid giving his warm approbation of the manner in which these gentlemen have uniformly conducted themselves while under his command, and of the gallantry with which they have redeemed the pledge they gave at the opening of the campaign to defend the country. The brothers Lafitte have exhibited the same courage and fidelity."

The Lafittes and the Baratarians were heroes and received pardons for their piracies and other crimes, real and alleged. But with the Battle of New Orleans came the end of the Baratarian empire, although by 1818 some pirates would again make it their home. Jean Lafitte, however, would not be one of them.

THE END OF AN ERA

For a while, the Lafitte brothers avoided privateering and piracy, and worked instead in another marginal trade, as spies for Spain. Known together as the "Number 13" by their spymaster, Padre Antonio de Sedella, they spied on Mexican revolutionaries, Pierre doing so in New Orleans and Jean on Galveston Island, Texas. Already a privateer base, Galveston Island had much potential, and Jean quickly reestablished a Barataria-like community there. And Jean Lafitte finally returned to sea. He commanded a privateer flying the Mexican flag, and went after slave ships, whose cargoes he delivered to smugglers such as Jim Bowie, who was later to die at the Alamo.

Again, it was not to last. In 1821 the brig USS *Enterprise* forced him without a fight from Galveston Island. For the next two years, Lafitte variously slipped secretly in and out of Galveston and New Orleans as, without a commission, he raided Spanish shipping in Cuban waters. Now there was no pretense. He was nothing but a pirate.

The attitude toward Lafitte and other "Cuban" pirates is best summed up by a note in an 1822 edition of *Niles' Weekly Register*. "It appears," the article reads, "that the famous Lafitte is at the head of some of those parties—that their business is increasing—that they often murder whole crews, and that some strong act of justice, after the manner of Jackson, must be committed to suppress these dreadful villanies, to which there seem to be parties throughout the island of Cuba." Sooner or later, the U.S. navy would probably put a noose around Lafitte's neck, as it was doing with all those who were left of the pirates of the Caribbean. The world of the sea and ships was changing: large-scale piracy was being eliminated, privateering soon would be, and the great age of steam power and iron ships was about to begin.

Lafitte, however, had one last trick up his sleeve after his near escape from Porto Principe the year before. He sailed to Cartagena, now a great city in the new nation of Gran Colombia. There he was commissioned in the Colombian naval auxiliary and given command of a small captured schooner, the *General Santander*, of only thirty tons (27 metric tons). He mounted the tiny vessel with a single eighteen-pound gun and a four-pound pivot gun, and crewed her with thirty men. As a privateer, the *General Santander* was capable of capturing common merchant vessels, but if she came up against a naval vessel or well-armed merchantman, her only defense would be to run.

Lafitte put to sea and now abandoned all scruples about attacking U.S. shipping. Perhaps he was angry that the U.S. navy was putting his kind out of business, or perhaps U.S. ships and schooners were simply convenient, for they now numbered far more than any other nation's in the Americas.

On February 4, 1823, while cruising for prey in the Bay of Honduras, Lafitte spotted two vessels, a schooner and a brigantine. Immediately he set out after them, for surely they were small Spanish merchant vessels. And even if they were not, he would likely capture them anyway, excepting only if they were Colombian. All day the *General Santander* chased. Pursuit at sea was often a long, drawn-out process. The chased vessel wanted to do but one thing: make it to nightfall where it had a good chance of losing the pursuer in the dark. Vessels were often miles away when spotted, and to overtake a swift vessel, even if it were a knot or two slower, could take hours. In this case, it took more than seventeen.

It was dark by the time Lafitte brought his small sloop near the brigantine and fired a warning shot. But the brigantine did not strike, and instead opened fire and signaled to its consort, the schooner. Unwittingly, Lafitte had fallen into an old trap, that of luring a pirate by running away, as a merchant vessel would. The pirate was caught between two well-armed pirate hunters, probably British or Spanish. The brigantine carried a dozen guns, the schooner six, and they quickly began to make splinters out of the *General Santander*.

And one of them, or even a grapeshot or musket ball, killed Jean Lafitte. He fell during the fight, wounded severely enough that he had to turn command over to his lieutenant. Throughout the fight he rallied his crew. They fought fiercely until after midnight, doubtless inspired both by the threat to their own lives as well as by the injury of their famous captain. In the darkness they escaped, but early the next morning Jean Lafitte died, probably forty-one years old, leaving his battered crew mourning for the loss of their famous captain.

Of course, there are many other stories about the death of the pirate Lafitte, but this one, recounted by historian Davis and based on a Colombian newspaper report, is by far the most likely. But no one wants heroes to die, and if they must, it should be gloriously, with the red flag of defiance flying, guns blazing, all surrender refused, and no quarter given. But it rarely ever happened that way.

Jean Lafitte was born to be a romantic hero. What else could he have become, this man who strolled the streets of old New Orleans, known today as the Vieux Carré, or the French Quarter; who ran a pirate empire, first from the Louisiana bayous, and then from Galveston Island, Texas; who later spied for Spain; and who ended his days as a sea-roving captain, as a prince of the sea? He truly was the last of two great ages—of the pirates of the Caribbean and of the pirates of the age of sail.

END NOTES

Chapter 1, Kheir-ed-Din Barbarossa
13 *Allah speed us!* Morgan, *Complete History of Algiers*, 618.
14 *Allah give you* Ibid.
16 *God forbid* Bradford, *Sultan's Admiral*, 8.
18 *killed some Christians* Morgan, *Complete History of Algiers*, 225.
21 *scoured the coasts* Ibid., 226-27.
21 *spread terror* Farine, *Deux Pirates*, 58.
25 *might be taken* Ibid., 41.
25 *O damned Turks!* Ibid., 42.
25 *firm heart* Ibid.
26 *There is no God but Allah* Ibid.

Chapter 2, Grace O'Malley
32 *May you be seven times* Quoted in Chambers, *Ireland's Pirate Queen*, 68.
32 *take this from unconsecrated hands!* Ibid.
33 *bulwark with gowns* Monson, *Naval Tracts*, vol. 4:105.
33 *good shot* Calendar of the State Papers Relating to Ireland, vol. 10: 436.
34 *impudently passed* William Drury, quoted in Chambers, *Ireland's Pirate Queen*, 74.
36 *Afterwards Griffith* Henry, *Chronicle of Ireland*, 187.
37 *comely, tall* Gernon, *Discourse of Ireland*, 357, quoted in Chambers, *Ireland's Pirate Queen*, 20.
37 *would rather have* Quoted in Chambers, *Ireland's Pirate Queen*, 53.
39 *their small-shot* Monson, *Naval Tracts*, vol. 4:105.
41 *entertained a skirmish* Calendar of the State Papers Relating to Ireland, vol. 10: 204.
41 *great shot* Ibid.
41 *horrible carnage and havoc* Anonymous, "Frenchman's Account," 438.
41 *mashing to pieces* Ibid., 439.
42 *ship anchored* Calendar of the Carew Manuscripts, 474.
42 *continuing roads* Calendar of the State Papers Relating to Ireland, vol. 9: 446.
42 *great spoiler* William Drury, quoted in Chambers, *Ireland's Pirate Queen*, 74.
43 *Are you trying to hide* Chambers, *Ireland's Pirate Queen*, 84.
43 *I went ther hence* Calendar of the State Papers Relating to Ireland, vol. 2:425.

Chapter 3, Francis Drake
47 *of strong limbs...broad breasted...his eyes rounde...well favored* Corbett, *Drake and the Tudor Navy*, 318.
47 *recompense* Drake, *Sir Francis Drake revived*, 233.
49 *fine roving* Ibid., 236.
49 *a pile of bars of silver* Ibid., 237.
50 *not finding his men* Vaz, *First Voyage*, 76.
54 *Yet there hardly escaped* Hawkins, "Here followeth," 94.
55 *the Minion aboord* Hortop, "travailes of Job Hortop," 454.

55 *forsook us* Hawkins, "Here followeth a Note," 101.
58 *Que gente?...Englishmen* Drake, *Sir Francis Drake revived*, 275.
58 *handy strokes* Ibid., 276.
62 *shotte at her three peeces* Pretty, "Famous Voyage," 241.
62 *our ship shall be called* Ibid., 242.

Chapter 4, Diego the Mulatto
72 *worst shark in the sea* Marx, *Pirates and Privateers*, 111.
77 *Do whatever you wish* López Cogolludo, *Historia de Yucathán*, 598. This line is paraphrased from the text. Translation by author and Mary Crouch.
77 *cut Rodríguez's nose and ears* Ibid. Translation by author and Mary Crouch.
81 *stately dinner* Gage, *Thomas Gage's Travels*, 316.
81 *remember him to her* Ibid.
81 *every possible remedy* Restall, *Black Middle*, 141.
82 *Pirate of Campeche* Exquemelin, *Buccaneers of America* (1684), 135.
83 *Christian Creole* Real Academia, *Memorial Histórico Español*, 474. Author's translation.
83 *Hoy por me* Gage, *Thomas Gage's Travels*, 316.

Chapter 5, Henry Morgan
88 *passed among the buccaneers* Exquemelin, *Histoire des Avantuiers*, vol. 2:2. Author's translation.
91 *every creek* Calendar of State Papers Colonial, 1669-1674, no. 293.
92 *with drums beating* Exquemelin, *Buccaneers of America* (1678), 107.
95 *If our number is small* Exquemelin, *Buccaneers of America* (1684), 136.
98 *One troop managed* Exquemelin, *Buccaneers of America* (1678), 113.
99 *in the usual manner* Ibid., 122.
100 *dunghill of the universe* Ward, *Trip to Jamaica*, 13.

Chapter 6, Juan Corso
102 *capitáns de corso* See for example Pinet Plasencia, *Península de Yucatán*, 345, regarding this designation in the case of Pedro de Castro.
105 *sons of whores* See for example Gage, *Gage's Travels*, 336.
105 *dark dungeon...close and stinking* Calendar of State Papers Colonial, 1681-1685, no. 303.
107 *barbarous and cruel* Dampier, *Voyages and Discoveries*, 149.
107 *mongrel parcel* Calendar of State Papers Colonial, 1681-1685, no. 1163.
107 *rogues culled out* Ibid., no. 1938.
109 *four or five glasses* Calendar of State Papers Colonial, 1677-1680, no. 1624.

109 *Spanish captain slighted* Ibid.
109 *hanging him up* Ibid.
112 *present all their small arms* Calendar of State Papers Colonial, 1681-1685, no. 1938iv.
112 *stress of weather* Ibid., no. 1938.
114 *one Bodeler* Ibid., no. 1198.
116 *burnt all the houses* Ibid., no. 1927.
116 *roasted on a spit* Oldmixon, *British Empire*, vol. 2:424.
116 *said to [i]crease* Ibid.
119 *of a weakness* Enríquez Barroto in Weddle, *La Salle*, 181.
119 *without wasting* Ibid.

Chapter 7, Bartholomew Sharp
123 *hulk and store-houses* Beeston, *Journal*, 298.
125 *if you will be unruly* Samuel Long, in Howard, "Earl of Carlisle's," 153.
128 *great disturbance...greatness...drought* Ringrose, "Buccaneers of America," 372.
128 *striking dory* [Povey?], "Buccaneers on the Isthmus," 108.
129 *vaporing* Ibid., 109.
129 *thirty paces long* Ringrose, "Buccaneers of America," 376.
129 *pitch, tar, oil* Ibid.
129 *fittest to march* Ibid.
129 *fig, olive, orange* Ibid.
129 *sugar-works* Ibid., 377.
129-30 *For they are a sort of men* Cicero, *Tully's Offices*, 3:29.107. Translation by Roger l'Estrange.
130 *coppers, cogs* Ringrose, "Buccaneers of America," 378.
130 *gave them their bellies* Sharp, *Captain Sharp's Journal*, 41.
130 *garden herbs* Ringrose, "Buccaneers of America," 379.
131 *saying thay had not* [Povey?], "Buccaneers on the Isthmus," 109.
132 *rich of gold and silver* Ibid.
132 *stout fellows* Cox, *Voyages and Adventures*, 39.
132 *affronts* [Dick], "Brief Account," 271.
132 *Thay had not all guns* [Povey?], "Buccaneers on the Isthmus," 110.
132 *to keep the longer from* Cox, *Voyages and Adventures*, 40.
132 *maintain his ground* Cox, *Voyages and Adventures*, 40.
132 *three of their chiefest men* Ringrose, "Buccaneers of America," 385.
132-33 *tracks of our feet* Cox, *Voyages and Adventures*, 41.
133 *placed at each door* [Dick], "Brief Account," 272.
133 *indifferent good brandy* [Povey?], "Buccaneers on the Isthmus," 109.
133 *delightsome garden* Ibid.
133 *old Indian woman* Ringrose, "Buccaneers of America," 387.
133 *very friendly together* [Dick], "Brief Account," 272.

134 *faint hearted* Ringrose, "Buccaneers of America," 400.
135 *in good fellowship* [Dick], "Brief Account," 282.
136 *savage Indians and pirates* Calendar of State Papers Colonial, 1681-1685, no. 1522.
136 *lit his pipe or wiped his breech* William Peniston, paraphrased in Ringrose, *Buccaneer's Atlas*, 32.
137 *misdemeanors...sworn allegiance* Burchett, *Complete History*, 579.

Chapter 8, Edward "Blackbeard" Teach

139 *They were prodigiously afraid* Roberts, *Four Years Voyages*, 91.
141 *with some of his own men* Johnson, *General History*, 58.
141 *cowardly puppies...he would neither give* "Abstract of a Letter from Mr. Maynard," reprinted in Lee, *Blackbeard*, 233.
141 *he was for King George* *Boston News-Letter*, February 23–March 2, 1719, excerpted in Lee, *Blackbeard*, 227.
141 *would let him alone* Ibid.
141 *dead or alive* Ibid.
141 *Damn you for villains* Johnson, *General History*, 53.
141 *You may see by our colors* Ibid.
142 *bid...I cannot spare my boat* Ibid.
142 *Damnation seize my soul* Ibid.
144 *uncommon boldness* Ibid., 45.
145 *When the pistols were ready* Ibid., 56.
145 *prostitute* Ibid., 49.
145 *liberties* Johnson, *General History*, 50.
145 *beard was black* Ibid., 57.
146 *tall spare man* Henry Bostock, quoted in Konstam, *Blackbeard*, 91.
147 *false optics* Roche, *Journals*, 99.
147 *got plunder* Johnson, *General History*, 45.
149 *very short of hands* Southey, *Chronological History*, vol. 2:212.
149 *about in his morning gown* *Boston News-Letter*, November 4–Nov. 11, 1717, excerpted in Konstam, *Blackbeard*, 70.
150 *almost naked* *Calendar of State Papers Colonial, 1717-1718*, no. 556.
152 *little sloop* "Abstract of a Letter from Mr. Maynard," reprinted in Lee, *Blackbeard*, 233.
152 *fell a-stern* Ibid.
152 *shot away Teach's gib* Ibid., 233-34.
152 *swan shot, spick nails* *Boston News-Letter*, February 23–March 2, 1719, excerpted in Lee, *Blackbeard*, 228.
153 *lie down snug* Johnson, *General History*, 54.
153 *several new-fashioned* Ibid.
154 *gave him a terrible wound* *Boston News-Letter*, February 23–March 2, 1719, excerpted in Lee, *Blackbeard*, 228.
154 *Well done, lad* Ibid.
154 *If it be not well done* Ibid.
154 *much wounded* Johnson, *General History*, 54.
154 *five shot in him* "Abstract of a Letter from Mr. Maynard," reprinted in Lee, *Blackbeard*, 234.
155 *belong'd to one of the sloops...had buried* Dowling, *Compendious History*, 124.
155 *Nobody but himself* Johnson, *General History*, 58.

Chapter 9, Bartholomew Roberts

157 *wait upon him immediately* Johnson, *General History*, 177.
158 *dispute was short and warm* Ibid.
158 *cross set with diamonds* Ibid.
158 *all the pleasures that luxury* Ibid.
160 *novelty...disagreeable superiority* Ibid., 212.
160 *since he had dipped his hands* Ibid., 168.
160 *a merry life and a short one* Ibid., 212
161 *courage, and skilled in navigation,* Ibid., 167-68.
161 *a most generous humane* Snelgrave, *New Account*, 174.
162 *severe revenge* Ibid., 173.
162 *sailed out of the harbor* Johnson, *General History*, 169.
163 *rich crimson damask* Ibid., 211.
165 *should be so served himself* Ibid., 195.
168 *stretched our larboard tacks* Atkins, *Voyage to Guinea*, 260.
169 *had depth of water sufficient* Ogle, *Historical Register*, 345.
170 *drubbed him* Johnson, *General History*, 236.
170 *negligent or backward* Ibid.
171 *with an hour-glass* Ibid., 202.
171 *upon a wind* Ibid., 211.
172 *vapoured* Ibid., 208.
172 *Solomon Grundy* Ibid., 172
173 *first rate oath...get clear or die* Ibid., 210-11.
173 *drunk, passively courageous* Ibid., 211.
173 *a man portrayed with a flaming* Ibid., 213.
174 *a sword in his hand* Ibid., 211.
174 *get up and fight* Ibid.
174 *made himself master of said harbour* Quoted in the *Weekly Journal*, excerpted in Breverton, *Black Bart Roberts*, 93.
175 *unfit for service* Johnson, *General History*, 211.
175 *Damnation to him* Ibid., 212.

Chapter 10, Edward "Ned" Low

176 *gave a most terrible relation* *Calendar of State Papers Colonial, 1724-1725*, no. 102.
176 *forced...whip't...behaved themselves* Ibid.
177 *without any ceremony* Johnson, *General History*, 292.
179 *knocked [several] on the head* Ibid.
179 *God damn...give him good* Ibid.
179 *little man...lusty* *American Weekly Mercury*, September 26–October 4, 1723.
181 *too apt to disagree* Johnson, *General History*, 285.
181 *weep plentifully* Ashton, *Ashton's Memorial*, 177.
181 *under the influence* Ibid.
182 *made a black flag* Johnson, *General History*, 285.
185 *always aspiring* Ibid., 280.
185 *came alongside of us* Ashton, *Ashton's Memorial*, 175.
185 *You dog you!* Ibid., 178.
187 *Nantucket Indians* *Boston News-Letter*, July 2, 1722, excerpted in Sewell, *Diary*, 307.
187 *large man-of-war* Ashton, *Ashton's Memorial*, 182.
187 *very name of man-of-war* Ibid.
188 *being a greasy fellow* Johnson, *General History*, 289.
188 *cut and mangled* Ibid.
188 *did not like his looks* Ibid.
188 *black flag with the figure* Ibid., 300.
188 *in the middle of which* Ibid., 317.
189 *deep blew flag* *Boston News-Letter*, July 23, 1723, excerpted in Sewell, *Diary*, 325
189 *five days and nights* Ashton, *Ashton's Memorial*, 183.
189 *swallowed up* Ibid.
189 *had no god but their money* Roberts, *Four Years Voyages*, 63.
190 *broiled* Calendar of State Papers Colonial, 1724-1725, no. 102.
191 *large range of teeth* Ashton, *Ashton's Memorial*, 186.
191 *chief companions* Ibid., 186-87.
194 *desperado...as soon as the others* *American Mercury*, June 20-27, 1723.

Chapter 11, Kanhoji Angria

201 *stately houses built with stone* Downing, *Compendious History*, 138.
201 *wrap their clothes around her* Ibid., 9.
204 *After Angria had taken this grab* Ibid., 7.
207 *whom he caused to be burnt* Burnell, *Bombay in the Days*, 89.
207 *marched and quartered* Ibid.
211 *Thus fortunate and invincible* Anonymous, "Authentic and Faithful," 455.

Chapter 12, Cheng I Sao

213 *keeping their eyes* Glasspoole, "Brief Narrative," 102.
213 *a stout commanding-looking man* Ibid., 103.
219 *male fear* Murray, "Cheng I Sao," 207.
223 *their defense [they are]* Ibid.
223 *Chin Chew* Turner, "Brief Narrative," 734.
224 *short sword* Glasspoole, "Brief Narrative," 117-18.
224 *Early in the morning* Ibid., 110.
225 *boxing master* Yun-lun, *History of the Pirates*, 46.
226 *in the whole village* Ibid., 47-48.
226 *tied behind their back* Glasspoole, "Brief Narrative," 114.
228 *No person shall debauch* Yun-lun, *History of the Pirates*, 14.
229 *was nailed to the deck* Turner, "Brief Narrative," 732.
230 *fixed upright* Ibid., 734.
230 *not being the red flag* Yun-lun, *History of the Pirates*, 25.
230 *and for this purpose* Hingston, *Maritime Geography*, 538.

Chapter 13, Jean Lafitte

240 *Captain La fette* Davis, *Pirates Laffite*, 28.
248 *of all nations and colors...gun vessels* Daniel T. Patterson in *Niles' Weekly Register*, November 19, 1814.
250 *Captains Dominique and Belluche* Butler, "General Orders," 478.
251 *It appears* *Niles' Weekly Register*, June 1, 1822.

SELECTED BIBLIOGRAPHY

CHAPTER 1

Bradford, Ernle. *The Sultan's Admiral: Barbarossa—Pirate and Empire-Builder.* 1969. Reprint, London: Tauris Parke Paperbacks, 2009.

Çelebi, Kâtip [Haji Kalifeh]. *The History of the Maritime Wars of the Turks.* Translated by James Mitchell. London: Oriental Translation Fund, 1831.

Currey, Edward Hamilton. *Sea-Wolves of the Mediterranean: The Grand Period of the Moslem Corsairs.* New York: Dutton, 1910.

Dan, Pierre. *Histoire de Barbarie et de ses Corsaires, des royaumes et des villes d'Alger, de Tunis, de Salé, & de Tripoly.* 2nd ed. Paris: Pierre Rocolet, 1649.

Farine, C. H. *Deux Pirates au XVIe Siècle: Histoire des Barberousse.* Paris: Paul Ducrocq, 1869.

Haëdo, Diego de. *Histoire des Rois d'Alger.* 1619. Reprint, translated by H. C. de Grammont. Algiers: Adolphe Jourdan, 1881.

Heers, Jacques. *The Barbary Corsairs: Warfare in the Mediterranean, 1480–1580.* Translated by Jonathan North. London: Greenhill Books, 2003.

Lane-Poole, Stanley, and J. D. Jerrold Kelley. *The Barbary Corsairs.* New York: G. P. Putnam's Sons, 1890.

Little, Benerson. *Pirate Hunting: The Fight Against Pirates, Privateers, and Sea Raiders from Antiquity to the Present.* Washington, DC: Potomac Books, 2010.

Morgan, J. *A Complete History of Algiers.* London: J. Bettenham, 1731.

CHAPTER 2

Anonymous. "A Frenchman's Account of the Gallant Behavior of an Englishman, in a Memorable Sea Fight." *In The Naval Chronicle of 1804,* Vol. 11, 431 – 441. London: J. Gould, 1804.

Calendar of the Carew Manuscripts. Edited by J.S. Brewer and William Bullen. London: Longman + Co., 1871.

Calendar of the State Papers Relating to Ireland of the Reign(s) of Henry VIII., Edward VI., Mary, and Elizabeth. 11 vols. Edited by Hans Claude Hamilton, et al. London: Longman, Green, Longman, & Roberts, 1860–1912.

Chambers, Anne. *Ireland's Pirate Queen: The True Story of Grace O'Malley.* 1998. Reprint, New York: MJF Books, 2003.

——. "'The Pirate Queen of Ireland': Grace O'Malley." In *Bold in Her Breeches: Women Pirates Across the Ages,* edited by Jo Stanley. London: Pandora, 1995.

Dan, Pierre. *Histoire de Barbarie et de ses Corsaires, des royaumes et des villes d'Alger, de Tunis, de Salé, & de Tripoly.* 2nd ed. Paris: Pierre Rocolet, 1649.

Gernan, Luke. "A Discourse of Ireland." In C. Litton Falkiner, ed., *Illustrations of Irish History and Topography, Mainly of the Seventeenth Century.* London: Longmans, Green, and Co., 1904.

Henry (of Marlborough). *The Chronicle of Ireland.* 1571, edited by Meredith Hanmer. Reprint, Dublin: Hibernia Press, 1809.

Little, Benerson. *Pirate Hunting: The Fight Against Pirates, Privateers, and Sea Raiders from Antiquity to the Present.* Washington, DC: Potomac Books, 2010.

Mainwaring, Henry. *The Life and Works of Sir Henry Mainwaring.* 2 vols. Edited by G. E. Manwaring and W. G. Perrin. London: Navy Records Society, 1922.

Monson, William. The Naval Tracts of Sir William Monson. 6 vols. Edited by M. Oppenheim. London: Navy Records Society, 1902.

Rixson, Denis. *The West Highland Galley.* Edinburgh: Birlinn Limited, 1998.

CHAPTER 3

Apestegui, Cruz. *Pirates of the Caribbean.* Translated by Richard Lewis Rees. Edison, NJ: Chartwell Books, 2002.

Cates, Thomas. "A Summary and True Discourse of Sir Francis Drake's West Indian Voyage, Begun in the Year 1585." In *Voyages of the Elizabethan Seamen to America,* edited by E. J. Payne. London: Thos. De la Rue & Co., 1880.

Corbett, Julian S. *Drake and the Tudor Navy.* 2 vols. London: Longmans, Green, and Co., 1898.

Drake, Francis. *A Summarie and True Discourse of Sir Francis Drakes' West-Indian Voyage.* London: Nicholas Bourne, 1652.

——. "Sir Francis Drake revived; Calling upon this Dull or Effeminate Age, to Follow his Noble Steps for Gold and Silver." 1626. Reprinted in C. Raymond Beazley, *An English Garner: Voyages and Travels Mainly during the 16th and 17th Centuries.* Vol. 2. New York: E. P. Dutton and Co., 1902.

——. *The World Encompassed by Sir Francis Drake Being his Next Voyage to that to Nombre de Dios.* Reprint, London: Hakluyt Society, 1854.

Hawkins, John. "Here followeth a Note or Declaration of the Troublesome Voyage made with the Jesus, the Minion, and Four Other Ships to the Parts of Guinea in the Years 1567 and 1568, by John Hawkins." 1589. Reprinted in C. Raymond Beazley, *An English Garner: Voyages and Travels mainly during the 16th and 17th Centuries.* Vol. 1. New York: E. P. Dutton and Co., 1902.

Hawkins, Richard. *The Observations of Sir Richard Hawkins, Knight in His Voyage into the South Sea in the Year 1593.* 1622. Reprint, edited by C. R. Drinkwater Bethune. London: Hakluyt Society, 1847.

Hortop, Job. "The Travails of Job Hortop." In Richard Hakluyt, *The Principle Navigations, Voyages, Traffiques and Discoveries of the English Nation*. Vol. 9. Glasgow: James Maclehose and Sons, 1904.

Monson, William. *The Naval Tracts of Sir William Monson*. 6 vols. Edited by M. Oppenheim. London: Navy Records Society, 1902.

Pretty, Francis. "The Famous Voyage of Sir Francis Drake, into the South Sea, and Therehence about the Whole Globe of the Earth, Begun in the Year of Our Lord, 1577." In *Voyages of the Elizabethan Seamen to America*, edited by E. J. Payne. London: Thos. De la Rue & Co., 1880.

Vaz, Lopez. "The First Voyage Attempted and Set Foorth by the Expert and Valiant Captaine M. Francis Drake Himselfe, with a Ship Called the Dragon ..." In Richard Hakluyt, *The Principal Navigations Voyages Traffiques & Discoveries of the English Nation*. Vol. 10. Glasgow: James MacLehose and Sons, 1904.

CHAPTER 4

Apestegui, Cruz. *Pirates of the Caribbean*. Translated by Richard Lewis Rees. Edison, NJ: Chartwell Books, 2002.

Calendar of State Papers, Colonial Series, America and West Indies, 1574–1738. 44 vols. Edited by Noel W. Sainsbury, J. W. Fortescue, et al. London: 1860–1969. (1669–1674.)

Exquemelin, A. O. *The Buccaneers of America*. 1678. 2nd ed. Reprint, translated from Dutch by Alexis Brown. London: Folio Society, 1969.

Fancourt, Charles St. John. *History of Yucatan: From its Discovery to the Close of the Seventeenth Century*. London: John Murray, 1854.

Fernández Duro, Cesáreo. *Armada Español desde la unión de los reinos de Castilla y de León*. 9 vols. Madrid: Sucesores de Rivadeneyra, 1895–1903.

Gage, Thomas. *Thomas Gage's Travels in the New World*. 1648. Reprint, edited by J. Eric S. Thompson. Norman: University of Oklahoma Press, 1969.

Haring, C. H. *The Buccaneers in the West Indies in the 17th Century*. 1910. Reprint, Hamden, CT: Archon Books, 1966.

Juarez Moreno, Juan. *Corsarios y Piratas en Veracruz y Campeche*. Sevilla: Escuela de Estudios Hispano-Americanos de Sevilla, 1972.

Little, Benerson. *The Buccaneer's Realm: Pirate Life on the Spanish Main, 1674–1688*. Washington, DC: Potomac Books, 2007.

———. *The Sea Rover's Practice: Pirate Tactics and Techniques, 1630–1730*. Washington, DC: Potomac Books, 2005.

López Cogolludo, Diego. *Historia de Yucathan*. Madrid: Juan Garcia Infanzon, 1685.

Marley, David F. *Pirates and Privateers of America*. Santa Barbara, CA: ABC-CLIO, Inc., 1995.

Marx, Jenifer. *Pirates and Privateers of the Caribbean*. Malabar, FL: Krieger, 1992.

Moreau, Jean-Pierre. *Pirates: Flibuste et Piraterie dans la Caraibe et les Mers du Sud, 1522–1725*. Paris: Tallandier, 2006.

Real Academia de la Historia (de Espana). Memorial Historico Espanol: Coleccion de Pocomentos, opusculos y Antiguedades. Vol. 16. Madrid: Imprenta Nacional, 1862.

Restall, Matthew. *The Black Middle: Africans, Mayas, and Spaniards in Colonial Yucatan*. Stanford: Stanford University Press, 2009.

CHAPTER 5

Ayres, Philip, ed. "Of the taking the Castle of Chagre." In *The Voyages and Adventures of Capt. Barth. Sharp and others, in the South Sea*. London: P. A. Esq. [Philip Ayres], 1684.

——, ed. "The True Relation of Admiral Henry Morgan's Expedition against the Spaniards in the West-Indies, in the Year 1670." In *The Voyages and Adventures of Capt. Barth. Sharp and others, in the South Sea*. London: P. A. Esq. [Philip Ayres], 1684.

Breverton, Terry. *Admiral Sir Henry Morgan: King of the Buccaneers*. Gretna, LA: Pelican, 2005.

Calendar of State Papers, Colonial Series, America and West Indies, 1574–1738. 44 vols. Edited by Noel W. Sainsbury, J. W. Fortescue, et al. London: 1860–1969. (1661–1688.)

Earle, Peter. *The Sack of Panamá: Captain Morgan and the Battle for the Caribbean*. New York: Thomas Dunne Books, 2007.

Exquemelin, A. O. *The Buccaneers of America*. 1678. 2nd ed. Reprint, translated from Dutch by Alexis Brown. London: Folio Society, 1969.

—— [John Esquemeling]. *The Buccaneers of America*. 1684. Reprint, New York: Dorset Press, 1987.

---- *Histoire des Avanturiers qui se sont Signalez dans les Indes*. 2 vols. Paris: Jacques le Febure, 1688.

Guzman, Juan Perez de. "Don Juan Perez de Guzman, his Relation of the Late Action of the English in the West-Indies." In *The Voyages and Adventures of Capt. Barth. Sharp and others, in the South Sea.*, edited by Philip Ayres. London: P. A. Esq. [Philip Ayres], 1684.

Haring, C. H. *The Buccaneers in the West Indies in the 17th Century*. 1910. Reprint, Hamden, CT: Archon Books, 1966.

[Heath, E.] "An Account of a Dreadful Earthquake, that Happened at Port Royal in Jamaica, on June the 7th, 1692; in Two Letters Written by the Minister of that Place." In Philotheus, *A True and Particular History of Earthquakes*. London: Printed for the author, 1748.

Little, Benerson. *The Buccaneer's Realm: Pirate Life on the Spanish Main, 1674–1688*. Washington, DC: Potomac Books, 2007.

——. *The Sea Rover's Practice: Pirate Tactics and Techniques, 1630–1730*. Washington, DC: Potomac Books, 2005.

Sloane, Hans. *A Voyage to the Islands Madera, Barbados, Nieves, St. Christopher's and Jamaica.* 2 vols. London: B.M. for the Author, 1707.

Ward, Edward (Ned Ward). *A Trip to Jamaica.* 1700. Facsimile reprint in Edward Ward, *Five Travel Scripts Commonly Attributed to Edward Ward.* New York: Columbia University Press, 1933.

CHAPTER 6

Calendar of State Papers, Colonial Series, America and West Indies, 1574–1738. 44 vols. Edited by Noel W. Sainsbury, J. W. Fortescue, et al. London: 1860–1969. (1680–1686.)

Dampier, William. *Voyages and Discoveries.* 1729. Reprint, London: The Argonaut Press, 1931.

Gage, Thomas. *Thomas Gage's Travels in the New World.* 1648. Reprint, edited by J. Eric S. Thompson. Norman: University of Oklahoma Press, 1969.

Laprise, Raynald. *The Privateer of Saint-Domingue and Louis XIV's Designs on Spanish America, 1683-1685.* Terrae Incognitae 39 (2007), 68-82.

Little, Benerson. *The Buccaneer's Realm: Pirate Life on the Spanish Main, 1674–1688.* Washington, DC: Potomac Books, 2007.

Marley, David F. *Pirates and Privateers of America.* Santa Barbara, CA: ABC-CLIO, Inc., 1995.

Oldmixon, John. The British Empire in America. London: J. Brotherton etal, 1741.

Pinet Plasencia, Adela, ed. *La Peninsula de Yucatan en el Archivo General de la Nacion.* Chiapas, Mexico: Centro de Investigaciones Humanisticas de Mesoamerica y el Estado de Chiapas, 1998.

Weddle, Robert S., ed. *La Salle, the Mississippi, and the Gulf: Three Primary Documents.* College Station, TX: Texas A&M University Press, 1987.

——. *Wilderness Manhunt: The Spanish Search for La Salle.* College Station, TX: Texas A&M University Press, 2001.

——. *The Wreck of La Belle, the Ruin of La Salle.* College Station, TX: Texas A&M University Press, 2001.

CHAPTER 7

Beeston, William. A Journal Kept by Col. William Beeston, from "His First Coming to Jamaica." In *Interesting Tracts, Relating to the Island of Jamaica.* St. Jago de la Vega, Jamaica: Lewis, Lunan, and Jones, 1800.

Burchett, Josiah. *A Complete History of the Most Remarkable Transactions at Sea, from the Earliest Accounts of Time to the Conclusion of the Last War with France.* London: W. B. for J. Walthoe, 1720.

Calendar of State Papers, Colonial Series, America and West Indies, 1574–1738. 44 vols. Edited by Noel W. Sainsbury, J. W. Fortescue, et al. London: 1860–1969. (1677–1680, 1681–1685, 1685–1688.)

Cicero, Marcus Tullius. *Tully's Offices (de officii)*, in Three Books. 6th ed. 3 vols. Translated by R. L'Estrange. London: D. Browne etal, 1720.

Cox, John. *The Voyages and Adventures of Capt. Barth. Sharp, and Others, in the South Sea*. London: P. A. Esq. [Philip Ayres], 1684.

Dampier, William. *A New Voyage Round the World*. 1697. Reprint, New York: Dover, 1968.

[Dick, William.] "A Brief Account of Captain Sharp..." In *The Buccaneers of America*, edited by Alexandre Exquemelin [John Esquemeling]. 1684. Reprint, New York: Dorset, 1987.

Howard, Charles (Earl of Carlisle). "The Earl of Carlisle's Answer to a Charge Against Him." In *Interesting Tracts, Relating to the Island of Jamaica*. St. Jago de la Vega, Jamaica: Lewis, Lunan, and Jones, 1800.

"Leter from Col. Cony to the Committee." In *Memorials of the Discovery and Early Settlement of the Bermudas or Somers Islands, 1511–1687*, edited by J. H. Lefroy, 549. 2 vols. London: Longmans, Green, 1879.

Little, Benerson. *The Buccaneer's Realm: Pirate Life on the Spanish Main, 1674–1688*. Washington, DC: Potomac Books, 2007.

——. *The Sea Rover's Practice: Pirate Tactics and Techniques, 1630–1730*. Washington, DC: Potomac Books, 2005.

Lloyd, Christopher. "Bartholomew Sharp: Buccaneer," *Mariner's Mirror* 42, no. 4 (1956): 291–301.

[Povey, Edward?]. "The Buccaneers on the Isthmus and in the South Sea, 1680–1682." In *Privateering and Piracy in the Colonial Period: Illustrative Documents*, edited by John F. Jameson. New York: Macmillan Company, 1923.

Ringrose, Basil. *A Buccaneer's Atlas: Basil Ringrose's South Sea Waggoner*, edited by Derek Howse and Norman J. W. Thrower. Berkeley, CA: University of California Press, 1992.

——. "The Buccaneers of America: The Second Volume." In *The Buccaneers of America*, edited by Alexandre Exquemelin [John Esquemeling]. 1684. Reprint, New York: Dorset, 1987.

——. "Captains Sharp, Coxon, Sawkins, and Others." In *The History of the Buccaneers of America*, edited by Alexander Exquemelin [John Esquemeling]. 1699. Reprint, Boston: Sanborn, Carter and Bazin, 1856.

Sharp, Bartholomew. "Captain Sharp's Journal of His Expedition." In William Hacke, *A Collection of Original Voyages*. 1699. Facsimile reprint, edited by Glyndwr Williams. New York: Scholars' Facsimiles + Reprints, 1993

Spencer, Thomas. *A True and Faithful Relation of the Proceedings of the Forces of their Majesties, King William and Queen Mary, in the West Indies*. 1691. Reprinted in *The Harleian Miscellany*, vol. 2, edited by Edward Harley. London: T. Osborne, 1744.

Taylor, John. *Jamaica in 1687: The Taylor Manuscript at the National Library of Jamaica*. Edited by David Buisseret. Kingston: University of West Indies Press, 2008.

CHAPTER 8

Calendar of State Papers, Colonial Series, America and West Indies, 1574–1738. 44 vols. Edited by Noel W. Sainsbury, J. W. Fortescue, et al. London: 1860–1969. (1717–1718, 1724–1725.)

Downing, Clement. *A Compendious History of the Indian Wars; with an Account of the Rise, Progress, Strength, and Forces of Angria the Pyrate.* London: Printed for T. Cooper, 1737.

Calendar of Treasury Papers, Volume 5, 1714–1719, edited by Edward Redington.London: Eyre and Spottiswood, 1883.

Johnson, Charles. *A General History of the Robberies and Murders of the Most Notorious Pirates.* 1726. Reprint, New York: Dodd, Mead, 1926.

Konstam, Angus. *Blackbeard: America's Most Notorious Pirate.* Hoboken, NJ: John Wiley & Sons, 2006.

Lee, Robert E. *Blackbeard the Pirate: A Reappraisal of His Life and Times.* Winston-Salem, NC: John F. Blair, 1974.

Little, Benerson. *The Sea Rover's Practice: Pirate Tactics and Techniques, 1630–1730.* Washington, DC: Potomac Books, 2005.

Oldmixon, John. *The British Empire in America.* Vol. 2. London: J. Brotherton, J. Clarke, 1741.

Roberts, George. *The Four Years Voyages of Capt. George Roberts; Being a Series of Uncommon Events Which Befell Him.* 1726. Reprint, London: The Traveller's Library, 1930.

Rocke, Jeremy. "The Journal of Jeremy Rocke". In *Three Sea Journals of Stuart Times*, edited by Bruce S. Ingram. London: Constable + Co., 1936.

Spotswood to Cartwright, February 14, 1718 (1719), "Virginia—Journal of the Council, The 11th day of March 1718(–9)," and Spotswood to Lords of Trade, May 26, 1719. In *The Colonial Records of North Carolina, Vol. II—1713 to 1728*, edited by William L. Saunders, 324–38. Raleigh, NC: P. M. Hale, 1886.

Southey, Thomas. *Chronological History of the West Indies.* 3 vols. London: Longman etal, 1827.

"The Trials of Major Stede Bonnet, and Thirty-three others, at the Court of Vice-Admiralty, at Charles-Town, in South Carolina, for Piracy: 5 George I. A.D. 1718." In *A Complete Collection of State Trials and Proceedings for High Treason and Other Crimes and Misdemeanors, Vol. 15, A.D. 1710–1719*, edited by T. B. Howell, 1231–1302. London: T. C. Hansard, 1812.

CHAPTER 9

The American Mercury, Vol. II, 1720–1721. Facsimile reprint, Philadelphia: Colonial Society of Pennsylvania, 1898.

Atkins, John. *A Voyage to Guinea, Brazil, and the West Indies.* 1735. Facsimile reprint, London: Frank Cass, 1970.

Breverton, Terry. *Black Bart Roberts: The Greatest Pirate of Them All.* Gretna, LA: Pelican Publishing, 2004.

Calendar of State Papers, Colonial Series, America and West Indies, 1574–1738. 44 vols. Edited by Noel W. Sainsbury, J. W. Fortescue, et al. London: 1860–1969. (1721–1722, 1722–1723.)

"Captain Ogle to Lords of the Admiralty, April 5, 1722." In *The Historical Register, Containing an Impartial Relation of All Transactions Foreign and Domestick*, vol. 7, edited by C. H. Green. London: H. Meere, 1722.

Johnson, Charles. *A General History of the Robberies and Murders of the Most Notorious Pirates.* 1726. Reprint, New York: Dodd, Mead, 1926.

Little, Benerson. *The Sea Rover's Practice: Pirate Tactics and Techniques, 1630-1730.* Washington, DC: Potomac Books, 2005.

Sanders, Richard. *If a Pirate I Must Be ...: The True Story of "Black Bart," King of the Caribbean Pirates.* New York: Aurum Press, 2007.

Snelgrave, William. "A New Account of some parts of Guinea and the Slave Trade". 1727. Excerpted in *Captured by Pirates*, edited by John Richard Stephens. Cambria Pines by the Sea, CA: Fern Canyon Press, 1996.

CHAPTER 10

The American Mercury, Volume IV, 1722–1723. Facsimile reprint, Philadelphia: Colonial Society of Pennsylvania, 1907.

Ashton, Philip, and John Barnard. *Ashton's Memorial.* 1725. Reprinted in *In the Trough of the Sea*, edited by Donald P. Wharton. Westport, CT: Greenwood Press, 1979.

Dow, George Francis, and John Henry Edmonds. *The Pirates of the New England Coast, 1630–1730.* 1923. Reprint, New York: Argosy-Antiquarian Ltd., 1968.

Calendar of State Papers, Colonial Series, America and West Indies, 1574–1738. 44 vols. Edited by Noel W. Sainsbury, J. W. Fortescue, et al. London: 1860–1969. (1722–1723, 1724–1725.)

"Extract of a Letter from on Board the Diamond Man of War, dated March 5." In *The Historical Register, Containing an Impartial Relation of All Transactions Foreign and Domestick*, vol. 11, edited by C. H. Green, 327. London: H. Meere, 1726.

"Jack Hall." In *The Complete Newgate Calendar*, vol. 2, edited by J. L. Rayner and G. T. Crook. London: Navarre Society, 1926.

Johnson, Charles. *A General History of the Robberies and Murders of the Most Notorious Pirates.* 1726. Reprint, New York: Dodd, Mead, 1926.

——. *Histoire des Pirates Anglois.* Utrecht: Jacques Brodelet, 1725. The Netherlands.

Little, Benerson. "The Origin of the Dread Pirate Banner, the Jolly Roger." *Pirates Magazine* 12 (April 2010), 9-14.

"New York, July 20th." In *The Political State of Great Britain*, Vol. 32, edited by Abel Boyer, 273. London: privately printed, 1726.

Roberts, George. *The Four Years Voyages of Capt. George Roberts; Being a Series of Uncommon Events Which Befell Him.* 1726. Reprint, London: The Traveller's Library, 1930.

Sewall, Samuel. *The Diary of Samuel Sewall, 1674-1729.* Vol. 3. Boston: Massachusetts Historical Society, 1882.

CHAPTER 11

Anonymous. "An Authentic and Faithful History of that Arch-Pirate Tulagee Angria." In *The Critical Review: or, Annals of Literature*, vol. 12, edited by Tobias George Smollett. London: R. Baldwin, 1756.

Beveridge, Henry. *A Comprehensive History of India.* London: Blackie and Son, 1865.

Biddulph, John. *The Pirates of Malabar and an Englishwoman in India Two Hundred Years Ago.* London: Smith, Elder & Co., 1907.

British Government. *Gazetteer of the Bombay Presidency, Volume 11: Kolaba and Janjira.* Bombay: Government Central Press, 1883.

Burnell, John. *Bombay in the Days of Queen Anne, Being an Account of the Settlement.* London: Hakluyt Society, 1933.

Downing, Clement. *A Compendious History of the Indian Wars; with an Account of the Rise, Progress, Strength, and Forces of Angria the Pyrate.* London: Printed for T. Cooper, 1737.

Hamilton, Alexander. *A New Account of the East Indies.* Edinburgh: John Mosman, 1727.

Kurup, K. K. N. *India's Naval Traditions.* New Delhi: Northern Book Centre, 1997.

Low, Charles Rathbone. *History of the Indian Navy, 1613–1863.* London: Richard Bentley and Son, 1877.

Mookerji, Radhakumud. *Indian Shipping: A History of the Sea-Borne Trade and Maritime Activity of the Indians from the Earliest Times.* Bombay: Longmans, Green and Co., 1912.

Naravane, M. S. *Battles of the Honourable East India Company (Making of the Raj).* New Delhi: S. B. Nangia, 2006.

Philoleutherus. *A Faithful Narrative of the Capture of the Ship Derby.* London: S. Osborn, 1738.

Saletore, R. N. *Indian Pirates.* New Delhi: Naurang Rai, 1978.

CHAPTER 12

[An Officer of the Caroline]. *An Account of a Voyage to India, China, &c. in His Majesty's Ship Caroline, Performed in they Years 1803-4-5, Interspersed with Descriptive Sketches and Cursory Remarks.* London: Richard Phillips, 1806.

"Diary of a Journey Overland through the Maritime Provinces of China, from Manchao on the South Coast of Hainan to Canton, in the Years 1819 and 1820." In *New Voyages and Travels: Consisting of Originals and Translations*, Vol. 6, edited by Richard Phillips. London: Sir Richard Phillips and Co., n.d.

Dikotter, Frank, Lars Laamann, and Zhou Xun. *Narcotic Culture: A History of Drugs in China.* Chicago: University of Chicago Press, 2004.

Glasspoole, Richard. "A Brief Narrative of My Captivity and Treatment Amongst the Ladrones." In *Yun-lun, History of the Pirates Who Infested the China Sea.*

Murray, Dian A. "Cheng I Sao in Fact and Fiction." In *Bold in Her Breeches: Women Pirates Across the Ages*, edited by Jo Stanley. London: Pandora, 1995.

———. *Pirates of the South China Coast, 1790–1810*. Stanford, CA: Stanford University, 1987.

———. The Practice of Homosexuality among the Pirates of China. In Bandits at Sea: A Pirate Reader, 244-52. Edited by C. R. Pennell. New York: New York University, 2001.

"Recent Exploits of the Ladrones." In *The Naval Chronicle for 1810*, Vol. 23. London: Joyce Gold, 1810.

Tuckey, James Hingston. *Maritime Geography and Statistics, or A Description of the Ocean and Its Coasts, Maritime Commerce and Navigation, &c. &c. &c.* 4 vols. London: Black, Parry, and Co., 1815.

Turner, J. O. "Brief Narrative of My Captivity Among the Ladrones; with Observations Respecting those Pirates." In *The Literary Panorama*, Vol. 5, edited by Charles Taylor. London: Cox, Son, and Baylis, 1809.

Von Krusenstern, Adam J. *Voyage Around the World in the Years 1803, 1804, 1805, and 1806.* 2 vols. Translated by Richard Belgrave Hoppner. London: John Murray, 1813.

Yun-lun, Yuan. *History of the Pirates Who Infested the China Sea from 1807 to 1810.* 1830. Translated by Charles Fried Neumann. London: Oriental Translation Fund, 1831.

CHAPTER 13

Allen, Gardner W. *Our Navy and the West Indian Pirates*. Salem, MA: Essex Institute, 1929.

Bradlee, Francis B. C. *Piracy in the West Indies and Its Suppression.* Salem, MA: Essex Institute, 1923.

Butler, Robert. Letter, "General Orders," January 15, 1815. In *Official Letters of the Military and Naval Officers of the United States During the War with Great Britain in the Years 1812, 13, 14, & 15*, edited by John Brannan. Washington, DC: Way & Gideon, 1823.

Chapelle, Howard I. *The Search for Speed Under Sail, 1700–1855*. New York: W. W. Norton, 1967.

Davis, William C. *The Pirates Laffite: The Treacherous World of the Corsairs of the Gulf.* New York: Harcourt, 2005.

Greene, Jerome A. *Jean Lafitte: Historic Resource Study (Chalmette Unit).* National Park Service, September 1985. www.nps.gov/history/history/online_books/jela/hrst.htm.

Niles, Hezekiah, ed. *Niles' Weekly Register*, November 19, 1814; April 22, 1820; and June 1, 1822.

ACKNOWLEDGMENTS

Writing a book is never entirely the work of a single person, and far too often the reader is unaware of those other than the author who have had a significant hand in getting a book to print. In particular, my many thanks go to Ann Crispin for pointing me toward Fair Winds, and to Will Kiester for providing the opportunity there. Editor Cara Connors worked tirelessly with me on each chapter, and her insistent attention to detail invariably improved my writing. She has not only my thanks but also my high regard. Likewise, I appreciated the diligent efforts of copyeditor Karen Levy. To Mary Crouch, my thanks, affection, and respect for her steadfast support, Spanish translations, suggestions, and more than reasonable patience in the face of my distraction and focus. As ever, my parents have my thanks for their support, far more than I can ever repay, and my daughters, for simply being there.

ABOUT THE AUTHOR

Benerson Little is the author of *Pirate Hunting*, and has written *The Buccaneer's Realm*, which examines the world of buccaneers in the 1600s, and *The Sea Rover's Practice*, a look at how pirates and privateers practiced their trade. Little is a former Navy SEAL, and now works as a writer and consultant in several areas with an emphasis on maritime and naval issues, particularly maritime threat and security. He has appeared in two television documentaries on piracy and has advised on several others. He lives in Huntsville, Alabama, and in his spare time he teaches modern fencing, researches historical fencing, and works on contemporary and historical non-fiction.

INDEX